French Impressions

Brittany

D0916135

George East

George East's French Impressions: Brittany
Published by La Puce Publications
e-mail: info@la-puce.co.uk
website: www.george-east-france.com

© George East 2010

This paperback edition 2010

ISBN: 978-0-9523635-9-0

The author asserts the moral right to be identified
as the author of this work.

Typesetting and layout by Harold Mewes of Red Dog Books

Printed and bound in Great Britain by Anthony Rowe Ltd,
Chippenham, Wiltshire

For Big Al. See you in the Paradise Bar, shipmate.

Other books by George East

Home & Dry in France
René & Me
French Letters
French Flea Bites
French Cricket
French Kisses
French Lessons

A Year behind Bars

and

Home & Dry in Normandy (compilation)

French Kisses (compilation)

A LA PUCE PUBLICATION
e-mail: info@la-puce.co.uk
web site: www.george-east-france.com

Author's Note

This is probably unlike any travel book or guide you have read.

Mostly this will be because we chose to spend a full year living in Brittany while I researched and wrote what my agent insists on calling a 'travel fusion' book. Apart from being much more comfortable than roughing it in a camper or living out of a suitcase, our excuse was that the static location would allow us to get a flavour of what it would be like for expat Brits living cheek-to-jowl with Brets.

An additional goal was to keep an eye open for a new home and business in the course of giving the reader an idea of the sort of things Brits abroad get up to. During our years in France we have bought, done up and sold a handful of properties, and always at a loss. We didn't plan it that way, but over the years developed a knack for buying at the top and selling at the bottom. Like most British expats below pension age, we also tried all sorts of ways to earn a living out of living abroad. Unfortunately, our anglo-gallic fusion pub, garlic-flavoured car deodorisers, back-to-nature weekends and metal-detecting competitions to unearth the miller's secret stash of gold were not profit-making concerns.

So apart from having an interesting year schlocking around Brittany, the aim of this book was to pass on at least an impression of the culture and history of the region, and what it might be like to own a property, live or run a business in this part of France (or other parts, come to that). For those readers with no such plans, I also wanted to give the armchair traveller a hopefully entertaining and certainly undemanding read.

Finally, we came to Brittany expecting it to be quite like the other parts of France in which we have travelled and lived. Now we know just how much it isn't. All the French regions have their own character and landscape and history and traditions, but are still, well, very French. Brittany begs to differ, and this book is a stab at trying to explain how, and possibly even why.

PS. *All the places, people and situations described in this book are real, except when they are not. In some cases, names and locations have been changed to avoid embarrassment, litigation or assault on my person.*

Acknowledgements

Hundreds of people helped this book come to pass, and not all of them are bar and restaurant owners. Special thanks are due to our ever-indulgent landlady Pandora, my private house detective and super-proofer Sally Moore, our indomitable ferret researcher Kris Hendrickson, Marie-Annick Cariou of the Brittany Tourist Board, property specialist supremo Pete Dwyer and his wife and my web mistress and computer fixer Sharon, Richard and Sarah of Anglo-info, Gareth and family of the Central Brittany Journal, Stephen Tuckwell and Gwyn Cherriman and Denis Pelloquin of Brittany Ferries, Welsh wi-fi wizard and cultural historian Tony Powell, justly proud Breton Phillipe Leost, our very special agent Benoit Dufour and, finally, all the British and Breton good eggs we met with and lived amongst during our stay. On the subject of helpful contacts for those wishing to visit, buy a house in, move over to or start a business in Brittany, you will find at the back of the book a list of organs and websites I found particularly helpful - or a good laugh.

Judgement Days

When editor of *Food & Drink* magazine, I took a pretty firm stance on how we handled restaurant and hotel reviews. Any critics who filed a harsh judgement were invited to return to the scene of what they thought had been the crime and give the place another try. My reasoning was that the reviewer might have caught the enterprise on a bad day for the business or himself, and it was anyway not fair to damn a place on the evidence of a single visit. I have tried to apply the same rules of engagement with the towns, villages and people mentioned in this book. So if I have been sniffy about a place, my unkind comments will usually have been based on several considered visits. Where I have been really sniffy about people, it may well have been dislike at first sight, and I have usually changed their names and locations for reasons already given. While on the subject, I must also apologise in advance for any historical and factual errors contained in these pages. There is never any real excuse for sloppy research, but digging up and passing on alleged facts from the past in foreign parts and in a foreign language can be a bit like a game of Chinese whispers, especially in a place like Brittany.

Also, it was never my intention to visit and review all the touristy towns and places in Brittany. That has been more than well done elsewhere. Nor did we set out to travel round and comment on places in any sort of geographic grouping or, as some might say, sensible order. We just wondered and wandered around the region as the mood or business took us. As my wife says, a map with one of those dotted lines following our progress would look as if a drunken insect had fallen in an inkwell, crawled out and then staggered about a bit.

Should you want to instantly check out any of the Breton, Breton-French (there is a difference) and 'Bretish' food and drink recipes, all have been made and tried by my wife or me to varying degrees of success...but always with great satisfaction.

A bit like Wales. Not.

As we travel together through these pages, I shall try to get to grips with some aspects of the complex historical, cultural and geographical factors that have combined to make the region unique. In the meantime, here's a sort of Brittany Life:

One of twenty-two* official regions of France, Brittany occupies the top left-hand corner of the country, and is often likened to Wales by British visitors and lazy travel writers like me. The comparisons are actually quite forgiveable, as both are about the same size, and at four million-ish, have a similar population.

The landscape and weather are not dissimilar, with lots of hills, trees, water and rain. Although it might not appear so from a quick look at a map, the two places are not too far apart on length of coastline. Wales has 2120 kilometres of beaches, bays and cliffs, while at 2,730 km, Brittany claims a third of the total coastline of France. An additional factoid of interest to those who like to see the sea at regular intervals and without too much hassle is that nowhere in Brittany is further than fifty miles from the coast.

Like Wales, Brittany is very Celtic, though nobody seems quite sure why. In another parallel, the Breton language and separatist culture were discouraged and even suppressed by the French government until fairly recent times, though the former is making a comeback and the latter never went away.

Another echo is that a lot of foreigners have made their homes in Brittany. Unlike in some parts of Wales, the Anglo incomers have generally been made welcome, and especially if they can claim a smidgeon of Celtic genes. British incomers are popular as they bring much-needed money to the community pot, are generally fairly well-behaved, and often seen as less foreign than the French. Also and unlike in Wales, there has been no shortage of ruins for Brits to buy and do up. As most young Bretons would not dream of starting married life in a former

---

* The exact boundaries, number and even names of the regions of France are often contested, and mostly by those who live in them.

cowshed with water running up as well as down the walls, there has been generally no more than a grade three shoulder shrug and a muted sigh of bemusement by the locals when confronted by what they see as a typically eccentric British penchant.

From a cultural perspective, Bretons appreciate greatly and like to practise art, particularly music. Two writers, three musicians, a sculptor and a bloke who makes life-sized blue plastic elephants just for fun live within a mile of where we were based in the mountains of Finistère. And that's with a population density not much above the most unfashionable areas of the Gobi Desert.

As further evidence of loving art for no more than its own sake, where else in France (or the rest of Europe) would hard-nosed farmers spend the time and trouble to make artistic tableaux from hay bales in their roadside fields just so that passers-by can enjoy them?

A final and, I think, significant statistic about Brittany is that the region boasts more independent (i.e. small and privately-owned) breweries than the rest of France put together. This is just one more reason we found ourselves so much at home here.

Lesmenez, April, Friday 18th.

Distant lights wink invitingly through the deepening dusk. A buttery full moon throws long shadows across the fields, forests and moorlands surrounding our new home. A sharp cry signals that a creature of the night has found or become supper. It is all splendidly bucolic as we sit by our rented lake and mull over how we came to be half-way up what passes for a mountain in Brittany.

This is the first time we have hired rather than owned (or more correctly had a huge mortgage on) a place to live in for forty years, and I am already enjoying not having to worry about maintaining this one. Earlier I noted a couple of tiles missing from the 300 year-old roof of the sprawling farmhouse, and it is good to know I won't have to replace them and cause other leaks in the process. Although the disparity is narrowing, sixty percent of French people still prefer to rent rather than buy property, and I can see their point.

Another unusual situation for us is that, having sold everything we owned in England, we now have for the first time ever what seems a huge amount of money in the bank. If it lasts, we will buy a home as a base in the land of my wife's ancestors. If not, we shall continue our wandering around the rest of France until it is time to pack it in and head for the old folk's home. We have given ourselves a deadline of a year to research and write a book about the region, and I am looking forward to finding out why so many Britons are attracted to visiting, buying homes or moving over here to live.

So far, all has gone smoothly for our small adventure. After saying a final farewell to England for the fifth time in twenty years, we and our mini-cavalcade arrived by car ferry at St-Malo in the early hours of this morning. Then it was due westward to the Finistère department, where we eventually found Lesmenez hiding behind a giant lump of rock in the midst of the otherwise desolate moors. Including ours, there are just five properties in the hamlet, and we are told by the letting agent that the average age of the residents is over eighty. This means there will probably be low levels of noise pollution, anti-social behaviour, murder, mugging, drug-dealing and other everyday events in today's rural Britain.

Now the dramas are done, we are here and I am experiencing that familiar mix of anticipation, excitement and even a little trepidation at the prospect of getting to know another part of our second favourite country. This time I hope we will find the perfect place to live and work, and not make any terminal financial cock-ups in the process. Given our record, it is quite possible we will get it all wrong again.

We began messing around in France nearly thirty years ago, when we bought a tiny cottage in Normandy from the proceeds of a dodgy deal. We never got to appreciate The Little Jewel, as I managed to sell it unintentionally while the paint on the walls was literally still wet. Our next home was a ruined water mill which was marginally more ruined when we left it more than a decade later. Then we went mad, borrowed oceans of money and bought a grand manor house at what we thought was a bargain price. It was, but that may have been because there was a thriving and very noisy dog kennels next door. The neighbours were a nice couple called Querville, who were from the Spanish borderlands. They owned the biggest and blackest dog I have seen as well as running a boarding house for another seventy.

After a series of misadventures including me trying to run a British pub by committee, we sold the *manoir* at a loss, said goodbye to the hound of the Basque Quervilles and returned to England just in time for property prices in France to rocket.

Once upon a time, only Francophiles bought a holiday home in or moved to France. That all changed as the property boom in Britain at the start of the new century made French houses look almost risibly cheap. It was not that a lot of Britons suddenly realised that France can be a lovely place in which to own a home or live. Many just looked at the property prices and could not resist buying a house and land for the same price as a lock-up garage in the UK. In what became known as *L'invasion*, a veritable army of Brits descended on France like booze cruise shoppers, buying ruined cottages and castles as they used to buy cheap wine and cheeses.

Then many of those Brits who went the whole hog and moved over to live in France realised that the cost of property should not be the sole reason for becoming an expatriate. If that were true, downtown Mogadishu would be full of British property owners. As well as the people coming over to settle with no work or transferable occupation, the second-home owners who had stayed in Britain learned the hard way that equity is not the same as disposable income, and that mortgages - even foreign mortgages - have to be paid. Then the French complicated matters further by wanting to get into the act when they saw what a crazy *rosbif* had paid Mrs Dupont for her tatty old place down the road.

So, having caused all the trouble and then found they were not as happy to own or live here as they thought they would be, thousands of fiscally or emotionally imperilled Britons put their homes on the market. This resulted in a glut of property for sale, and a passing Martian might be forgiven for thinking *À Vendre* to be a very popular house name in France.

Nobody knows exactly how many Britons are now living in France full-time, but coming up for a third of the 240,000 foreign-owned secondary residences are owned by British nationals. Another unknown figure is how many Britons are living in France and wish they were not.

But we love it, and have arrived with the intention of starting again, and finding the best and cheapest property or business in the region. We shall also be seeking a sense and place of belonging in this part of France.

It is an initial irony that, although we have not begun our search for a perfect place to live in France, we are already technically in Paradise. The farmhouse is called 'Bihan Baradoz', which is Breton for Little Paradise, and so far the place seems to be living up to its name.

The main room downstairs is about the size of a tennis court, and everything except the curtains appears to be made of stone and slate. This is granite and slate country and the houses are naturally made of the same material as the craggy peaks thrusting through the thousands of acres of moorland around us in the Monts d'Arrée national park. Massive slabs of slate from the Black Mountains deck the floor, and almost the whole wall at one end of the room is taken up by a majestic fireplace. We are told it grows breathtakingly cold in winter at this altitude, but I reckon the hearth would take half a tree trunk with ease.

Outside, several acres of obedient lawn surround the house, with a long tree-lined drive from the lane. There is a big pond fed by water from the mountains, a small wood of mostly Douglas fir, and a busy stream and tumbling cascade which reminds me of our former home in a Norman water mill. All in all it is a wonderful picture-postcard sort of place, but for us the real treasure of this house lies in its precise location.

From the side door, a winding track leads past the homes of our nearest two neighbours and to the moors and jagged cols of the *Landes de Cragou*. Looking at the map, it is clear we could walk all day without encountering a road, and according to the guide books, we could walk all day without encountering another traveller.

There will be time for unpacking and introducing ourselves to the neighbours and exploring beyond the area in the coming days, but already I think we have done very well in finding Little Paradise and Lesmenez. The English physicist and mathematician James Jeans is generally credited with the observation that it is often better to travel in anticipation than to arrive, but I have a feeling that we have, for a change, chosen our destination well, and that our time here may even live up to all our expectations.

*

There is an old Breton saying that the day belongs to the living, and the night to the dead. As Britain has its ASBO-ignoring mini-yobs and binge drinkers infesting the dark hours, this part of rural France is traditionally home for all manner of almost as scarey ghouls, ghosties and other-worldly beings. The grim reaper Ankou stalks the land with scythe in hand, while his *lavandières* busily prepare shrouds for his clientele. As yet we have seen no sign of him or his ghostly washerwomen, but our first night in this fey-ish land is already living up to its promise of tales of mystery and imagination.

An hour ago we heard the clatter of approaching hooves, then watched dumbly as two gloriously golden and almost iridescent horses cantered along our drive and down a grassy slope to disappear into the woods beyond the stream. Brittany overflows with stories of animal apparitions arriving to presage momentous events, and the two palominos fitted the bill perfectly. Their white-rimmed eyes flashed and their breath and bodies steamed in the chill air as pale manes and tails floated wraith-like in the twilight. On investigation, the piles of horse pooh they left in their wake seemed real enough. While my wife fetched a bucket and spade to take advantage of the windfall, I pulled on my Wellington boots and headed for the woods.

*

The mystery is solved and we have already become acquainted with one quarter of the population of Lesmenez. Our near-neighbours and unretired retired farmers are Mr Goarnisson and Madame Messager. The use of separate surnames is not because they are living in sin or that Madame is an ultra-feminist, just an old countryside tradition.

Finding the horses playing hide-and-seek in our copse, I backtracked and followed the trail of manure to a field, the entrance to which had originally been fenced off by a length of blue string. As anyone who has lived in rural France will tell you, blue baling twine is imbued with magical properties. Even for the largest farm animals, it has about the same impenetrability factor as the force field of the star ship Enterprise on maximum setting. This piece of magic string was lying on the ground, and the horses had obviously felt empowered to escape. Across the lane, a faint light glowed through a glass panel set in the door of an otherwise darkened farmhouse. People generally go to bed early in the countryside of any country, but I was sure the owners would want to know their horses had done a bunk.

My tentative knocking eventually summoned an elderly and very small lady in a big nightgown. As I began my tale, her bemused, faintly irritated and very pained look took me instantly back to the time I started trying to communicate with the French in their own language.

Having listened for as long as she could bear, the lady looked fleetingly towards a shotgun hanging in the hallway before turning and shouting at someone who, going by the language she used, was Klingon. Moments passed as I waited for Mr Worf to come lumbering down the stairs, but I was to be disappointed. The man who appeared was a trifle shorter than the lady of the house, and, together with the same pained expression, was wearing an interesting combination of striped pyjamas, countryman's cloth cap and wooden clogs.

As he joined in with the open-mouthed gurning, I realised that I was trying to make myself understood to a couple to whom French was a second language. It was not Klingon they had been speaking, but Breton.

Another echo of my early days in France came as I resorted to sign language, giving what I thought was a passable impression of a runaway horse by neighing, tossing my head and prancing up and down outside the door while slapping my backside. More silence followed as I pawed the ground and blew heavily through my lips and the lady studied the shotgun.

Eventually, the man looked across the lane at the empty field opposite, and understanding spread like dawn across his weathered features. He said something to his wife which I assumed was the equivalent of 'You forgot to put the force field on again', and she disappeared and reappeared with rubber boots and a couple of rope halters. I pointed at the pooh in the lane and at the entrance to our driveway, then beckoned, remembering not to slap my backside, whinny and prance as I led the way. There will be plenty of time for the neighbours to get to know us, and I would not want to start by giving the impression that the newest member of the community is not only foreign but thinks he is a horse.

*

The moon sails serenely on a sea of cloud, and all is calm. An owl hoots advice as my wife tends my bramble scratches with calamine lotion and we take a nightcap beside the silvery pond. Cows look curiously over the fence from the field alongside as they discuss the excitement of the past hour. From what I can hear of their conversation, they speak with a standard French rather than Breton dialect.

The horses are back where they should be, the force field string is back in place, and I have been rewarded for my help in the round-up. As I left her at the doorstep, Madam switched to a Breton version of French, casually mentioning she had skinned a beaver that evening and enquiring if I would also like to have a crap. After I reassured her I had had a good one on the boat, her partner took over. Although having an even more impenetrable accent, he had obviously appointed himself as official translator. In the way of these things, his method was to loudly repeat exactly what his wife had said, but even more quickly. While I was thinking of the best way to respond without causing offence, the lady of the house returned from a trip to the kitchen. As I nodded like a Victorian explorer trying to look grateful for the present of a freshly dressed monkey's head, Madame handed me a bowl of wallpaper paste and a brown brick. If I had not enjoyed a crap before, she said - or I thought she said - I certainly would after eating her little present. She had also added a block of condensed beaver.

Now and as we discuss the promise of our new location, the silence of the night is rent apart by an agonized howling. People who do not live in the countryside do not understand just how noisy a place it can be; it sounds as if a local cat has fallen foul of a fox, or Madame is rendering down another beaver.

Then I realise the noise is some sort of musical instrument, and what it is producing is similar to the sound of Scottish bagpipes, only worse. My wife, who is part-Welsh and has Breton ancestors, so knows about these things, explains that someone in the hamlet above ours is playing a set of Breton pipes. The tune of the region's national anthem is apparently the same as the Welsh favourite, Land of My Fathers, but the player is having a problem hitting the notes. Or rather he is playing all the right notes but not in the right order.

I think about finding the source of the noise and hitting the player with the crap brick, but decide tomorrow is another day, and assault on a local even from another hamlet might not be a good way to start our time here. We gather up our glasses, the wallpaper paste and brick and head for the farmhouse. It is a beautiful night, but tonight we will sleep with the window shut. If this moonlight serenade is to be a regular performance, I shall unpack my penny whistle and respond in kind with some traditional sea shanties and we will see who has the most staying power.

Saturday 19th

We have been exploring our new surroundings, and it seems we have stumbled upon hidden treasure.

Walking around the hamlet at twilight was, corny as it sounds, like passing through a time portal. A lot is written and said about isolated French rural communities where time has stood still and life is virtually unchanged, but this is invariably not true. We have visited hundreds of isolated dwelling places and no matter how old or quaint, they are inevitably of their time. Cars on the road or on bricks dominate what planners like to call the street scene, and satellite dishes, garden furniture and even childrens' toys and bikes remind you of when as well as where you are.

But our immediate neighbours have no cars, their children have long grown and gone, and Lesmenez seems to be doing its best to live in the past. The gardens grow grass and flowers and vegetables and not plastic furniture and toys. The lane past our farmhouse is unmetalled, and if you ignore the power cables and telephone lines overhead, the handful of cottages appear little different from how they would have looked a couple of centuries past.

But the most noticeable reminder of how things would have been here a hundred or more years ago is the utter silence. I have lived in the busiest of cities for the past two years, and, to my urban-trained ears, walking here is like watching a film with the sound turned off. Anywhere in England is not far from a busy highway, and a newspaper recently ran a competition to try and find a spot where there was no noise from people, cars and planes. They had to cheat by putting a limit of a few minutes on the silence, and still had a job finding somewhere completely quiet. Every evening when the Lone Piper is not welcoming the dusk, it is almost eerily still here.

Also enhancing the quietude this evening is the lack of movement. There is not a breeze, and no human or animal activity. The birds have gone to bed, and the residents are preparing to take to theirs. Light leaks through the odd unshuttered window, but there is no other indication of habitation or life. For the first time in years, I can hear silence, and it is almost unnerving. It will take me a while to become acclimatised to our new surroundings, but I suspect I will find that no hardship.

Monday 21st

Another close shave with Ankou and becoming an entry in France's road fatality statistics.

Before we travel any further down this road, it is important to get things straight about what may appear to be my xenophobia vis-à-vis French driving standards. But I speak here of what I know, and have driven in town and countryside all over the world. Without a jot or scintilla of doubt, the great majority of French drivers are totally useless and should not be allowed on the road.

There are, of course, all sorts of bad drivers in Britain. In France, nearly all drivers are completely bad, mad and very dangerous - and in different ways. In Britain we have boy and, nowadays, girl racers; in France it is as likely to be a toothless granny whizzing by you at top revs on a blind bend or as a hump-back bridge looms.

The totally pants standard of driving and general road use in France is also not just my opinion, but a verifiable fact. And here is the incontrovertible evidence:

In a country nearly four times the size of England (so with much less congested roads) and with about the same number of cars with the same safety features and even more stringent rules of the road and penalties for disobeying them, French drivers manage to kill coming up for twice the number of people we do.

I have driven the distance to the moon and back on French roads, and count myself lucky to have lived to tell the tale. For

21

many years we drove a British-registered car in France and thought local drivers were harrying and generally persecuting us because we were foreigners. Now we have a Brittany-registered left-hand drive car, and realise we were actually being treated with caution by other road users when we were in our English car.

Local knowledge

As reported earlier, Brittany is about the same size as Wales or, if you want to be more continental, Belgium. According to who you believe, there are four or five departments or counties in the region. This is because, once upon a time, Nantes was the capital of the duchy of Brittany. Then Rennes took over as the seat of the supreme court, and there was all sorts of rivalry and aggro until the region was carved up during World War II, making Nantes the main town of a new pic'n'mix region to be called Pays de la Loire. Now, embittered or sentimental unificationists say that the law of the land may be based in Rennes, but the heart of the region still lies in Nantes.

For our purposes, the four departments of Brittany are Ille-et-Vilaine, Côtes d'Armor, Morbihan and Finistère. The name of the department in which we stayed means 'the end of the earth', which is how a lot of French people still regard this wild and often wet and windy place. Older Bretons recall the times of ancient and rival fiefdoms with evocative names like Léon and Cornouaille, but nowadays the region is generally divided more simply into the *Armor* (land of the sea), and the *Argoat*, (land of the woods).

On a touristic note, Brittany is the most popular French holiday destination for Britons. It is also popular with tight-fisted French holidaymakers who want to be able to enjoy the glorious landscape and coastline for free while camping or caravanning.

Brittany has been a territory or province of France since 1532, and many Bretons are still not happy about that. Arguments abound on the origins of the race, but all sides agree that Bretons are one of the six so-called Celtic Nations. Interestingly, the province was at one time allegedly called

'Lesser Britain' from where it is said that the name of Great Britain originates.

Around 300,000 Bretons are said to speak the amalgamated version of their once regionalised language, which to the untrained ear sounds like a bitter disagreement on the bridge of a Klingon battle cruiser. Breton is said by linguists to be similar in cadence and rhythm to Welsh. Some words are the same in each language. In fact, some Breton words like 'labour' (as in work) are the same as in English, which further deepens the mystery of where the Breton tongue originated. For my money, Star Trek creator Gene Roddenberry either holidayed in Brittany and thought a similarly belchy language would sound suitably alien and aggressive for the warlike Klingons, or it was a spookily complex case of art imitating life. In a Chariots of the Gods sort of way, the Klingon empire could have established an outpost in Brittany in pre-historical times and taught the natives their language, and introduced them to the Klingon hobby of sticking stones in the ground for absolutely no purpose other than the *craic*. Then along came a sci-fi series producer, and the rest is televisual history.

Further connections with Wales include the fact that Brittany lies to the west of its host country, that there are lots of mountains, and that the French like to make jokes about thick or miserable Bretons ('potato heads' is one of the politer descriptions, while President Sarkozy won no friends here by allegedly using a much ruder comparison).

Interestingly, as Scotland palled up with France against England, Brittany often sided with England against France in the Middle Ages.

As mentioned earlier, Brets also love to make music and their bagpipes are even more tuneless than the Welsh or Scots versions. They are also great believers in the supernatural, and there are a number of well-subscribed pagan groups operating in the region. Some of them like to burn down chapels or deface churches as a weekend treat.

Brittany is France's premier agricultural and fishing region, but seems to have something against keeping sheep and inventing a national cheese.

Home cooking

As every non-biased observer knows, the French are - or like to appear - very fussy about their food. Unlike their liberal attitudes towards all matters sexual and things like farting and peeing in public, they are narrow-minded and even prudish about what may or may not be put in one's mouth in the food line. Some would say they are obsessed with being accepted as the arbiter, authority and even originator of all dishes worth eating. Who else but the French would name the humble cottage pie after the man they say invented it?

I find attitudes refreshingly different in this region; Bretons seem much more down to earth and modest about their cuisine. I am sure lots of people from other regions would say they have much to be modest about.

While the coastal areas are known for dishing up anything that comes from the sea and moves (and quite a lot of things which do not), inland Breton cuisine seems based mainly on bread and butter and salt. Or rather flour and butter and salt. The wallpaper paste Madame gave me for helping with her horses was in fact a standard crêpe mixture. The brown brick was *bouille d'avoine*, a regional delicacy used to make what we would call gruel.

In the old days, Breton peasants would gather round a cauldron bubbling with *yod kerc'h*, or oats and water. When it was judged ready, the head of the household would make a hole in the sludge and add a lump of butter. There would then be a free-for-all to see who could get a spoonful from the buttery bit. This slap-up treat would be washed down with *lez ribot*, a Breton variety of buttermilk, and on holy and high days a glass of cider might be added to the pot.

Nowadays, *bouille d'avoine* is sold as a luxury item in supermarkets with specially reinforced shelves. I am told Breton gourmets (which seems a bit of an oxymoron) fry it with sesame seeds, but I reckon it would be more suitable for repairing the soles of clogs.

Unlike the residents of most other regions, Bretons like their butter salted, and a number of traditional recipes recommend eye-wateringly and artery-clogging amounts. For some reason Brittany was exempted from a tax on salt right up till the Revolution, which is perhaps why Bretons have always been so liberal in its usage. Predictably, there was also a healthy trade in salt smuggling across the border.

The basic Breton crêpe is, for all the fuss some people make about it, no more than a thin pancake of buckwheat flour. These were made by literally whipping the batter by hand, then cooking both sides on a flat stone or a rimless cast-iron pan called a *bilig*.

Although crêpe is the familiar generic name, in Brittany it is generally limited to pancakes with sweet fillings, while the savoury versions are called galettes. Arguments rage about the exact type of flour mix or type to use for either variety, but I do not want to get into that angels-on-a-pinhead type of debate as life is far too short. *Galette* is also a term used for flat cakes or other confections, but that is another place I do not wish us to go. Suffice it to say that Bretons will put almost anything savoury in a galette, and the Breton version of a bacon and egg sarnie can be bought at most markets; the knack of eating one without decorating your shirt front is a skill which marks out locals from visitors.

The knack of making such an apparently simple thing as a crêpe/galette also takes a bit of acquiring. If the mixture is too thinly spread in the pan it will break up when you try to turn your nascent crêpe over or remove it from the pan; if you have put too much batter in the pan, it will be rubbery when it comes out. Do not despair if your early attempts do not work out well, as we have found that practice does make perfect; If I can make a proper-tasting and looking crêpe, anyone with two hands can.

Should you fancy trying your hand at knocking up a bunch of basic galettes/crêpes, here's a typical recipe. In Brittany it is usual to make a big batch of around 30 pancakes, so be sure to invite some friends along to try them (or adjust the measures accordingly):

Ingredients:

6 ounces of wheat flour
1lb of buckwheat flour
3 eggs
5 oz salted, melted butter
Half a bottle of dry cider (approximately a pint)
2 litres of milk (go on, use full-fat just this once)
Some cold water and fresh or packet yeast.
A teaspoonful of salt

Method

Put the flour and salt into a mixing bowl and break the eggs into a well in the centre. Start mixing the batter with a wooden spoon (or your fist if you want to be faithful to the original recipe) and gradually add the milk and cider. Finish off by adding some water (if necessary) and the yeast, but beware of making the batter too runny. Melt half the butter and add to the mixture.Find a suitable flat stone, or failing that, gently heat a small frying pan which has been greased with some cooking oil. When the pan is really hot, ladle enough batter in to cover the surface of the pan. Leave for a couple of minutes or until the surface starts to bubble, then turn over and lavish some more butter on it. (N.B. keep the mixture beaten between the making of each crêpe.) You are now ready to experiment with fillings, which should be enclosed in the galette so that the finished article resembles a deflated Cornish pasty.

Sporting note

Thankfully for the maintenance of world peace, the record for galette throwing is held by a Breton. Along with apricot stone spitting and beret tossing, new attempts on the crêpe-chucking record take place at the small town of Mahalon each July, but so far no-one has come near to equalling the tally of 7.45 metres established in 2000 by local hero Fabien Le Coz.

Dietary concerns

A common Breton recipe for long life and good health comes out as *debri mad, kousel mad, kaohad mad*. In keeping with their view of the important things in life (after art and drinking), the maxim translates as 'eating well, sleeping well, shitting well...'

Finistère Fact File

What has been most noticeable about our visits to the four departments of Brittany is how different they are, topographically speaking. Generally, it is as if the authorities drew the boundary lines based on geological rather than political considerations.

To the Romans, the bit of Brittany we stayed in was literally the end of the earth (*Finis Terrae*), while to the inhabitants it was *Penn-ar-Bed*, or Head of the World. This area was settled by Celts in the 5th century BC, conquered by Rome in 56 BC, and invaded by Anglo-Saxons from the 5th century until and including the present day.

As far west as you can go without falling into the Atlantic Ocean, Finistère is the remotest Brittany *département* (county). Being physically furthest from the rest of France may account for why it seems furthest from French influence. Whatever, it is said that more Breton is spoken here than in the other departments. As with most enclosed or remote areas, people have married mostly within their community or tribe. This is why in some small towns, one person in every five will have the same surname. Within a mile of where we live, there is LeGoff the dentist, LeGoff the plumber, LeGoff the postie, LeGoff the Pratt, and our nearest neighbour Alain LeGoff.

When last counted, the static population of Finistère was around 870,000, with an average age of 40 years, living in a land area of 6,755 sq. kilometres. This results in a population density of 131 per square kilometre. Mind you, the mountain and moors area surrounding us would probably average no more than one man and a dog.

The department of Finistère runs from the north to south of the west of the region, so boasts a varied and stunning coastline of 1,200 km. In the north, the old pastimes of smuggling, ship robbing and even wrecking by luring ships on to the rocks off the 'coast of iron' were particularly popular, and some villages in that area are said to still be proud of their past activities. Such is the inverted status that some villages miles inland claim to have been ship-wrecking communities. Perhaps the legends of a turbulent and elemental past helps explain why, in an otherwise deeply religious region, paganism is said to flourish.

Due south by more than a hundred kilometres of Cornwall and also benefitting from the Gulf stream, Finistère has a similarly wet and warm-ish temperate and what the boffins call an 'oceanic' climate. Average temperatures in summer are 17.5 degrees C, and 5.6 degrees C in winter. Sun freaks and worshippers would probably not find Finistère sufficiently broiling in the summer, but then the winters here are correspondingly mild compared to many so-called French hotspots where Hell could freeze over in some landlocked areas. Weather snobs claim it is always raining in Brittany; the true facts are that the region averages 813mm precipitation a year compared to 824mm in sunny Nice and 850mm in baking Bordeaux. So there.

The biggest, liveliest and definitely newest-built (or rather, re-built) county town in Finistère is Brest, though the administrative centre is to be found in much posher Quimper.

MAY

Huelgoat, Le Cloître-St-Thégonnec, the lake at
Brennilis, the chapel of St-Michel at Brasparts,
St-Jean-Trolimon , Lake Guerlédan, Bon Repos,
Les Forges des Salles, Mur-de-Bretagne, Pontivy,
Loudéac

All the auguries promise a fruitful summer. Nature has obviously followed to the letter her own recipe for the mix of rain and sun at just the right times, and the verges and hedgerows are aglow with verdant colour. There are swelling seas of dandelions and oceans of buttercups yellowly lining the lanes around our new home, and the pinewood copse is carpeted with harebells mingling with the modest beauty of Solomon's-seal. Taken together with other indicators like the stiffness of our nearest neighbour's left elbow, these colourful displays are flagging up the promise of good times to come.

In the meantime, we have been taking up our indulgent landlady's invitation to make ourselves at home on her land. The deal is that we will keep an eye on the grounds, plants, streams, mini-lake and woodland and in return may make reasonable use of the terrain for our crops and animals. The distant owner of these premises is a keen gardener and animal lover, and obviously likes the idea that her land will be put to fitting purpose. A good deal is when both sides are content, so I think we have struck a very good deal indeed by choosing to rent Paradise for a year.

A vegetable garden has been dug and fenced off, and a contented quartet of chickens are sizing up their new surroundings and each other to see who is going to be at the top of the pecking order. So far my money is on the little Sussex Red. As in human societies, it is often the smallest and noisiest who emerge as leaders and sometimes dictators.

We have never lived in the countryside without keeping chickens, and do not see how we could be without their company.

I once worked out that each egg from our hens costs more than a dozen from most supermarkets, but this way we know not only when they arrived, but how. And illusory as it probably is, they taste so much better straight from the hen.

We picked the four birds up at a local market yesterday after I had made them a luxurious home in the old stables alongside the barn. Donella is fussing around the new arrivals like, well, a mother hen, and has already given them suitable names. The warlike Sussex Red is now to be known as Brunhilde, the large and placid speckled grey is Griselda, the huge white and obviously soppy bird will be known as Blanche, while we have called the black one Whitney. This is not only because of her colour, but because she is already showing signs of divadom and likes to make peculiar movements with her beak whilst squawking.

*

Night comes slowly in this elevated area, and there is a luminous quality to the light as I sit beneath the ancient *calvaire* which marks the boundaries of the hamlet and the beginning of the track up to the moors and mountains.

It is unlikely there is a settlement in Brittany which did not have one of these sombre stone creations, clearly erected to remind the inhabitants that they and their behaviour were being watched. This one may have a particular significance, as a great battle between the forces of good and evil is said to have been fought on this spot a thousand years and more ago. The remaining bits of the slain good guys were taken to a holy place nearby, which is where the abbey of Le Relec got its name. Or, of course, the story might be a lot of codswallop, dreamed up by our neighbour or the Finistère Tourist Board of 1347.

Curiously, though they are decidedly Christian in intent, some of the most unfussy and even primitive-looking *calvaires* have a pagan, polytheistic feel. If not topped with minimalistic crosses, they may display complex Celtic-style stone knots or gargoyle-like faces, and I have seen one with what looks like a pair of spread buttocks mooning at passers-by. Brittany has more calvary crosses than anywhere else in France, and the oldest is

30

in the south Finistère town of St-Jean-Trolimon. The level of intricacy and stone filigree work on a *calvaire* normally denotes the alleged piety level of the inhabitants, and it is interesting that the one we sit beneath is almost totally devoid of frills and curlicues. The base is made of large, roughly-dressed blocks, from which rises a central column. There is some small detail at the top, but centuries of moorland weather have made it unrecognisable. The base is a good place to rest after a walk across the moors, and the blocks are comfortably indented from the wear and tear of ten thousand bottoms.

My reverie is interrupted by the pained roar of a mistreated engine, and a battered Range Rover lurches around the bend of the track leading to the neighbouring hamlet of Kernelec. It is strange how intrusive is the noise of a car in this pastoral setting, while a tractor roaring by is just an agreeable part of the rural scene.

I am particularly irked by the intrusion as the passer-by is Lady Muck. She is the daughter of the elderly couple who presented me with the brown brick on our first night here, but appears not to approve of the presence of outsiders on her territory. It says much about her view of her status that she drives a vehicle more associated with haughty county and country ladies in Britain than French hill farmers.

Lady Muck and her husband farm most of the surrounding fields, and because generations of her family have lived on and off the land here, she seems to regard the two hamlets and network of lanes and tracks as part of her private estate. This is not an uncommon attitude, and also why it is rarely a good idea to buy a spare house or barn from a farmer who is going to continue working and living nearby. Many forget about the money they got for their former property, and thus view the new owners as squatters.

Wanting us to be seen as friendly and unthreatening incomers, I tried waving and smiling when the lady of this manor first bucketed by, but that seemed to make her even more unhappy. Then my friendly wave changed to a two fingered version when she refused to acknowledge us beyond a curt nod. Now, when she passes I sweep off my hat, tug my forelock and make an exaggerated bow, but I think the irony is lost on her. Once I contrived to be peeing into a hedge as she approached, and turned as if by accident as she passed. There was no more than a flicker of acknowledgement, and I thought I detected a look of condescending pity before remembering she owns a prize bull and keeps an awesomely-equipped Breton shire horse in her top field.

Now the coast is clear, I walk along the lane and over the hump-back bridge to leave a handful of dried dog food under a hazel bush. Since we got the chickens, I have been trying to establish a telepathic rapport with the local fox so we can come to an agreement. The basic conditions of the compact are that I will provide breakfast and dinner each day, and he or she or members of the immediate family will not eat our hens.

I know the locals would think me deranged, which is why I leave the food when there is nobody about. But I believe I can establish sympathetic contact, and so far our contract has been upheld. The fox will certainly know there are chickens in the area, as someone at Kernelec keeps a cockerel and this is the best advertisement for the presence of hens. We have not met yet, but I and my dog have felt his presence at dusk. Last week I saw a flash of grey in the woods above the lane, and have never seen Milly react so dramatically to a fox. Although the locals would consider me mad for even thinking it, it is just possible that there is a wolf living in the pine forest at the foot of the moors. Books were written as recently as 1875 about the pleasures of wolf-hunting in the Black Mountains*, and that massive ridge of slate lies directly to the south. On the other side of the moorlands and at the gateway of the Monts d'Arrée, Le Cloître St-Thégonnec has cornered the wolf fascination market. An impressive stone carving of a family of wolves sits at the heart of the village, and there is a museum devoted to the history, biology and legends surrounding the species' activity in Brittany. The reason Le Cloître feels entitled to be the authority on all things wolf-like is that the last recorded killing of one in the Arrée mountains was by villager Pierre Berrehar on the 6th of October 1884.

Whether because of its location or the nature of its localised claim to historical fame, the village certainly has a timeless feel about it. There is a very good bakery and grocery shop, and a classic rural *bar tabac* and eating place run by a young, single and attractive woman. This may account for its popularity as a gathering place for men of all ages. A more debatable issue is why Le Cloître has one of the best-maintained and preserved churches in the area, yet like all other smaller places of worship hereabouts, it will be closed on Sunday. In a very Roman Catholic region of France, this is a puzzle, especially when one sees the church brooding sulkily and the bar across the square packed to the doors.

Thursday 1st

Today is a public holiday, or rather *the* public holiday. Curiously, only May 1st (Labour Day) is on the statute books as an official day off for all French workers. The rest are granted by what is called a collective convention, and the convention often seems to be that there are more days off than on. Few saints are forgotten when it comes to looking for an excuse to take a break from work, and a popular device is 'the bridge'. This comes into play when there is a public holiday anywhere near a weekend and it is not deemed worth going back to work for the day or two in between the official day off and the nearest Saturday or Sunday.

The total for time away from work for most French people over the course of a year takes no account of sickness (the French are demonstrably the most enthusiastic hypochondriacs in Europe) and the standard five weeks holiday in the summer. Nor do the statistics take into account all the strikes and unofficial stoppages.

Because it is not only public servants and people working for big companies who enjoy public holidays, nearly all shops and many bars and restaurants and other places of entertainment will be closed, leaving those on a day off with

---

* Wolf-Hunting and Wild Sport in Lower Brittany by EWL Davies is a rollicking read and a freely available digital copy is to be found at: www.archive.org/details/wolfhuntingwilds00davirich

nothing to do away from home. This is perhaps why there is a law banning the use of mowers on public holidays, and why everyone with a garden ignores it.

Saturday 3rd

Elsewhere in France, the Monts d' Arrée would be seen as little more than hilly ground, but Bretons like to make the most of their natural assets. Anyway, the moors and craggy tors surrounding our new home have more to offer than mere height above sea level.

In keeping with the Breton love of myth, mystery and supernaturality, this is the kingdom of Ankou (literally 'Mister Death') the aforementioned reaper of souls. Also to be found here are any number of mischievous sprites and will o' the wisps, including whole tribes of vengeful trouble-making Korrigans.

Running in a north-easterly slant and punctuated by giant granite outcrops, this rugged part of the Breton landscape forms the border between the ancient areas of Léon and Cornouaille. From the top of the highest crag above Lesmenez, one can see toy-like ferry boats steaming in and out of harbour at Roscoff, and, on an especially clear day, waves crashing against the cliffs of the Pink Granite coast. From this vantage point, there is also much evidence of the diversity and sometimes breathtakingly monumental style of the Breton landscape. A couple of miles to the south is the great lake at Brennilis, surrounded by some of the oldest and biggest peat bogs in Europe. At a mile across and more than a thousand acres in surface area, Brennilis matches a fair-size Scottish loch or Cumbrian mere. The lake was once claimed (probably by a rival commune) to be the watery path to the gates to Hell. This may also be why they built the now redundant nuclear reactor on its shores.

Further afield towards the town of Brasparts is the tiny chapel of St-Michel, sitting atop what is thought to be a giant Celtic tumulus and approached from one side with a step for nearly every day of the year.

They farm high in this part of Brittany, and patchwork fields of rape and cereal share the rugged terrain with peat bogs, scrubby gorse and pastureland. The county of Finistère is big on beef and dairy cattle, but there is a curious absence of sheep. According to our nearest neighbour, this is because they cannot survive wet and cold winter conditions.

Alain LeGoff has obviously never visited Wales, and we are told that the real reason sheep are not kept here is because there is little money in raising them. Not that I would suggest this to our neighbour, as after twenty years of close encounters I think I know how to best handle aged French countrymen, especially the unmarried variety.

Growing up in an isolated community free of television and cars and most other outside influences must obviously have an effect on the individual's character and philosophy. Certainly, it seems to me that all the older French countrymen I have met share some commonalities. While apparently innocent or at least unknowing of the ways of the modern world, they seem to compensate by developing a level of cunning which would make a particularly crafty fox jealous. Bachelors are the most extreme of the genre, and invariably rigidly fixed in their ways and views. Even when they don't, they have an unshakeable belief that they know all there is to know about the countryside, and that your originating from any town or part of Britain will guarantee you to be completely clueless about all rural matters.

Our nearest neighbour is a little over eighty, and is thus the youngest permanent resident of the hamlet. He was born in Lesmenez and lives alone in a small house behind his impressively distressed ancestral farmhouse, which has been uninhabited and uninhabitable for the best part of a century. Alain helped his father build the new house when he was ten, and the granite blocks were brought by wagon the twelve rocky miles across the mountains from the quarry at Huelgoat.

We met the day after our arrival, when I thought I had surprised an off-piste korrigan in the copse by the pond. Then the figure emerged from the undergrowth and I saw that, except for the footwear, he was wearing standard French aged countryman's outfit. Topping off a face with the texture of a well-weathered Cox's pippin was the inevitable time-shiny cloth cap which would probably take a surgical operation to remove, and below the neckline was the usual ensemble of tightly-buttoned suit jacket over collarless shirt and extremely lived-in trousers. This being Brittany, the footwear was specific to the region, with carpet slippers sheathed in traditional wooden clogs. The only thing missing was the roll-up cigarette welded to the lower lip.

As we should have expected, our nearest neighbour seems unaware of any boundaries or town-grown taboos on dropping in unannounced and is apt to appear like a pantomime genie at any time and anywhere. So far he has not materialised in the bed or bathroom or toilet while we have been using them, but it can only be a matter of time. Though the sudden manifestations can be a little unnerving and even dangerous when I am using a chain saw or halfway up a ladder or both, we like the informality, and the open-door policy also applies to his domain.

Yesterday, Alain materialised in our kitchen as we were trying to relieve the suffering of an ailing hen. Griselda went off lay last week, and it is pitiful to hear her keening cry as she lies forlornly and eggless in the nesting box. As she grew more and more moribund and miserable, a visit to the vet confirmed she was egg-bound and we were offered three solutions. The first, said the affably honest Mr Tanguy, was to buy from him an exceptionally expensive ointment to ease the passage for the egg from inside to outside Griselda. The second would be to try the undignified but sometimes more effective ruse of holding her over a pan of boiling water so that the steam would act as a lubricant. The third and most obvious solution would be to cut our losses and eat her.

It was while I held poor Griselda above the steaming pot and Donella pulled on her rubber gloves that Alain made his entry. For a moment, we held the silent tableau, then before leaving to report the weird goings-on to the rest of the village, he cleared his throat, gave a mini-shrug and observed dryly that, in France, though people like their food as fresh as possible, it is considered normal to kill and pluck a chicken before cooking it.

Friday 9th

From his bar stool, Clint Eastwood surveys his surroundings with that trademark part-puzzled, fully angry squint. At his shoulder, a man with a purple head is arguing with himself about whose turn it is to buy the next round. From a nearby table the mad monk Rasputin is giving us the evil eye.

On the terrace, a coach-load of tourists is pretending to be entertained by a man wearing a monogrammed dressing-gown and an oversized pair of boxing gloves. He ducks and feints and shuffles adroitly as they smile weakly in a very English way. What they do not know is that the man is reprising the action on the night he claims he nearly won the area finals in the Breton boxing championships of 1976. The locals know he is a former Latin teacher, and some say he lost his reason trying to conjugate a particularly ticklish irregular verb for his bored pupils. The more cynical say he is merely a compulsive attention seeker and very mean, and that he wears the boxing gloves so as to be unable to get his hands in his pocket when it is his turn to buy a round.

From what we have learned, this is just another average night in Huelgoat. It is our first official run ashore, and we have obviously come to the right place for local colour and interesting characters. Armed with some stunning natural attributes, a few made-up legends and lots of places to take drink, Huelgoat is a very popular tourist attraction. Huelgoatians also clearly like a drink, as for a static population of only a thousand there are seventeen licensed premises which remain open all year round. As well as the facilities in the betting shop and camping gaz outlet, there are even well-appointed bars in the two bakeries in case customers become faint with thirst while waiting for their daily baguette.

Claims to fame for Huelgoat ('High woods' in Breton) include a large lake, hundreds of acres of forests ringing the town, a world-renowned arboretum and a fascinating valley trail called The Chaos. This forest and riverside walk is littered with giant rocks said to be thrown around when the giant Pantagruel stubbed his toe and lost his cool while passing through. I reckon it more likely he was staggering home after a night on the batter in Huelgoat and felt like a bit of full-on giant-sized vandalism.

Like a hundred others around Europe and even further afield, the town also claims to be a favourite stopping-off place for King Arthur, with the alleged remains of his camp to be found high in the forest. Later and more verifiable residents of note include the ancestors of American Beat Generation poet, novelist and artist Jack Kerouac. Impressionist painter Paul Gauguin is said to have painted the lake from the attic studio above a shop just off the square, but as the premises sells painting and art materials that could be a marketing ploy. TV archeologist Sir Mortimer Wheeler often dug here, and it is a much-told story that actress Jane Fonda once cooked a crêpe for her then boyfriend Roger Vadim in the kitchen of a hotel in the square.

Pagan groups are said to prance regularly around in the forest, and it is claimed by those who also claim to know about these things that Huelgoat sits on a confluence of ley lines, giving it a mystical significance and special appeal to people of a spiritual nature. This may actually be true, and I do believe there is something special about the town. It might be the force of nature, or it could just be the number and variety of bars on tap which attracts so many unusual people. Huelgoat certainly seems to have its fair share of weirdos, which is why my wife says I feel so instantly at home here.

Our guide and future gossip correspondent for this part of the region is Allan Bevan, a former naval master-at-arms in the Royal Navy who now runs a bed and breakfast establishment near the square. Or rather, his wife Ann runs the B&B, while Allan absorbs the ambience and red wine and researches the book he will one day write about his life and times in Huelgoat. As he says, if and when it is done it will have to go in the fiction department, as nobody would believe it to be about real people and circumstances.

As the evening revs up, we learn that, as usual in situations like these in rural France, all is not as it seems at first sight. Clint Eastwood is actually a local plumber who has long tried and failed to make a living as a lookalike of the rangy Hollywood star. I am puzzled by his lack of success as, unlike nearly all lookalikes

I have seen, he really is the spitting image of Eastwood during his Dirty Harry years. Then Claude/Clint climbs down from his stool, disappears from sight behind it, and his severe lack of inches explains the reason for his lack of bookings.

As Allan explains, the man with the purple head is a local artist who enjoys the company of an imaginary friend, while the mad monk is a former car sprayer and now part-time Druid who lives in a caravan in the forest with - he claims - a tribe of Breton wood elves. The reason for the baleful stare is apparently that we have not taken out the insurance cover offered to British visitors which involves buying him a drink to avoid their holiday being cursed.

As to the size of the crowd, the reason the bar is so busy is that the premises are under new management.

The locals have turned out in force to check out such important issues as the ease and level of credit rating and what the new patrons are made of, and Madame is doing her best to show them. She would be tall even without her towering stiletto heels, and is wearing a very unpractical and flimsy dress which clearly leaves very little room for underwear. What looks like Christmas tree baubles hang from her ears, but all male attention is focused on the spheres struggling to escape from the plunging neckline of her blouse. Each time she leans forward to attend to a customer, there is an appreciable stiffening in the bar and a sudden falling off of conversation. Allan says a sweepstake has already been set up to estimate the exact date and time her breasts will escape from their billet, and other side wagers include estimating their individual and combined dimensions and weight. To get some inside information, one of the local sculptors has offered to create a life-size statue of her to go in the bar window, but her husband has said he would prefer it to be a bust. Allan points to where a middle-aged man is leaning on the bar, obviously studying form. He must be favourite for winning one of the side bets, says our host, as he is the owner of the town grocery store and renowned for his ability to gauge weight without the aid of a pair of scales.

We have been enjoying a very Breton rite of spring at the hamlet which looks down on the rooftops of Lesmenez. Kernelec is a bigger and racier dwelling place than ours as there are more than a dozen residents and some are below retirement age. Lady Muck lives here, as does the sculptor whose life-sized plastic elephant guards the border between us and them.

We are venturing into rival territory because we have befriended an English couple who have a holiday home in Kernelec. Their little stone cottage is everything one would hope for in its eye-pleasingness, and made more attractive by the sorely distressed property across the lane. The man who lives in it is clearly someone who likes to start projects and not finish them. Since we arrived, his cottage seems to become ever more distressed as bits are knocked down and not replaced. Even he has realised the threat of an imminent collapse, and the plastic elephant has recently been shifted to help support the sagging gable. This rearrangement has started a promising village feud, as the lady of the cottage opposite says she resents waking each morning to look out of her window and up an elephant's arse. Tonight she will be happy, as the blue elephant has been moved to provide a static ride for local children. Our dusk piper has been performing, and still cannot get the tune of the regional anthem right. The elephant man is putting on a marionette show, and guest of honour will be an exhibition of impromptu Morris dancing, put on by the holiday home-owning Brits. They are an unusual couple, even for these parts. With a suitably Dickensian name, Morley Friend is a man of huge size and heart, and with his rumpled, baggy clothing and giant, slow moving amiable bulk, he brings to mind the elephant across the road. He is clearly a man whose depth, sensitivity and understanding of the world match his size, though he likes to pretend otherwise. His sensitivity is probably why he so often hangs his head and sighs at the ironies and perversities of life and follies of Man and the former Milk Marketing Board.

Sue Friend could come from Central Casting as an apple-cheeked farmer's wife, and is as small and straightforward as her husband is vast and complex. The couple are dairy farmers who live in a remote part of Devon, and are in the painful process of handing the running of the farm over to their son. Upcott Farm has been in Friend hands for five generations and as retirement age approaches, it is time for Morley to step back. His health is not good, and like many vigorous and powerful men, he resents bitterly the depredations of age. Last week he let out a gale of a sigh, shook his great shaggy head and told me that if he were one of his own animals he would shoot himself.

Sunday 11th

I have misjudged Lady Muck. Far from being stuck up and xenophobic, she is just shy. She also does not like the job which occupies almost all her waking hours, which explains her preoccupied and distant air when she races by. Mary-Jo arrived at the kitchen door yesterday to see if we would like to buy a stake in one of her soon-to-be slaughtered steers. She was taking orders in advance, and would put our name on any parts not already spoken for. When I persuaded her to come in and risk an English coffee, she became quite talkative. After I had remarked how many people would envy her life, she said they might find it not as bucolically attractive as in slushy films and novels. Mary-Jo is the only child of Mr and Mrs Goarnisson, and felt she had no choice but take over the farm when her parents reached official retirement age. Contrary to what a lot of civilians think, she said, spending one's life up to the ankles in cow shit is not all it is cracked up to be. Waving as she drove off and back to a life she resents, I thought how easily we make assumptions based on our own beliefs or prejudices. When you are also communicating in a language which is foreign to one of you, it is even easier to jump to the wrong conclusions.

Monday 12th

We have been visiting the next-door department of Côtes d'Armor to view an isolated farmhouse and its almost inevitable gite 'complex' (usually code for one other building apart from the owners' accommodation). The premises are up for sale, and the indulgence of a spare designer home which nobody lives in may well be the reason.

A major challenge for many Britons buying a wreck in France is to discover how expensively they can turn the former pig sty, cattle byre or other unsuitable ruin into a guest house which will cost more to do up than it could earn from visitors in two lifetimes. I believe the real reason most Britons spend so much on gites is not because they believe them to be a commercial proposition, but so the women can have even more bathrooms and toilets to not use. I have noticed how the number of bathrooms in their new homes seems to be of increasingly crucial importance to British owners, and it is not uncommon for them to total more than the bedroom count. The property we are looking at has four bedrooms, five bathrooms, a shower room and three separate toilets. Apart from having become a place of thanksgiving to the local plumber, the property is said to be a real bargain; this usually means it will not be, for some undisclosed reason, but for us the journey is a good excuse to take the measure of the surrounding countryside.

Finistère is often likened to Cornwall, while Côtes d'Armor's undulating hills, vales and less dramatically craggy coastline calls Devon or Dorset to mind. It is a place of rolling green sward, fenceless fields and ancient deciduous woods and forests. This glorious setting naturally makes it a favourite buying place for Brits who think they would like to live in a place which reminds them of how they think England used to look. Côtes d'Armor also has the appeal of being the cheapest department for property, for which I have been unable to discover any other reason than common-or-garden snobbery.

From what we have seen, the views and coastline and weather and other pro and con factors in this department equal if not surpass those in the other three, but just as in Britain, unfathomable fashion sets the agenda and the house prices. It is interesting how Britons take their tribal prejudices and preferences with them, even or especially when buying or moving abroad. On the boat from Portsmouth, a slightly drunk property agent told me he could always tell in which part of Brittany his

British customers would buy just by looking at the make and vintage of their cars. Those pulling up in a convertible BMW or similarly flash car would most likely choose the coastal area of Morbihan, or swisher parts of Ille-et-Vilaine. Couples from the north of Britain who arrived in battered vans would like the look of property prices in Côtes d'Armor, while those crusty Brits favouring beards, lived-in clothing and even more lived-in Volvo estates would always be taken with Finistère. When I asked him where he thought we were bound for, he said my beard and decaying body-warmer were a dead giveaway, and he bet we had a Volvo on the car deck and were heading for the furthest reaches of the end of the earth. He was spot-on, but we also like the look of Côtes d'Armor, and especially the property prices.

Whatever we think of the farmhouse which is up for sale, it seems we will be spoiled for choice across the whole region. Thousands of very expensively restored and improved properties have recently been put up for sale by Britons who have realised that living in a foreign country is not for them. Sadly it is a common and usually very costly mistake to think it would be even better to live full time in a place that you love visiting for a couple of weeks a year.

There are a number of factors causing the current Dunkirk-like retreat of so many expatriate or second home-owning Britons. Some Brits are going home for purely financial reasons, which can be fairly blamed on the current recession. Others would have committed fiscal *hara-kiri* at any time by coming over to buy a modest holiday home then borrowing shedloads of foreign money for a much bigger and more expensive place.

Then there are those who fled to France to escape the bad bits about life in Britain only to discover how much they miss the good bits. There is no shame in finding that you do not like living in a foreign land, but it has become taboo for expatriates to admit it to other people - or even themselves. Health reasons or missing friends and family are the most common excuses for retreating Brits, and I know of those who have claimed marital breakdown rather than admit they just don't like living in France or with the French.

The couples who seem most successful in adapting to and even relishing living with the old enemy are those with strong relationships, enquiring minds and a generally philosophical outlook. Most valuable of all is a sense of humour and proportion, especially when accepting how differently and sometimes even badly things are done in your host country.

*

We will not be putting in an offer for the farmhouse. If the place was restored by British craftsmen, I think they must have been graduates of the Channel Crossing University of Construction. It is a standing joke that there is an office on board all ferry boats to Brittany and other French ports which offers instant certification in all building trades. Whether or not this is true, many Britons who wish to start a new working life in France board the ferry as graphic designers, car dealers, lorry drivers or aromatherapists, then disembark as allegedly expert plumbers, carpenters and general builders. I have seen some extreme examples of their work, and still have bad dreams.

Strangely, I have also seen even grosser acts of vandalism practiced by the people who own the properties than the dodgy Brit builders they might have employed. For while the instant converts to builderdom learn the ropes on other people's properties, some British home owners are happy to practice on their own. It can be traumatic for the visitor to see what horrors can be wrought by an enthusiastic amateur whose previous experience in DIY has been limited to screwing a shelf to a wall. Curiously, most of those afflicted by the compulsion to Do It Themselves Very Badly are, like the parents of ugly children, unable to see their handiwork as others do.

Apart from the appalling and often lethal standard of the work, the property we visited was not ideally located. Instantly identifiable as British-owned by its silly name, Les Deux Tournesols stands just up the road from a busy pig-rearing and slaughtering facility, though the owner assured us it is only noticeable when the wind comes from the east or the carcass lorry goes by every Thursday. Also, he felt obliged to point out that the garden behind the property belonged to someone in the next village who had gone on record as saying he would never sell it. What the owner's wife thought of their new home and life in rural France we could not tell, as the man looked wistfully out of the window for a while before saying she was in England visiting family and friends.

Sadly, this, as we have already learned, is often expat code for 'She's left me…'

*

Driving through a small town this morning I had to take to the pavement to avoid a vehicle charging out from a minor side road. It was coming from the right, so I was in the wrong. Had there been a stop sign, the driver would have been required to heave to and wait till the main road was clear before entering it. As the minor road was little more than an alleyway, had no cautionary markings and was virtually concealed by the communal Christmas tree which had been obviously kept and put there for camouflage purposes, the driver was entirely in his rights to charge out and dare me to collide with him.

This is because, in the land of Descartes, Simone de Beauvoir and a host of other big-hitting philosophers and allegedly logical thinkers, there exists an ancient yet unrepealed driving law so bizarre that even French drivers generally ignore it unless they are in a really bloody mood.

In essence, the law requires any 40-tonne Euro-lorry barrelling down a main road to give way to any vehicle emerging from any minor passageway to the right. As if the old *Priorité à Droite* code was not crazy enough, it also applies to some roundabouts. Not all, but some. In effect, that means that you have to give way to traffic joining one of these roundabouts rather than vehicles already on it. The situation is further complicated by most French drivers ignoring or not knowing the law, but others calling it into play depending on the situation, local custom and the driver's mood at that moment.

Officially, any communes exercising their right to employ the old priority-to-the-right ruling must say so in the form of a prominently displayed notice. In fact, most are carefully hidden or placed in the most obscure positions, to be seen only after the visitor has passed through the danger zone. The advice given to foreign drivers is to be prepared to respect the current priority usage when on a main road, but not to expect others to respect it when they are coming out of a side road. In the case of this morning's incident, the attacking vehicle was an ambulance. It could be that the driver was a stickler for tradition, that the mayor of this town has decided to observe the old law on alternate weekdays, or that the ambulance was merely touting for trade.

*

The jewel in the tourist crown of Côtes d'Armor, Lake Guerlédan is the largest stretch of inland water in Brittany, and looks it. Its electricity-generating powers were created in the 1930s by flooding the valley where the Nantes to Brest canal meets the Blavet river. Together with four hundred hectares of woodland, a number of houses and lock-keeper's cottages were swallowed up in the process, providing an ideal opportunity for local tourist officials and other interested parties to hint at ghostly sights and sounds emanating from beneath the waters. More credible stories surround the founding of the Cistercian abbey of Bon Repos, which sits alongside the canal at the western end of Lake Guerlédan. Here are staged regular regional events and sometimes really spectacular *son et lumière* spectacles. Close by, Les Forges des Salles is in a much better state of preservation, and was an entire village devoted to the art and practice of blacksmithery. Surrounding the lake and its miles of walks and cycle tracks is one of the biggest private forests in Brittany.

Facing the ruined abbey on the other side of the canal is what comes close in my book to being the perfect bar. Until last year it was owned by an eccentric (even for Brittany) Breton who made a unilateral declaration of independence and claimed his bar to be the official hostelry of the principality of Bon Repos. I do not think there were any tax, duty free or other advantages to the scheme, as he opened and shut exactly when he liked and seemed completely immune to infection by modern customer service principles.

We thought he would be a very hard act to follow, but the new owners are equally as eccentric in a different way. Madame restricts her self-expression mainly to purple hair and some beguiling combinations of short skirts and heavy boots, but the patron is particularly interesting. Working from a kitchen alongside and no bigger than the unisex toilet, he offers hundreds of dishes and daily specials, each with his own signature styling. He also demonstrates his artistic sensibilities by a penchant for white see-through tops and trousers, and, set free, his hair would reach his waist. He also smokes a cigarette more creatively than any Frenchman I have seen, and that is saying something. Unusually for a rural French bar, he also serves snacks. On our last visit, my wife's slice of *gâteau de fromage blanc* was garnished with a segment of tangerine, three sculpted grapes, two currants and a drizzle of raspberry sauce. Sticking in the top as the *pièce de résistance* was something like a miniature cheerleader's razzle-stick.

Although a pale imitation of British-bred cheesecake in taste, it was a rare treat, as the serving of snacks in many rural French bars is regarded by their owners as akin to dealing in class 'A' drugs. It is my wife's theory that the disinterest in coffee and cake breaks is what keeps older French women so noticeably slim, and examples of their abstinence are everywhere. There is a very traditional Breton bar and restaurant in the grounds of Le Relec, and each day of the summer dozens of coaches laden with mostly middle-aged or older ladies arrive in the car park. After walking around the abbey and grounds, the ladies push their way past the seating outside the bar and climb on board the coach. In England, there would be quite intense hand-to-hand fighting to win a place at table for the holy rite and right of huge slices of carrot and cheesecake with a cup of tea or coffee.

Recently, we were given a classic demonstration of this cultural phenomenon. Every day, the bar and restaurant at Brennilis serves hundreds of superb lunches. It was towards the end of the lunchtime session and my wife was feeling hungry, so I asked if there was any cake to go with our coffee. The owner - normally a kindly and affable man - looked as if I had asked if he would like to buy some dirty pictures of his wife, and said rather curtly that there was no cake available. A few minutes later, a lady customer emerged from the restaurant area to pay her bill. As we left, the owner asked pointedly if Madame had enjoyed her cake. He did not add that she had eaten it for dessert in the proper place at the proper time, but what he meant was clear. Things are changing even in France *profonde*, but it is good to see some old habits dying so hard.

*

With its nose-in-the-air stance, Mûr-de-Bretagne looks out of place in the most down-to-earth county of Brittany. Although solidly built there is an ineffable air of upmarketness about the town which reminds me of a twee village in the Cotswolds. Contributing to this air of comfortable middle-classness is a very good English bookshop and coffee house in the shadow of the church, where the owner is still recovering from our request for a cup of coffee of the instant variety.

There is an evening market at Mûr during the summer months, with the expected top-end comestibles on sale around the square and most of the shops staying open more than usually late. A mixture of pop and traditional Breton music comes from local bands, and the end of the season is marked by a grand *grillade* barbecue. Another suitably trendy feature of Mûr is that the tower of the church is used to teach abseiling.

Further along the edge of the great lake is the village of Caurel, where there is a very well-stocked and satisfyingly old-fashioned English grocery store. It is very popular with British expatriates, though some are said to pick their orders up under the cover of darkness. It has long puzzled and irritated me how Britons living abroad are supposed to give up their favourite foodstuffs for fear of ridicule and condemnation by the chattering classes. The same people actively encourage settlers in Britain to pursue the traditions and preferences of their home country, and would be horrified at the thought of a French person living in England developing a taste for sliced white bread and Marmite. But the idea of a British expat seeking out proper baked beans and peanut butter spread is for some reason viewed with

48

contempt and even horror by those who like to tell us what we should eat and drink as well as what we should think.

*

Like other mid-range Breton towns, I think Pontivy would be a pleasant place to live if you were old or young. It is big enough to have all the facilities you need at each end of the age spectrum and the town has a comfortably refined but non-snotty feel about it. This is probably down to the quality and tone of the ancient buildings and modern shops ranged around the medieval walkways. A huge bonus to Pontivy's appeal is that it sits on a confluence of canal and riverways and boasts a really classy fortified *château*. As any tourist knows, there are castles and castles, but the one at Pontivy is the real deal and looks and feels as if it means business. Work started on the fortress in the 17th century at the behest of one of the great Lords of Rohan. I cannot report if the inside matches the exterior, as on the day we called it was shut for lunch. A minute before two o' clock I followed a pretty young woman through the small door beside the great gates, but found myself in the staff toilets rather than the courtyard.

Leaving Pontivy we passed through Loudéac, and, by and large, that seems to us to be the best thing to do.

For absolutely no good reason, we find this central Côtes d'Armor town depressive and oppressive. It might be that our two visits were on a bad day for the town or us, but on the first occasion we were so menaced by a group of drunken yobs that we felt we had been teleported back to Britain. The next time we got much less than a warm welcome in a bar, and saw not a single Loudéacan smile during our time there. As all restaurateurs quickly learn, one bad experience is all it takes to put a visitor off. This should not apply to a whole town and we will give Loudéac a third chance, but not in the near future. For those who want to see how wrong I have it, there are five major horseracing events each year and a considerable forest near to hand to explore. Each Easter the Palais de Congress et Culture is transformed into Jerusalem for the Passion of Loudéac, so someone obviously feels strongly positive about the town.

Wednesday 14th

There is often something about the eyes of survivors of wars or tragedies. Whether they want to or not, they still must look back and recall the horrors. This preoccupied and even haunted look is also found on the faces of some Britons who have decided to run a pub or restaurant in France. Sometimes they also wear the expression of someone who has just realised it is not a good idea to put your hand in a chip pan to see if the oil is boiling yet.

Of all strange and inexplicable compulsions, taking on a pub or eating-place abroad seems right up there with self-mutilation. Who in their right mind would come up with the idea of starting a business in which they had absolutely no experience, and in a foreign land to boot? Then there is the slight handicap of not speaking the language, and the fact that pubs and restaurants head the bankruptcy lists of French enterprises when run by French people, let alone foreigners. There is a saying amongst embittered Britons who have set up shop in France that the best way to make a small fortune in this country is to start with a large one, and nowhere is this more apt or applicable than when trying to make a go of a bar or restaurant here or in any foreign land.

My wife and I know what the true cost of running a pub on either side of the Channel can be, and Donella is under strict instructions to hit me very hard with the nearest blunt instrument if I even mention the idea of taking on another licensed business. But, as I said to her this morning while she eyed a nearby lump hammer, it does no harm to look, and we owe a duty to my readers to consider all sorts of businesses taken on by Brits in Brittany.

The pub for sale is in a village remote even by rural Brittany standards, and comes complete with spacious accommodation, a large garden, several spectacularly distressed barns, a grocery shop and the garage and service station next door. Behind the workshop is a former ballroom still equipped with mirrored glitterball, and allegedly used by the French Resistance for covert meetings during the Second World War. Another intriguing piece of information not included in the property information details but passed on by the current owner is that a number of German officers went out of the back door of the ballroom with pretty local girls and never returned. The all-in asking price for all the properties and potential businesses is less than a hundred thousand Euros. The proprietor is a down-to-earth Scot who had run successful country pubs in England. Over a beer he told us candidly that when he took the place over he could just about get by on the twenty regular customers the bar attracted. In the last three years, several of his thirstiest punters had died, and with it his bar business. All the motorists in the village went to the local supermarket for cheap petrol, and as his wife refused to learn how to be a motor mechanic at 68, he could offer no other services at the service station.

Saturday 24th

Anglo-Info is a very popular website franchise which provides information and contacts for those Brits wishing to move to or buy property in different regions of France. The Brittany version is particularly well-run and useful, though you might not want to share a cab with many of the regular forum users. Like most on-line clubrooms, this part of the site is dominated by a sometimes breathtakingly opinionated clique. Most of them have obviously learned to type but not to think. To enter the forum on most of these sites is akin to pushing open the door of an unfamiliar village pub and hear silence descend as the debating society at the bar turn to look down their noses at you, the intruder. The irony is that as well as being contemptuous of visitors, the members of these cabals seem to dislike each other and their opinions even more.

Asking a simple question about how to register a British car in France will result in a dozen contradictory replies before the senders abandon the point of the exercise and descend into a verbal punch-up

There are, however, pearls to be found in the accounts of those expats or holiday home owners who have fallen foul of an ordnance from the make-it-up-as-we-go-along department of their local town hall. This morning I came across a corker from a bemused Brit who related how, some years before, he and his wife had applied for permission to erect a shed in their back garden in Morbihan. The okay was duly given, and the couple got as far as laying the concrete base before being distracted by other more pressing matters. Recently, they decided to finish the job off, and anxious to go by the letter of the law, contacted the town hall to ensure all was well with their intentions. Back came the reply that the couple could not in fact put the shed on the concrete base, as their garden had been declared a nature reserve.

*

We have set a first by weeding a stretch of water.

According to our landlady, the previous owner drained the big pond to claim his fish before leaving. Grass seeds had taken root before it was re-filled, and, now the growing season has begun, it looks like a neglected paddy-field.

After hearing the owner's cautionary tales about the muddy depths and finding a single Wellington boot rooted in the shallows, we tried a number of solutions. An improvised raft sank before I got aboard, and a pair of garden shears tied to a broomstick proved unsatisfactory as a long-distance pruner. After much practice, we found a garden rake with a length of rope tied to the handle did the trick. It was inevitable that our nearest neighbour would appear just as I was casting the device at a dense patch of zoysia grass by the inlet channel. After watching me haul in the line and untangle my catch from the tines of the rake, he shook his head, adjusted his cap and went off to tell the other residents of Lesmenez about the curious manner in which the English like to fish.

Monday 26th

Our village now has its own Rites of Spring celebration, and I am the unintentional creator.

I don't know who counted them or how, but impeccable sources have it that there are around a ton of earthworms for every acre of soil in Britain. Each year they pass ten tons of soil through their bodies, though the report does not say if that is in total or each.

Aristotle described them as the intestines of the earth, and Darwin thought that few creatures had played such an important part in the history of our planet as the lowly earthworm. As well as being amazingly industrious, the earthworm can put an ant to shame for feats of strength, and can shift stones up to sixty times its own weight.

This may be so, but it would be some sort of earthworm which could take on the granite rocks lying just below the surface in this part of Brittany. I dug up at least sixty times my bodyweight to make our vegetable patch, and this may be the reason that the chicken compound seems to be a no-go area for worms. Yesterday evening I tried an old fishermen's trick by laying a sheet of plywood on the ground and jumping up and down on it. Worms, like moles, are said to be attracted by vibration and sound, so I accompanied my foot stamping with a burst of Walking the Dog on my blues harmonica.

It was of course inevitable that our nearest neighbour would arrive to see what was going on, and equally inevitable that he would show me the proper Breton way to jump up and down. Our combined efforts attracted our part-time neighbour and Parisian Mr Vitre, who despatched his wife to fetch a bottle of wine and alert the rest of the village that there was a party going on. An hour later and the home-made cider and bootleg apple brandy was flowing, we had been joined by the Breton bagpiper and Lesmenez was staging its first *Fest Noz*.

Dancing Lessons:

For those not familiar with the event, a Fest Noz ('Festival of the Night') is a sort of barn dance without the barn. And often without the dancing, come to that. The tradition dates back to at least the Middle Ages, and its origins and purpose are unclear. Mind you, given the amount of drink that is consumed at these bashes, that is not surprising. Officially, it is thought that the event was to mark and celebrate the completion of a new house. The owners would invite their neighbours to a shindig as a thank-you for their help on the building, and also to act as a sort of mass human steamroller. When everyone had drowned their inhibitions with copious draughts of home-brew firewater, it was time for the ceremonial Fest Noz dance. This was quite literally a knees-up, with no formal steps or intentions other than jumping up and down a lot on the spot. The crafty part was that as well as being good fun, the repeated impact of several dozen pairs of clog-clad feet on the earth floor made it instantly fit for purpose.

To spur the guests on to (literally) greater heights in this ancient forerunner of punk pogo-dancing, everyone was supplied with unlimited quantities of chouchenn. What Ancient Brits probably knew as mead, this innocuous-sounding but lethal infusion is basically fermented honey and water. Sometimes the brew was livened up with cider, and often with the corpses of the bees themselves to add to the texture and taste. The result was an interesting concoction which weighed in at (at least) 14 percent alcohol by volume.

When you think that the average beer or cider would be around 4-5 percent strength, you can see how a pint or two would encourage the guests to jump about with some abandon. Having tasted the stuff, I reckon it also had another valuable function. Any leftovers could be thinned down a bit and used as glue to waterproof the roof of the new building.

Franco Files

It is not recorded how many expatriate Brits try to start a business in France, but there is a better (or worse) than 90 percent failure rate, and most fail in the first year.

More people visit France on holiday than inhabit England.

A recent academic investigation identified 43 gestures made uniquely by the French.

An Internet survey registered 3579 people who said they hated the French. The figure for those hating the English was more than 4000. Only 756 German-haters bothered to register.

Home cooking

Without wishing to sound too Little Britain-ish, I have to say that the Bretons (or the French in general, for that matter) do not seem big on the complexity or variety of their regional pastries and cakes. In England we can choose from Bakewell tarts,

Eccles cakes and Bath and Chelsea buns, and in my home county of Hampshire there's the wonderfully accurately entitled lardy cake. In Brittany, there is *Kouign-Amann*. In the practical way the Bretons like to identify things and places, this translates as cake of butter, which pretty well nails the contents. It is straightforward to make, and in taste terms very nice and… buttery, and rather like our lardy cake without the lard.

Ingredients

1lb of plain flour
A sachet of baker's yeast
12 oz softened butter
One lightly beaten egg yolk
Some sugar
Salt to taste
Some tepid water

Method

Mix flour, yeast and salt and add some tepid water to make dough. Shape into a ball, cover and leave in a warm place to rise (usually around half an hour).Using the heel of your hand, fashion the dough into a sort of pizza base circle of about a foot across. Spread half the butter on the surface, leaving an unbuttered border.Fold in the four edges to make a square and press to seal, then leave the dough in a cool place for another half an hour.Roll the dough out and spread on the remaining butter and fold again. Brush the top with the egg yolk and sprinkle on some sugar. Place on a baking sheet and cook in a preheated oven at 220°C/425°F or gas mark 7 for half an hour, when the top should be caramelized and nicely browned off. Serve warm with a nice cup of tea or shot of bootleg apple brandy.

Close-up on Côtes d'Armor

A tad larger than Finistère yet with not much more than half the inhabitants and a head count of just 79 people per square kilometre, this is the most sparsely populated department in

Brittany. A place of undulating, wooded greenery and great lakes, there are parts of Côtes d'Armor where you can drive for many a mile and see no sign of human habitation. You are also not likely to see too many pigs or chickens scratching around as they will be confined to the giant *élevages* or rearing barns which are a hallmark of the county. As the name suggests (*Armor* is old Breton for 'the sea'), the county has a long and spectacular coastline, and there are many tucked-away coves and inlets that time and tourists seem to have overlooked. The county town is St-Brieuc, an interesting mix of ancient and modern architecture which overlooks the eponymous bay. Here there is a huge nature reserve and long and leg-stretching rambling paths. The climate in Côtes d'Armor is virtually the same as in the neighbouring department of Finistère, and property is reckoned to be cheaper here than anywhere else in Brittany. This area has its own particular surnames, and in Brittany many were physically descriptive rather than occupational or geographic. A common name in Côtes d'Armor is LeMoal, which means bald. My wife's ancestors come from Guingamp and were Moals, and looking at the lack of hair on the male side of her family, you can see how genes travel through time. I recently met a Breton whose name roughly translates as Big Willy. I followed him to the toilets after a couple of beers, but have to report that the poor chap seems to have missed out on his rightful inheritance.

June

Plounéour-Ménez, Pleyber-Christ, Morlaix, Brest, Le Conquet, Plouyé

Our nearest town is Plounéour-Ménez. 'Menez' is Breton for mountain, and 'Plounéour' is Breton for Plounéour.

It is a comfortable, sturdy and unflappable place with three bars, a betting shop and tobacconist, a chemist's shop and bakery. This shows it has got its priorities right for the average Breton country dweller. For more frivolous shopping needs, locals and people in the surrounding settlements need to travel elsewhere.

Five miles across country from our hamlet and straddling the main route to Roscoff's ferry port, Pleyber-Christ is twinned with Lostwithiel in Cornwall. I have known of sleepy fishing ports in the south of France matched with sprawling coal mining towns in the midlands, and often wonder what criteria is used when the jumelage committees decide on who they wish to link with, and why. In the case of Pleyber-Christ and Lostwithiel, however, I would say the committees got it just about right comparison-wise.

Both are unremarkable and even, in places, pug-ugly towns. Both have a population of around three thousand, and both find themselves in the way of a constant stream of heavy traffic which wishes to be elsewhere.

With an almost straight face, Lostwithiel claims to be Cornwall's hidden treasure, which is the line that desperate tourist bosses come up with when they can think of absolutely nothing positive to say about a place. Pleyber-Christ has, as far as I know, no advertising slogan. If it did, it might be something like 'A Great Place To Pass Through'.

But, as with some people, if you ignore first impressions there is much of value to be found beneath an indifferent facade. With its range of shops and down-to-earth attitude to getting on with life in a rural area, I would think Pleyber a pleasant enough place in which to live or do business. The town also has a savagely effective arrangement for gaining revenge on motorists who are passing through and not stopping to spend money.

As with so many areas of activity, there is a strange ambivalence in the French authorities' attitude towards speeding and those who practice it. Unlike the tradition in Britain, drivers in France are always warned when approaching a speed camera. This shows they have been put there to achieve their alleged function of slowing traffic down rather than acting as sneaky and huge revenue-earners. On the downside, those who make the rules of the road like to play some funny games with drivers entering a restricted speed zone.

The thousands of cars and Euro-juggernauts approaching Pleyber from the south at full breakneck speed every day find themselves suddenly presented with a 70kph sign, and ten yards beyond that a sleeping policeman almost as tall as some standing French coppers I have seen. Distracted by struggling to regain control of the vehicle and staunch the blood flow from the top of his or her head, it would be hard for any driver to spot the 50kph sign immediately beyond the hump. Spotting it is made even more unlikely as it is positioned on the other side of the road and facing the wrong way. Every other Monday, the same shapely young policewoman hides behind a poster hoarding just beyond the sign with her camera gun at the ready, and must pay for her wages a hundred times over in that single shift. There is a sort of natural justice to the arrangement, as locals know that she will be there and often exchange waves and pleasantries as they chug by. Those just passing through must pay the price of falling into the carefully constructed trap. We have already been caught out, and know that the only safe time to go over the limit here is between noon and two, when the lady and every other law enforcement officer in the area will be taking lunch.

A dramatic if ineffective attempt to get drivers to think about the consequences of bad and mad driving can be seen in the grim black silhouettes standing on the verge facing oncoming traffic. Each shape of man, woman or child represents someone killed in a road accident at that spot. These figures appear at roadsides across the nation, and are most poignant when a whole family of cut-outs is clustered forlornly and eternally together.

Today, we are passing at a suitably slow pace through Pleyber-Christ to visit the weekly market and look at a house for sale in one of our favourite small-big towns in France.

If the ancient town of Morlaix were a woman, I think she might be a sophisticated, elderly but still game former university lecturer in fine art. Madame Morlaix would have a very developed sense of style and presence, a bit of a past, and a penchant for smoking the odd spliff.

Sitting at the end (or beginning if you think that way) of an estuary opening on to the north west coast, Morlaix has an unusual and rather twee inland port. Once upon a time, the medieval quay allowed barges to pick up and discharge their cargoes for and from Paris. Nowadays, the old tobacco factory is a trendy business centre overlooking an even trendier marina. Posh yachts pass through the lock gates when the tide is right, and make their way into the great bay named for the town. The Rade de Morlaix is dotted with islands bearing forts, very exclusive homes and what the local tourist board claims to be the tallest lighthouse in all France. The tourist board representing the lighthouse on the Île Vierge along the coast a bit would beg to differ. Along the shorelines are thriving oyster farms, a number of interesting villages with restaurants specialising unsurprisingly in food from the sea, and some belting coastal path and clifftop walks.

Back the other way, trains run over the soaring viaduct which overlooks some near-perfect examples of unspoiled *colombage* beam-and-plaster-fronted buildings around the old market square. From the town centre, cobbled lanes or *venelles* climb woozily and steeply up to the surrounding heights.

Morlaix got an early taste of booze-cruising Brits in 1522, when an English raiding party sacked the town. According to legend, the raiders gained entry by dressing the most attractive of their number as women, who talked their way through the gates and let the rest in while the guards were admiring what they thought were the comparatively hairless legs and underarms sported by English females.

Obviously already knowing a bit about the British attitude to and tolerance for strong drink, the surviving locals waited until the raiders drank themselves insensible, then killed them all. This encounter is said to be the origin of the town's motto, which is along the lines of Bite Us and we Bite Back.

Nowadays, Morlaix is more welcoming to British visitors, and obviously a town very much at ease with itself. Its artiness rating is almost off the scale and indicated by the number of older men wearing carefully cultivated apparently uncultivated beards, pony tails, voluminous overcoats and interesting hats. Many of the older women dress as artfully, but most eschew the beards. Morlaix also continues the peculiar Breton tradition of having more lookalikes to the square kilometre than any other region of France. So far today we have been served coffee by Robbie Williams, bought a newspaper from Sacha Distel and seen Jo Brand and Graham Norton indulging in some heavy petting on a bench outside the public toilets.

It is a rare interlude when there are not several concerts, exhibitions and other festivals and celebrations of the arts happening around the town, and every Saturday, Morlaix stages what is acknowledged by many to be the biggest and best market in the department. On that day there will also be a variety of artistic happenings and at least a couple of protests and demonstrations to entertain market–goers. Last week, I sat on the terrace of a café in the square as a jazz band arrived by vintage charabanc. While they were belting out a Gallicised version of Muskrat Ramble, a stunningly beautiful young woman in a bridal costume and long veil appeared at the entrance to the Town Hall. She watched the band for a moment, then threw her bouquet at a startled passer-by, picked up her skirts and ran off through the stalls. This being Morlaix and France, it could have been an artistic event or an act of pure and genuine impulse, and I am saddened that I will never know the reason for the lady's spirited sprint, or how the story ended.

While here we will be looking for bargains at market, though the opposite will apply to the majority of visitors. Of all regional markets I know, Morlaix is a classic example of how the French will pay wildly varying prices for the same thing, depending on where they buy it. No motorist would dream of paying over the odds for a litre of fuel because the petrol station was in a trendy area, yet market shoppers happily pay through their noses for goods which would be half the price in a supermarket just down the road.

Smiling apologetically at a succession of ever-optimistic and very tall black men selling bongo drums, and short Bretons selling horrendously expensive berets, we make our way to a narrow alleyway in the least fashionable area of the town centre. Ignored by those who like to pay over-the-odds for an item, this small corner is favoured by those who, like us, delight in paying the least. It has not yet become chic to treasure-hunt for fashionable labels in charity shops here, though the melee around the line of tables heaped with clothing shows that violence amongst bargain hunters is not confined to British shoppers.

*

It says something of the general uninquisitivity levels of the French and the cosmopolitan nature of this town that nobody gives a second glance at a man strolling through the market square on a warm spring day in a fully quilted, day-glo orange ski suit complete with gloves, goggles, bobble hat and Hannibal Lecter style plastic mask. Being half-Scottish and fully mean, I love a bargain and, in the opposite way to a Gallic price snob, will buy something just because it is ridiculously cheap though I neither want nor need it. I have no plans to go on any alpine activity holidays in the near future, but it gets very cold in the mountains here and a top quality winter ensemble for twenty Euros is an offer I could not possibly refuse.

As we reach the car, I see I am not alone in the high-profile clothing stakes, and nominate a passing lady for our Pussy Pelmet of the Month award. It is yet another French paradox that while the rest of the world acknowledges their country as prime leader and opinion former in all matters of style and fashion, millions of rural and provincial French women would be barred from joining the Dolly Parton Appreciation Society on the grounds of the vulgarity of their dress, hair, make-up and overall appearance. In the same way that so many provincial French businessmen think a lime jacket, orange shirt, blue tie and persimmon slacks represent the epitome of subtle colour co-ordination and style, a lot of French women like to dress as if for a Vicars and Tarts fancy dress party.

This month's short-odds contender for the title is a lady who will not see forty again. While probably a perfectly decent woman and loving mother and perhaps grandmother, she is dressed like a rebellious teenager who wants to send her parents into cardiac arrest. The white floor-length, fur-trimmed plastic overcoat has been left open to reveal a belt masquerading as a skirt above a pair of black, thigh length shiny boots with huge platform soles. The lady is also more adorned with baubles and shiny things than an overdressed Christmas tree, though none of them is actually flashing. The number of rings on each finger makes it hard for her to hold her brace of mobile phones to her ears. Somehow she is having a conversation with two people at the same time, and possibly wants all passers-by to know that she has more than one friend.

As a visual antidote and as if to demonstrate the contradiction in terms of style that is France, a young woman passes us on her way in to a bar. She is wearing an army greatcoat over denim trousers rolled carelessly up to mid-calf above highly polished hiking boots. On her head is a blue beret worn at a coquettish angle, and the bobbled ends of a matching scarf trail in her wake. From a shoulder hangs a voluminous and obviously elderly Gladstone bag of classy leather. Her entire ensemble could have been bought for a handful of Euros from the cheap stall we have just left, but she makes it and herself look a million dollars.

*

In any historic town centre in southern England, the house we are looking at today would be valued at more than half a million pounds. In some areas of London, the asking price would be a couple of million. Here in Morlaix, the going rate for a characterful four-storey, three-hundred-year-old former merchant's home is below that of a beach hut in some parts of Cornwall.

Things are changing, and *le mortgage* has become a familiar fixture for young couples, but in general the French have not become as obsessed with property as the British. The transition stage has caused some interesting inconsistencies, with the typical street a mixture of trendily done-up houses and long-neglected wrecks held upright by their neighbours.

The house we have been looking at falls between the two types, and is proof that even though they have been at it for a much shorter time, the French can be as bad at DIY as the most creatively incompetent Briton. A good example is the mouth-watering 15th-century front door with oversized hinges and studwork into which the owner has fitted a modern metal letterbox and one of those weird oriental-style hanging cowbells which were all the rage in Britain in the 1970s.

Inside, the house continues the same awkward fusion of classic architectural features embellished with more modern fittings. It also doubles as a war museum. The owner is a tall and strangely intense young man clad entirely in black, and every room of the house is filled with memorabilia of World War II, or rather memorabilia of the uniforms and weapons of one side. In the hallway is a mannequin dressed in the uniform of a German stormtrooper, and in the downstairs toilet I find myself eye to eye with the Fuhrer in life-size poster form.

As we leave I say to the owner that his door would be worth at least a thousand Euros in any antique shop in London. He raises an elegant eyebrow and offers to fetch a screwdriver and sell it to me at half that price. Laughing, I lift my arm to bid him a cheery farewell and acknowledge his joke. As if in instinctive response, he starts to raise his hand skywards with fingers rigidly extended, then looks around almost guiltily, lowers his arm and contents himself with a click of heels, a nod and the thinnest of smiles.

Tuesday 3rd

A close encounter with Farmer Grumpy and his even more disgruntled dog this morning. Guiltily avoiding eye contact with a veal calf as I walked down to the stone cross to give the fox breakfast, I saw that all entrances to the fields alongside the lane had been sealed off with lengths of blue string. This happens when a transfer of cattle is about to take place, and the string is to make sure the half-ton creatures do not stray from the planned course. Some of the entrances and gaps in hedges were double-stringed, so there was probably going to be a particularly bad-tempered bull with the herd.

Farmer Grumpy is young, but has the fully-developed misanthropic attitudes of a much older man. Pope John XXIII is said to have said that men are like wine, with some improving with age and some becoming vinegar. Farmer Grumpy seems to have gone straight to the vinegar stage. As I found out recently, as well as suffering permanently with a bad back, he is also a bachelor. It is one of life's ironies that so many men are unhappy because they are not married and thus cannot know how much more miserable they might be if they were.

Apart from sealing off fields and keeping trousers up, another use for the magic blue twine is to hold old or damaged farm machinery and vehicles together. Yards of it have been used on Farmer Grumpy's old Renault, the most decrepit and abused car I have seen which still lives. Most farms are graveyards for dead cars, but the curious thing about this vehicle is that the author of the life-threatening injuries to the car is its owner, and I believe few of them to be accidental. If there were a law against the abuse and maltreatment of motor cars, Farmer Grumpy would now be doing a life sentence without the option. There is not an inch of the surface of the Renault which has not been kicked, beaten or otherwise damaged by being driven into a suitably immoveable object. I do not think for a moment Jean-Luc mistreats his animals, and he certainly seems to think more of his cows than the rest of humanity. I suspect that, like a Gallic Basil Fawlty, he takes out his dissatisfaction with his life in general on the car. There are also other manifestations of our neighbour's discontent with his situation and status, and what he considers the reason for it.

Alongside the road leading down to our hamlet is a very big and rusty water tank, upon which Farmer Grumpy has painted some not very complimentary comments about British beef.

When we first passed his cottage and waved, he turned his back on us. When I walked by with Milly a week later, his dog rushed out and attacked her. If anything, the cross-collie appeared more unsociable than its master, and is one of the very few dogs to have snarled at me as if he really meant it. It was not until I mentioned these incidents to Alain that I learned Jean-Luc and his dog are misanthropes rather than xenophobes. It is not that they do not like foreigners and especially British foreigners; they simply do not like anyone.

Thursday 5th

This morning I drove past a field in which a man dressed as a pirate was serenading a pile of burning leaves with an alto saxophone. I could have pulled over and asked him why, but I feared there may just have been a mundane explanation which would have spoiled the moment completely.

*

We have been lost for an hour and do not have a clue where we are, so the people responsible for directional road signage in this area can feel pleased with a job well done.

An important thing to remember as a visiting driver is that the basic raison d'être of all road signs in France is to confuse rather than inform. I do not make the accusation lightly, and am allowing for the fact that all motorists complain about road signage in their own as well as other countries. Like accusing your wife of holding the road map upside down, blaming misleading or non-existent road signs is a convenient way of shifting the blame. But, in France, whoever is in charge of telling drivers where to go is either awesomely incompetent or heads a committee charged with ensuring that all signs either mislead or completely confuse.

A classic example is the Primrose Path Syndrome. This is where you are assured every fifty metres that you are on the right road to your destination, then the information is suddenly withdrawn when you get to a roundabout or the rural French equivalent of Spaghetti Junction.

Even more annoying are the signs which can't make up their mind the way they should be pointing. It must take ages to fiddle with all those millions of directional placards until they are in exactly the right position to confuse and misdirect the victim.

Another extremely irritating thing is the way that more means so much less in road sign terms here. If there is the slightest excuse to put up a superfluous sign, the French will take it, especially if they work for the Department of the Very Bleedin' Obvious. Where else would you have a sign warning drivers entering a motorway that it is illegal to do a three point turn and then drive in the opposite direction against all the oncoming traffic on your side of the crash barriers? In the same way, the authorities also think it necessary to put a similar sign up to tell those already on the motorway that it does not recommend them doing a sudden U-turn and driving up the slip road against any oncoming traffic.

Friday 6th

More evidence that it is not only the locals who are eccentric. We were invited to tea today by a Briton and his partner, who live contentedly in an even smaller hamlet than Lesmenez. What makes the former Northumbrian coal miner qualify as being a bit off-centre is that his chosen partner in domestic quietude is an alpine goat. I do not think there is anything perverse about the relationship, and our new friend says she is good company, eats anything she is offered, and is certainly more easy on the eye than his former wife. Our host has also recently adopted a Highland ram, just so that he can introduce it as Colin, the black sheep of the family...

Monday 9th

The French have a saying about an unwanted visitor turning up like a hair in the soup, and our nearest neighbour has a way of appearing just as I am doing something he will enjoy criticising. This morning I was finishing off a new bird table when Alain arrived with his poking stick poised for action. All Breton countrymen beyond a certain age carry one, and Alain takes his hazel cane everywhere. The home-help lady who looks after him says he sleeps with it.

As an anteater uses its tongue to gauge the promise of an old tree trunk, elderly countrymen use their poking sticks to investigate anything new or unfamiliar, or of which they do not approve or think may be suspect. When I am doing some rough carpentry or running repairs to the outside of one of the buildings, our neighbour will invariably appear at my shoulder, look at my handiwork with deep distrust, then poke it with his stick. Usually he will poke it in exactly the right spot to make it collapse. Having achieved his self-fulfilling prophecy, he will sniff, look down at the ruins of my work and tell me how it should have been done. After demolishing my bird table with a single poke this morning, he asked if I would like some acorns for my window sill to keep the storm away. At least, that is what I think he said. I hope Alain has not had a stroke, but in the last week it has become increasingly difficult to understand him. He has turned the rules and usages of regional pronunciation upside down by enunciating all the letters in any word like a native of the Languedoc. When he talks about tomorrow, the usual northern French *demah* becomes *demayne*, and when he wants us to pick up a loaf of bread from town, it is not *du pah* but *du payne*.

When I looked at the sky and said the weather forecaster on TV had said nothing about a storm and I would anyway prefer a lightning conductor to a handful of nuts to protect our home, he grunted grimly and stumped away in a very you'll-be-sorry way.

Tuesday 10th

As I should have been able to predict, the officially unforecast storm arrived last night. We sat up and watched in awe as the Breton gods of the air fought a pitched battle over the mountains. The three-storey-high pines in our patch of woodland swayed and danced like whirling Dervishes but stayed upright. We have been without power all day as a surge after a giant clap of thunder has melted the fuse board. Worse, it travelled through the telephone line and has eaten most of the insides of my computer. We had to go over to Alain's house to use his phone and call for assistance. While there, I told him I had changed my mind and would be most grateful for a handful of his acorns for our window sill.

Thursday 12th

I am making an unsteady way home, and the reason for my meandering gait is that I have been involved in a friendly neighbourly ambush. One of my favourite local bars is called the Embuscade, and it is a very suitable name for a pub which specialises in lock-ins.

Apart from Alain LeGoff and the Parisian holiday-home owner, our only other neighbours in the lane leading to the mountains and moors are retired farmer Jean-Yves Madec and his wife.

Jean-Yves has lived in Lesmenez since almost before the handful of cottages became an official hamlet. At eighty-six, he is the senior member of our community, but only by a couple of years. He has a perfectly round and friendly face with a countryman's roseate complexion, and looks as fit and sturdily built as a man thirty years younger. These attributes he puts down to a lifetime of hard work on the land, and regular infusions of good food and red wine. Nowadays, he needs a stick to get about and is profoundly deaf, but bears his handicaps with dignity and fortitude. Jean's wife is restricted to her bed, and although his children and grandchildren visit regularly, I feel he is sometimes lonely. I see him at the window when I take Milly for a walk on the moors, and I know his much-loved collie died a few years ago. His quiet fortitude is good for me, as whenever we meet and I complain of a twinge or inconvenience, he just looks at me steadily with his faded blue eyes and I am reminded of how comparatively healthy and lucky I am.

The cause of my downfall this evening has been an introduction to the Breton version of moonshine apple brandy. In Normandy, where they claim to have invented it, the legal distillation is called Calvados, and the far rougher and much, much cheaper bootleg variety is known as *calva* or simply *goût*, as in 'taste'. This is either a complete misnomer or an in-joke, as a few glasses of the really fresh stuff completely removes all sense of taste and feeling. Think how your jaw feels (or rather doesn't) when the dentist has numbed your gums and you will get the idea.

I believe it is no coincidence that Normandy registers the lowest sales of toothbrushes in all France. Those who regularly augment their breakfasts with a *café-calva* or two claim that the spirit cleans the teeth better than any fancy-dan toothpaste, but I have noticed that most of the people who say this are usually very low on tooth-count. Here in Brittany, *lambig* is one of the names given to brandy made from apples, and is, allegedly, more used for cooking than drinking. It takes a full barrel of cider at 225 litres to make just twenty bottles of hooch, and I suspect most Bretons would prefer to go for quantity over head-banging strength.

Apart from doing dentists out of work, another magical quality of bootleg apple brandy is its ability to bestow upon the drinker total fluency in any known language. In the same way that science fiction films always have a magic little box which enables Venusians, Martians and Altarans to converse freely, after my first encounter with the local hooch I instantly found myself able to speak fluent Norman patois. Tonight, I discovered that the same trick works with the local moonshine. For the past three hours I have been chatting to my neighbour in not only Breton, but the local version of Breton. Or at least I think I have, as Jean-Yves made no response, and was merely nodding and smiling regularly as I told him about our past lives in Normandy and plans for the future. I did notice his hearing aid was on the hall stand as I left, but think it may have been a spare.

Saturday 14th

The mystery of Alain's new way of speaking his own language has been solved. When I asked him if his old friend had suffered a stroke or was having problems with running-in a new set of teeth, Jean-Yves explained that Alain has actually been speaking French with an English accent to help me understand the language. In the way that some Britons will put on a cod French accent when trying to communicate with a French person in English, our neighbour has been trying to help us out by speaking French with what he imagines is an English accent. It is fascinating to think that, though we can instantly recognise a French, German or Russian by the way they speak our language, we have no idea of what an English person speaking French sounds like to a native. Going by the look on the faces of most French people I speak to in their tongue, it cannot be a pleasant tonal experience.

Monday 16th

A pleasant afternoon in Brest, celebrating a friend's birthday at a Chinese restaurant. The new system of oriental *buffet volante* (help yourself) outlets has taken France by storm, which is another indicator of how things are changing here. My first visit to a Chinese restaurant in France was twenty years ago, and the Cantonese owners had obviously adapted their food and serving methods to suit the host culture. Each item on the menu was being served as a separate course, with long breaks for a cigarette and discussion on the quality and suitability of the chosen wine. When we asked for seven different items to be served at the same time, the place fell silent and the customers watched open-mouthed as we piled our plates high with curry and rice and noodles and sweet and sour pork and, of course, chips.

Nowadays, younger French people like the casual way of eating where you make as many visits to the buffet as you wish, but they are still very French about it. In England, any eat-as-much-as-you-like-for-a-set-price deals are often seen as a challenge. Our table was for six, and I think it would be a close run thing as to whether we made more visits than the rest of the diners combined on a busy Friday afternoon. As everyone tries to get into the game, the appearance of new Chinese *buffet volante* restaurants seem to match the closure rate of village stores. Some do not last or are run by inexperienced or even unscrupulous entrepreneurs. I recently heard of one new outlet which had been closed down after the disappearance rate of local cats rose quite dramatically.

Finistère's biggest town reminds us of our home city of Portsmouth, where most of the ancient buildings were taken out by the Luftwaffe on their frequent awaydays in search of the naval dockyard in our localised version of The Blitz. On this side of the Channel, the Allies were responsible for the near-total destruction of Brest during the course of flushing the occupiers out, so large areas are covered with immediately post-War and depressingly unimaginative buildings and blocks of flats. Possibly because of this, Brest, like Portsmouth, has a certain air of edginess, though you are much more unlikely to be accosted, mugged or murdered here.

When we first approached the high-rise skyline, we looked across the bridge and turned back. But since crossing the bridge and getting to know the town better, we have come to like the if-you-don't-like-us-sod-off feel of Finistère's largest metropolis.

I quite often find my first impression of a town or city can be hopelessly wrong, though curiously not so much with people. This may be because I usually give a place a fair chance to prove me wrong, but arrange and interpret my observations of individuals to suit the prejudices I have already formed.

For us, the docks area of Brest is a satisfying mix of commercial and leisure activity, with rusty scows cheerfully rubbing shoulders with disdainfully sleek yachts, and an equally varied selection of bars, restaurants and scruffy shipping offices lining the quayside. The trouble with most waterside areas is that they eventually get gentrified and homogenous, and as boring as they are overpriced. Here, tattoo parlours and tough-looking dockside boozers sit at ease alongside trendy café bars where the beau monde comes for a lunch and the weekly turnover is more than the building would have fetched a couple of decades ago. A favourite local of ours is McGuigan's Bar, for once named for the real owner, who is even more unusually actually Irish. Dan McGuigan is from Belfast and specialises in offering local workers value-for-money lunchtime meals. The boss also employs some of the prettiest waitresses in the region, which does no harm to trade.

Though with a population of 140,000 it is the largest town in Finistère, the title of capital is awarded to Quimper, which is probably because it scrubs up better and appeals so much more to French snobbery. Brest arrived on the map as a major seaport in the 17th century, when the clever Cardinal Richelieu saw its potential and ordered the construction of a major harbour of wooden wharves. Großadmiral Erich Raeder also saw the value of the towns' strategic location at the start of World War II, and Brest became a major U-Boat base. The town was said to have only three buildings left standing when the Allies had finished liberating it, and the German government paid several billion Deutschmarks in compensation even though they were technically not responsible for the damage.

Nowadays, Brest earns a good living from being the nearest French port to the Americas. Though Nantes and St-Nazaire can handle bigger shipping, the great Rade or Bay of Brest offers sheltered accommodation to all sorts of vessels. Although the Battle for Brest left so little of the old town standing, there is one visitable ancient castle and tower, and modern attractions include the Oceanopolis marine centre. For bridge buffs, the Pont de Recouvrance is the largest example of its type in Europe.

Another claim to fame for the town is that Jane Birkin of the famous handbag and orgasmic groans on the breathy 1960s hit *Je T'aime... Moi Non Plus* made with her Svengali–style lover Serge Gainsbourg, is a Brestian. Now a composer, singer and campaigner, what the subject of ten million male fantasies is getting up to nowadays can be learned by visiting www.janebirkin.net

*

We are as far as you can go westward on mainland Brittany. Le Conquet is a small fishing port which dubs itself The Port at the End of the World. Le Conquet was founded around the tenth century, and probably because of its strategic location not far from the *goulet* or bottleneck of Brest. All it got in the way of recognition and, as the name suggests, was to be sacked repeatedly by Norse and then English attackers. Le Conquet is one of the ports serving the pinprick island of Molène and its comparatively giant neighbour, Ouessant. To sit on the old wall here and look out from the land is to get an inkling of just how much sea there is around our shores, and how unfriendly it can be.

Tuesday 17th

We have been looking at a home and business for sale, and there is obviously money to be made from chicken feed, or rather feeding chickens.

Brittany is big on meat production, and provides more than half the pork eaten in France. Cattle rearing supplies fifteen percent of the country's needs, and though poultry farming is the third largest agricultural activity in Brittany, it produces more than three quarters of chickens consumed by the French. Everywhere in Brittany, and particularly in Côtes d'Armor and Finistère, there are enormous farm buildings which are remarkable by their lack of windows. If they do not house pigs, inside each of these aircraft hangar-like buildings many thousands of chickens will live their short lives. Unlike the common method in Britain, the birds are not confined to a cell, but fairly free to wander around. After two months of rearing, they are taken away for killing and processing while the vast hangars are cleaned out and made ready for the next batch of fluffy chicks.

In spite of the mind-numbing numbers produced here, chickens are not cheap in Brittany. From a butcher, a free-range corn-fed bird with a more detailed and accurate provenance than many a valuable antique could set you back twenty Euros; in a supermarket the cost of a small dressed bird will be twice what you would expect to pay in Britain. This is because it will not have led such a miserable existence or suffered the final indignity of being pumped full of water postmortem. This is also why it will taste much better.

The *élevage* we looked at is licensed to rear fifty thousand chickens at a time. The system for looking after the birds is very high-tech, and the feeding and lighting and heating is all controlled automatically from one panel. The owners are a kindly couple who are retiring and the farm is in a beautiful, remote part of the department, but Donella says she would not want to go into chicken–rearing on that scale. Not only would she find it impossible to send her charges off to meet their fate, she admitted that even she would find it very difficult to think up different names for fifty thousand chickens, let alone remember each of them.

Friday 20th

Most people who move abroad like to hang on to at least some scraps of their national identity. Some try to pretend they are still living where they came from. Spain is full of Britons who live in a world peopled by and run for their own kind.

At the other end of the spectrum, there are those Brits who go native when they move abroad. Rather than integrate, they turn their back on their heritage and try to become what they can never be. For some reason, these strange hybrids are always contemptuous of all things and people from their own land, and treat any fellow countryman they encounter much in the way a vampire reacts to a shaft of sunshine.

In this part of France, the situation becomes even more bizarre, as there is the added dimension of Brittany seeing itself as apart from the rest of France. So the challenge to the expatriate who comes here and would subsume himself in his new surroundings and cut off all links with his natural past is not only to become French, but Breton-French. To get the full risibility of the proposition, imagine if a Frenchman were to move to Scotland and adopt all that country's customs, traditions and irritating prejudices. Would he start to talk in Gaelic, wear a kilt and develop a liking for haggis and chips and headbutting any passing Englishmen? I think not.

A classic example of the British-Breton runs one of my favourite pubs in Finistère, but he is Welsh so already more than qualified for victimhood.

Byn Walters has been in charge at the Ty Elise at Plouyé for more than a quarter of a century, and is in danger of becoming a regional treasure. His pub oozes character and is a customer magnet simply because the owner does not give a stuff (or appears not to give a stuff) what the people who enter his domain think or want. He has done the place up to suit himself, and that is just how it should be.

Inside the single stone-walled bar it is satisfyingly forever twilight. An irritable-looking dragon looks down its nose from a huge Welsh flag tacked to the ceiling, and customers walk beneath it and an equally intimidating Breton flag across a gloriously uneven stone and baked mud floor and past a selection of mismatching benches, chairs and rickety tables to the bar. Behind the counter, the landlord and entry examination await.

Byn looks to be a tall man, but this is because of the sheer force of his character and presence; the impression of height is also because of the old French custom of installing a platform behind the bar so the server can look down on the served. The beer, like the conversation and the ambience, is very strictly Breton, though well-behaved and suitably deferential British customers and non-locals may be tolerated.

The first time we visited the bar I made the mistake of asking for a glass of lager, which obviously did not agree with the licensee's idea of what I should be drinking in his pub. Making polite conversation and trying to curry favour as he ignored my order and started pouring a pint of local brew, I said how we had recently discovered the glory of Breton sausages, and that it was a pity we had not seen them on sale elsewhere in France. As silence descended and our host ceased in mid-pour, several customers drank up and left, while others made for the toilets and one man hid beneath his table.

For the next half hour we were treated to a harangue on the exact composition, proper method of cooking and serving and the ubiquitous availability of the Breton sausage and its links with the development of all areas of Breton culture. We eventually repaired the damage by apologising humbly for the offence we had given and buying the owner lots of beer, and have become regular customers at the Ty Elise. There are too few pubs and landlords like Byn's left anywhere, and we shall be poorer without them.

(Shortly before going to press with this book, the Ty Elise was razed to the ground. At time of writing, no cause for the blaze has been announced. Tributes to Byn and the bar were already flowing in from around the civilised world, with plans afoot for the Ty Elise to raise phoenix-like from the flames).

The Breton beer we had at Byn's bar was from the Lancelot brewery. Brittany has small breweries like Normandy has cheeses, and more of them than anywhere else in France. The tradition of small brew-it-yourself enterprises beginning on farms is similar to ours, but did not develop as in England. There is also a strong tradition of Celtic brewing throughout Europe, and probably the best known Breton brand is Coreff ('Korev' is old Breton for 'beer'), with the company HQ in Morlaix. Coming in light or dark varieties, it is the nearest you will get to cask-conditioned ale in France, though made from wheat and a tad sweet for some tastes. The Maison des Bières Bretonnes at Locronan boasts 75 varieties of bottled beers brewed in the region, but I have not yet tried them all.

Double standards

Being Celtic and thus enjoying healthy debate or, as some would say, a good verbal punch-up, some Bretons are still arguing over which of two versions is their rightful flag.

The simple black cross (*Kroaz Du*) on a white background has been around since at least the Middle Ages. It can be any size and is commonly displayed on Breton fishing vessels, especially when in foreign (i.e. French) waters.

The more elaborate version is known as the Gwenn ha Du, or White and Black, and shows nine black and white stripes and what is called a scattering of stylised ermines. The black stripes represent the dioceses of the eastern part of the region, and the white those of the western part. According to one of many legends about the subject, a 10th-century Breton duke was inspired to take on and defeat a raiding party of Vikings when he saw an ermine turn on a fox which was attacking it. Another common symbol of Breton-ness is the triskele (see cover), a classic Celtic three-legged spiral symbol said by some experts to represent Life, and dating back to at least the Bronze Age. Nowadays it is a popular name for Breton bars.

Speaking in Tongues

Until relatively recently, a Breton speaker from one end of the region would have little chance understanding someone from the other, as there were distinctly different versions of the mother tongue. It was decided in 1908 to unify the Breton dialects of Cornouaille, Léon and Trégor and create a true *lingua franca*, but some signs (and people) stubbornly keep to the old differences. In eastern Brittany, Breton gives way to the totally different Romance language called Gallo.

Home cooking

Dropping in to see if Alain needed anything from the shops, I found him eating what looked like cold Yorkshire pudding dotted with prunes. He told me that it was another greatly prized delicacy called *Farz Fourn*, which was old Breton for 'Flour Oven'. I tried some and found it tasted like cold Yorkshire pudding with prunes in it. To be fair, the taste was improved by the prunes having been soaked in best moonshine apple brandy for a couple of days. My assessment was also not far off the mark, as Farz started off in the 18th century as a savoury accompaniment to a meat course. Anyway, here's how Alain's twice-weekly visiting housekeeper (*femme de ménage*) makes a meal of it:

Ingredients

250 grams plain flour
150 grams caster sugar
Six eggs
A litre of milk
250 grams dried prunes (or apricots or raisins)
Some vanilla essence
A tot of dark rum
Butter for greasing the tin

Method

If using whole prunes, cut in half and remove the stones, then place on the baking dish, cut side up. For the best results, the fruit should have been marinated in the rum (or preferably home-brew apple brandy) overnight. Mix the flour, sugar and eggs, adding the eggs one by one. A food processor is handy for this, but use your hands if you really want to be traditional. Now add the vanilla essence and gradually blend in the milk. Having added the tot of rum (or hooch), pour into the dish and bake at 180 degrees C for an hour...or until the custard is set in the middle. If the mixture starts to over-colour, cover with foil. Serve hot or cold, and preferably with a glass of ice-cold cider.

Sugar, Sugar

Like most Celts, the Brets seem to have a sweet tooth. Unlike in the rest of France where expensive oils are used to anoint any salad, a traditional Breton favourite is a mix of sugar and vinegar. This ancient sweet 'n' sour combo may sound unappetizing, but try it before you condemn. A good tip is to use quality wine vinegar, which makes the contrast between sharpness and sweetness even more interesting.

July

Carhaix-Plouguer, Plouescat, Port Launay, Châteaulin, the isle of Ouessant, Plougastel-Daoulas, Logonna-Daoulas, Bindy Point, the Crozon peninsula, Locronan, La Gouesnière, La Roche-Bernard

Although France abandons all pretence of work for the first three weeks of August, from Nature's point of view the summer is already over. The midsummer solstice is a memory, and the nights draw in. It is a strange, limbo-like time of year as the holidaymakers have not arrived and the various pagan tribes are resting after their round of saluting the gods of summer and burning down the odd isolated chapel.

Across Brittany, more conventional groups are rehearsing for the awesome schedule of fetes, festivals and other excuses for a knees-up which have to be crammed in to the next couple of months. In the smallest villages there will be celebrations of fish, cheese, meat, vegetables and even milk. Summer is also the time when the artistic community like to show off the results of a long winter's work. Painters and sculptors will organize their own exhibitions or get together to commandeer a town or village hall for a group offering.

By its nature, Brittany is not only well-stocked with native talent, but also attracts artististically inclined people from other lands. Today we are going to view the latest work of a British painter. Penny Lancaster produces striking impressionist and abstract works. She lives and works with her picture-restorer husband Simon and her enchanting mother in a small and creatively distressed cottage in the midst of the Arrée Mountains.

Penny's exhibition is being staged at the eye-catching medieval building which houses the tourist office in the centre of Carhaix-Plouguer. Unlike other visitor information centres, the bureau at Carhaix is open throughout the tourist season, literature is in English as well as French, and the staff admit to speaking English.

Carhaix is a very interesting town, and has been knocking around in one form or another since Roman times. For me, if Morlaix would best be represented by a retired university teacher, this town suggests a once-beautiful hooker now ravaged by time, activity and circumstance, but still with a heart of gold.

At the junction of several Roman roads and with a recorded history of occupation since those times, Carhaix is not a mélange of ancient and modern buildings; rather it is a mélange of ancient and post-war buildings. Unlike in many provincial French towns, there are no gleaming glass and concrete creations uneasily rubbing shoulders with medieval structures, just a jumbled progress from fifteenth to early twentieth century architecture.

The main shopping thoroughfare is also the main route through the town, with a phalanx of shops fronting a long and narrow road through which thousands of vehicles charge every day. Being France, parking is permitted on both sides of the road, leaving no more than six inches freeway when two cars pass. When one of the vehicles is a large car or lorry or bus, it adds much to the interest and enjoyment of pedestrian shoppers.

The term-time presence of three thousand students gives Carhaix a youthful, academic and sometimes edgy buzz, and explains the number and quality of kebab shops and pizza takeaways. But Carhaix's real claim to fame comes each August when the population of just under eight thousand increases thirtyfold as top acts headline at the world-renowned open-air music festival. The organisers pride themselves on catering for all musical tastes, and previous acts at the Vieilles Charrues have included Charles Aznavour, The Killers and ZZ top. Last year American rock supremo Bruce Springsteen was headlining, and all tickets were sold before they were available.

Other attractions in and around Carhaix include the proximity of the Nantes to Brest canal (the remnants of the old inland port and railway system are still on show) and the alleged remains of a Roman aqueduct. I say alleged because we have explored the town on many occasions and found nothing remotely resembling an aqueduct of any age. There are many tourist plaques claiming to show the way, but, like so many French road signs, they peter out conveniently at the first roundabout or crossroads.

Saturday 5th

We are now a two-goat family.

My wife's reasoning behind the latest addition to our menagerie is that goats will keep the grass down at a fraction of the cost and maintenance demands of a motor mower. We both know that to be completely untrue, but, for reasons of domestic harmony, it was not a point I wanted to make a stand about. That their arrival would push me down the household pecking order was also not up for consideration. The only consolation is that the pair will not be a permanent overhead and responsibility, as I have formulated what is thought to be the first rentagoat arrangement in this part of Brittany.

In the way of these things, the deal was done over several drinks on neutral territory. The broker was a new friend who is almost as fond of animal husbandry as my wife. Georges LeMoal owns a small hamlet of two quite spectacular ruins and one marginally less-dilapidated cottage in a part of the mountains which is so remote even the regular postman often loses his way there. By day, Georges is a stone mason; at other times he and his wife Vonette collect animals like some people collect beermats. The tally to date includes five dogs, a giant Breton workhorse named Laurette whose constant companion is a Shetland pony, and a menagerie of over a hundred domestic, farm and semi-feral creatures which live around and often in the LeMoal cottage. Visitors are often met by a fortunately amiable bull called Lulu. Georges' wife Vonette is an accomplished folk singer, and a regular performer at festivals across the region. The couple are great hosts, the kindest of people and rival my wife in their tenderness towards any animal.

To strike the deal, we gathered in the hotel in the square of a village near Plounéour, and nobody seemed to think it odd to see two goats bellying up to the bar. There are usually more tractors than cars in the parking spaces, and we have yet to see or hear of a guest staying there. The imposing building was allegedly bought at a knock-down price by a couple of townies who wanted to bring gourmet cooking and four star accommodations to this remote part of the region. The hotel is on the road to and from nowhere, and its lack of potential trade is probably why it was such a bargain buy. The complete lack of anything except very local trade also explains why our host looks so glum when on duty behind the bar or standing forlornly in his chef's whites gazing morosely at the deserted dining room. It is not only Britons who think the low cost of property is a good enough reason to buy a hotel or bar, regardless of where it is or how much they know about the hospitality business.

Georges having made the introductions and explained the circumstances and rules of engagement, we learned that the man with the goats at the end of a length of rope was not actually their owner. In the way that Georges was our self-appointed broker, agent and minder, the goatholder was acting on behalf of a farmer who lives in a neighbouring village. It would have been easier and quicker and much cheaper to have walked down the lane and asked the owner about buying or borrowing the pair, but that is not how things are done in rural France, and matchmakers are highly valued here. Last week, the owners of half the homes in Lesmenez descended on us to make hard work of buying a rusting bicycle that Alain had spotted in our barn. As official translator and intermediary, he told us Mary-Jo's eldest daughter needed a bike for getting to and from her new school. Although the girl was not present for the bargaining process, her grandmother had come along to make a bid, and Jean-Yves was there to see fair play. Interestingly, whether the old bike was for sale was never questioned.

The proceedings in the hotel bar ran along the lines of the bicycle deal, and followed a strictly observed rite applied throughout rural France

First comes the polite conversation over a couple of glasses of wine, then the would-be buyer reluctantly broaches the subject of price. This request is always treated as if a complete surprise to the vendor, who will act as if it had never occurred to him to have a figure in mind. After a suitable bout of head, brow and nose scratching, puffing out of cheeks and a wander around the arena, the seller will be persuaded to name his price. This will be the signal for the buyer and his backers to go into near-cardiac arrest or pantomime a series of rapidly assumed expressions of shock, horror and disbelief which would make a silent movie actor look as if he were underplaying his role.

In the case of the goat deal, the farmer's broker chose the popular method of writing the price down on a piece of paper and sliding it across the table as if passing on the solution to the Da Vinci code. This ploy allows the injection of even more drama and facial contortions before, during and after the unfolding of the slip. In this case there was no need for any play-acting, as the price being asked for the two goats would have bought a reconditioned sit-on mower with accessories and turbo-booster. I was now in real trouble, as the goats had identified the soft target and worked their magic on my wife; they and we all knew there was no way she would be leaving the bar without them. So, in desperation I came up with the rental suggestion, and we now have Molly and Mandy on permanent lease-back. The weekly payment (to be handed over in the local bar each Friday evening) would buy us a new car on tick. But, as Alex the fairly honest broker says, we are free to hand the nanny and her baby back at any time if my wife becomes weary of looking after them. He is obviously a shrewd judge of character, and knows that there is as much likelihood of that happening as me winning a deal with a French countryman.

Tuesday 8th

Alain materialised by the rhubarb patch yesterday morning to announce he had bought a black cat and called it Bisdu. When I asked what the name meant, he looked at me as if I were half-witted and said it was Breton for 'black cat'.

The cat has already worked out her place in the community, and came to an agreement with Milly shortly after they were introduced. If in the mood, she will allow our dog to chase her. If not, she will stand her ground, arch her back and thoughtfully regard the claws on one paw as Milly skids to a stop. If in a really provocative or bad mood, she will chase Milly into the kitchen and eat everything in her food bowl.

Wednesday 9th

To Plouescat, a trendy resort town on the north-western coast, to look at a bed and breakfast enterprise.

Our part of Brittany alone has more than a thousand kilometres of varied and often stunning coastline, but this is not a favourite stretch of ours. There are some pleasant walks along the dunes, but the area is too blandly flat, commercial and busy for our tastes. There is a saying that the French will always pay for a view, and pay through the nose if the view is of the sea. That seems particularly true in Brittany, where properties on the coast will fetch UK prices. Quaint and very small fishermen's cottages will sell for more than the original occupant would have earned in several lifetimes. It also appeals to French snobbery (and, contrary to common perception, they can effortlessly outsnob the English) to pay a fortune to live in the former home of someone they would normally have crossed the road to avoid.

According to fairly recent history, it seems the commune leaders at Plouescat are unusually prudish. In the suitably named Guandong province of China, a major tourist attraction is a huge rock which looks exactly like an erect penis. In 1987 it was pointed out that a rock off the coast of Plouescat also looked like a rampant if more modestly-sized willy. Determined not to embarrass future visitors, the town council had it dynamited. Since then a lot of local people have said what a cock-up the destruction of what could have been a major tourist attraction was, but it is too late to do anything with the remains of what has inevitably become known as the Plouescat Prick.

The bed and breakfast business we had come to see was not worth considering further, as it was running at an occupancy rate of less than twenty percent, and you would have had to climb on to the roof to enjoy the sea views as advertised on the property details.

Friday 11th

Brittany is known for its prehistoric standing stones or menhirs, and can claim the origin of the word which is used around the world. *Men* is 'stone' and *hir* is 'long' in Breton. Menhirs are always big and usually monolith (single) stones, often tapering at the top, and are found just about everywhere in the region. Brittany seems to have cornered the market, and there are 1200 known menhirs in north-western France. They date from different periods of pre-history, and represent part of a Megalithic culture which flourished throughout Europe.

There are almost as many theories about why they were erected and what they were used for as there are menhirs. Some think they were sacrificial altars for a Druidic culture; others believe they were celestial or earthly calendars. Menhirs should not be confused with dolmens, which are usually single-chamber megalithic tombs which look like a giant's dining table.

Like everywhere else I have travelled in rural France, Brittany has its fair share of standing men. Most are single and unemployed, and have not much else to do but stand and wait for the local bar to open. This morning I walked across the moors to Plounéour and saw a figure by the traffic lights at the crossroads. I thought at first the man was trying to hitch a lift, then recognized him and realised he was waiting for The Bar of the Bounty to open, or as the locals say, be unwrapped.

Though of middle age, Thierry is a child in his mind, and lives alone in an apartment paid for by the commune. He had a forlorn air as he stood on the edge of the pavement watching a steady stream of monstrous lorries roaring on their way to Roscoff. Their slipstream tugged at his clothing, and it looked as if he might step off the kerb at any time. Some drivers were sounding their klaxons in warning as they thundered by. At each blast the man would hold his arms straight out from his body and sway even closer to the road, and it seemed as if he was trying to find companionship through his proximity to the giant lorries. I have seen men like him throughout rural France, and though they are well looked after by the communes it is sad to see their loneliness.

Wednesday 16th

Like some restaurants in this part of France, the supermarket at Pleyber-Christ shuts for lunch. The management also ensures that there will be no check-out queues at closing time by stationing bouncers on the doors a quarter of an hour before the deadline. Across the Channel they would be doing their best to persuade customers to come on to the premises; here they physically turn them away as the lunchtime break approaches.

Another vagary of the French supermarket system is how the check-outs are staffed in inverse proportion to customer levels. The general rule at our branch is to start each day with all six check-outs fully functional, then close one station for every hundred customers arriving. But there are variations on this theme, depending on the creative flair of the management team. In our local there is a sort of goon tower next to the wet fish counter, from where the manager can monitor the car park and aisle density levels, then make the fine tuning and adjustments to cause maximum havoc at the check-out. The busier the store becomes, the more staff are withdrawn, and one occasionally hears a muffled cheer from the tower when there is a complete logjam. In England this would be the cause of unrestrained violence, but here I think it is actually part of a drive towards increased customer satisfaction.

Whereas there is no word for 'queue' in their vocabulary and most drivers would die rather than stay in line (particularly when approaching a deadly hazard), I have found that the average French customer is never averse to waiting in a shop, garage or post office. This is a paradox of the highest order and one for which I can find no explanation. In Britain the slightest delay at the front of a queue leads to exasperated sighs and pantomimes of frustration. Here, the shoppers waiting their turn actually seem to enjoy watching the action, particularly if there is a chance of a small drama developing.

Thursday 17th

A revealing day as to just how tough the market is becoming for those who sell houses. In general, I am much in sympathy with property agents, especially in France. It is a thankless job and many agents have to endure sometimes breathtaking rudeness and inconsideration from their British customers. I have found property agents on this side of the Channel to be accurate in their descriptions, but as the market slows there has been a noticeable increase in hyperbole. Often it is the British owners and not their agents who are responsible.

To me, ponds stop and lakes begin somewhere above an acre of water. Copses are increasingly spreading overnight into woods according to some property details, and we arrived at a house recently to find an alleged forest made up of six fir trees and an overgrown shrubbery. Going by the number of allegedly stately homes on sale in our region, every square kilometre must have contained at least a dozen manor houses, and there must have been more former presbyteries and nunneries in our region than religious orders to fill them.

Another ruse is the over-indulgent use of the 'could-be' scenario, where the vendor paints romantic word pictures of what could be done with any building to unlock its potential if no consideration is given to suitability or cost. Thus a rotting barn 'could be' a covered swimming pool, or a rambling chicken farm could transmogrify into a twenty-gite holiday complex with no more than a relative handful of Euros spent on the makeover.

Today, we saw what was described as a mini-*château* in its own grounds. According to the blurb, the Art Deco-influenced house had been built by an eccentric Parisian and boasted an underground spring feeding the lake; the property also boasted five bedrooms and a library in the turret. Far and away the most attractive feature was the price, which was ridiculously low even by French standards.

We arrived to find the place in the shadow of a grand *manoir* we had hoped might be the property for sale. The grounds were a small if admittedly neat garden, and the lake was no more than a pond. It was also in the hands of an even odder descendant of the eccentric Parisian. The lady greeting us at the door was wearing what looked like a full length ballgown over Wellington boots, and had the same make-up technique as Joan Crawford on a particularly sloppy lipstick day. She also had a disturbing way of laughing at secret jokes as she showed us around, and I could not but wonder if her amusement level reached cackle-point as we reached places where former viewers were buried.

The underground 'living' area had no freshly-dug earth floors or concrete patches, but was no more than a cellar. When we had inspected two rather pokey bedrooms on the first floor and I asked about the other three, Madame took a giant crochet hook from a cupboard and advanced down the passageway. As I sheltered behind my wife, the owner reached up and pulled down the loft hatch from which a sliding stepladder emerged. Upstairs, we gathered next to the water tank and looked around at row after row of ball gowns and elaborate dresses. Not wishing to cause trouble but feeling I should make the point, I said that we were gathered in what by any stretch of the imagination could be called no more than a floored attic, and that there were no three bedrooms or a turret, let alone a turret with a library in it.

After a long silence and as the agent started clambering down the loft steps, the lady drew herself up to her full height and adjusted her elbow-length gloves before saying in an almost perfect imitation of Peter Sellers in The Pink Panther: 'Zat may be technically true... but zere could be.'

Friday 18th

More disappointment this morning when we looked at what was described as a whole village for sale and found it to be a dishevelled farmhouse surrounded by a handful of even more dilapidated outbuildings. Because the property had a name and stood in isolation, villagehood has been bestowed upon it by the agency.

It is a shame that the ancient dwelling place did not live up to its description, as it stood far away from any roads and within a genuine stroll of the Nantes-Brest canal.

Though the distance in a straight line would be much less, this erratic combination of rivers and artificial waterways takes more than 360 kilometres to get from the old capital to the north-western seaport of Brest.

Work on joining these two important towns started at the beginning of the 19th century after the authorities had been talking about it for around four hundred years. Problems with bad or non-existent roads and latterly the British raids on Breton ports were spurs to come up with a way of moving goods more efficiently and safely across the region. What makes this canal so unusual and attractive is that only around a fifth of the distance is made up of man-made cuts. The rest of the journey meanders alongside eight rivers on their eccentric way from the Erdre at Nantes to the Aulne estuary at Brest. Because of the undulating countryside, it took more than 200 locks to even-out the watery highway, and what would be a formidable engineering task in any era was forty years in the making.

At our end of the canal are two interesting, complementary but very different towns.

Port Launay is the smaller, with a population of less than five hundred, and is every tourist's picture of how a quaint former fishing village should look. But unlike the way it happens across the Channel, posh yachts rub shoulders with battered old scows, and the owners working on their boats reflect this agreeable diversity. So do the properties lining the quayside, and it is good to see the odd neglected building standing out like a bad tooth in an otherwise gleaming smile. It is here that, after wending its way past the frontages of *chambres d'hôtes*, restaurants and former fishing cottages at Port Launay, the Nantes-Brest canal ceases to be. Beyond the impressive and fairly new flood barrier at lock 273, the Aulne widens and drifts lazily past wooded hillsides and vast maize fields on its lazily winding journey to the sea.

Going against the flow and to the south-west of Port Launay, you pass almost immediately into Châteaulin - or Kastellin as more traditionalist Bretons call their home town. Where Port Launay is a picture-postcard setting, Châteaulin is more of a getting-on-with-it place. Although a historic settlement dating back to at least the 10th century, the town is obviously a busy modern place of work and leisure. Cars stream by on either side of the river and over the ancient bridge, and many will be on their way to the giant Leclerc hypermarket which sits unashamedly amongst a row of quality houses overlooking the waterway.

Deeper into the town are some satisfyingly quirky streets sporting a jumble of restaurants and bars. There is a thriving market and thousands of tourists find Châteaulin a good starting point to explore the nearby Crozon Peninsula, where a former volcano called Ménez Hom offers panoramic views of the west coast area.

There are 5000 or so Châteaulinoi, and one of the town's famous sons is an emblem of war-time resistance. Wherever you go in France, there will be a street, fountain or public building (if not all three) named for Jean Moulin. More locally, there is a Rue Jean Moulin in Carhaix-Plouguer, and the next street is named for the IRA hunger–striker Bobby Sands. As far as I know, there are no streets in Brittany named for Protestant martyrs, but that is perhaps not surprising.

*

As arranged, we met today's house-finder on the bridge at Châteaulin. She recognised me because I had been fairly honest in describing myself, and I recognised her because she is typical of the modern female French property agent. Young and smartly dressed, she displayed a clipboard as if it were a fashion accessory and walked very quickly and with determined tread towards us. Once upon a time, most provincial French property agents were males who liked to dress like colour-blind gameshow hosts. As elsewhere in an increasingly homogenised Europe, things have changed. Martine was obviously a very self-assured modern French woman, and, as we discovered to our complete unsurprise, she drove like a complete lunatic.

Before returning to our cars I made the mistake of asking her to remember we were following and did not know the area, and she probably took that as a challenge. Or worse, what we took as her often suicidal careering was actually more restrained than normal to allow for her being followed by a couple who were not only old but foreign.

90

From outside, the house and its setting looked attractive enough, but we shall never know the feel of the inside. We have had some unusual viewing trips in France, but this was the first time we were not allowed to enter what we might be buying. As we screeched to a stop in a shower of gravel behind our agent's car, the English owner of the house emerged to explain that his wife was allergic to just about everything the modern world had to offer. Without wishing to give offence, it was likely that, to her super-sensitive nose, our clothes would reek of cigarette smoke, remnants of food and bodily odours. The hairs from our dog and cat would also be clinging to our clothing, and any proximity within twenty feet would bring his wife out in a severe rash, make her nauseous and likely to pass out. She was at the moment resting in a darkened room, but we were free to look at the house from outside; to further assist us, he had constructed a virtual tour of the inside on his lap-top computer.

This was how we came to be sitting on a terrace, looking at photographs of the inside of the house directly behind us. Our agent had also never been allowed inside, and was particularly fascinated by the size and range of the fixtures in the kitchen, particularly as the lady owner did not allow them to be used in case of the discovery of other allergies. Looking at the photographs of the eight-burner stainless steel cooker and a fridge freezer the size and shape of a very large wardrobe, Martine said it was peculiar how the first thing British people who bought houses through her offices did was fill the kitchen with lots of impressive and expensive equipment they never seemed to use. As my wife explained, it is a curious fact that though the British cook less and less at home, they own more cookbooks and watch more advanced cookery shows on TV per head than any other race on earth. They also compensate for any feelings of guilt by buying more and more extravagant items to show they could feed an army if they wanted to.

Sunday 20th

Now I know why the Lonely Goatherd was a Norman No-Mates. Goats are even more smelly and messy and noisy than I had thought possible. Also, with our rentagoat arrangement it seems we have bought or rather rented a pig in a poke. Or been sold a pup, or, more actually, been kidded. Whoever said that goats were hardy, durable animals who keep grounds neat and tidy by eating all the brambles and rubbish obviously never kept one, or our pair are not as other goats.

Capra hircus was amongst the first genus of animals to be domesticated or kept by Man, around 9000 years ago. There are more than two hundred varieties and over 400 million living around the world. One of the most common myths about goats is that they will eat anything including old tin cans and other rubbish. Ours turn their noses up at anything but a balanced diet of fresh corn and even fresher nettles, which must be chopped up to a precise length and proffered like a slave presenting a titbit to a Roman Emperor. Goats are obviously also very highly strung and delicate creatures. Ours have been taken to the vet twice so far at a cost of more than a hundred Euros, and we now have a very expensive selection of food additives and special diet sheets. Our goats are clearly exceedingly independent and rebellious animals, and we now owe Mr Vitre a shrub and a goodly section of his hedge. When Alex recommended we stake and chain the wayward couple in our grounds and move them when the grass was cropped, Donella said that, like the chickens, they should be free to range. The problem is their idea of a good outing is to clatter up the lane and attack our neighbour's hedge, shrubberies and even the upholstery of his car. Our Alpine duo could also crap for France, and I spend at least an hour a day cleaning up after them.

Worst of all, Molly and Mandy are not, as was claimed, mother and daughter. They are totally unrelated, and Molly attacks the kid whenever she comes near. This aggression and neglect makes Mandy very unhappy, and she cries all day and night for her new mother, who is of course my wife. I now have to solve the problem before I have to share the bed with a baby goat as well as my wife and a dog and cat.

Monday 21st

We saw Alex in the bar last night and it has become increasingly irritating how he lifts his glass and leers at me, then turns back to have a snigger with his cronies. Obviously, he likes telling the story of how he lumbered us with the goat rental scheme, and I suspect that not all the rental fee I pay him reaches the owner.

Tuesday 22nd

As well as the longest coastline in France, Brittany has one of the most varied. We find the west coast particularly attractive and reminiscent of Scandinavian fjords with hundreds of filigreed inlets, coves and small secret places.

We have been working our way along the coastline from the pink granite coast to the north-west of Morlaix, and today covered a stretch between Brest and the Crozon peninsula.

The coastal waters of Brittany can be a yachtsman's nightmare, and the region seems to specialise in very dangerous rocks which hide just beneath the surface at high tide. There are also many big enough to be called islands whether or not they are inhabited. As far as I know, nobody has counted the number of habitable islands around Brittany, but the Gulf of Morbihan (Breton for 'small sea') claims one for every day of the year. Actually, there are around forty, depending at what time of tide you count them.

A handful of communities live in the sea off the westernmost point of Brittany, and the largest island is Ouessant. Said to have the most powerful lighthouse in the world, the island is also distinguished by being the only place in Brittany with its own English name (Ushant). It features in my favourite sea shanty Spanish Ladies, and an old Breton proverb predicts doom for those who try to navigate its rock-strewn coastline and ten-knot tide. The island is around eight by four kilometres, with a little under a thousand inhabitants having plenty of personal space. As the menfolk were at sea fishing, the running of the island's affairs was traditionally handled by the women. The modern-day islanders may be isolated, but can never feel lonely with thirty thousand ships passing each year. Unlike in the rest of Finistère, sheep are big on Ouessant, and the island has its own breed. Understandably, the traditional meal on the island is mutton stew.

Today we drove from Brest across the impressive Albert Louppe bridge and high above the estuary of the Élorn and on to Plougastel-Daoulas. This unassuming place is for some reason the epicentre of strawberry production in Brittany. Further down the coast is Logonna-Daoulas, where our walk began near Bindy Point at a giant former paper mill and fish canning plant called Moulin de Mer. The first of many tree-lined coves has its own islands, and sitting smugly along the winding clifftop walk are houses which look directly out and across the ever-varying seascape. Passing them on a stormy day is one of the times I wish I were rich enough to buy the privilege of that sort of setting and view.

Today, all was calm, with placid clear water reflecting an unbroken tent of blue sky. A mini-flotilla of dinghies, yachts and fishing boats bobbed at their moorings, and the slapping of wavelets against their hulls and the odd cry of a gull was all that broke the silence. Then, glittering in the near distance we saw what looked like a beach made of pure mother-of-pearl, and left the clifftop to crunch across a million oyster shells. In the shallows were thousands more, and all alive.

As we were filling our pockets, a man and his dog walked by. In England we would at best have been warned of the health and safety risks. Here, we were told where to find even bigger and better specimens. When I asked if they were edible, the man smiled wryly and said only if we had a bottle of suitably cold white wine, some brown bread and good Breton butter, and a dressing of exactly the right proportions of olive oil, wine vinegar and finely chopped shallots. As he suspected we had not come equipped with these accessories, he asked if we would like to bring our catch to his house on the cliffs above, where he would provide them in return for a share of the oysters and some conversation to help improve his abysmal English. We said we certainly would, and did. It is these small and unexpected encounters which remind us how France can be such a satisfyingly informal place to live.

*

Replete with oysters, and wine and good company, we decided to work our lunch off by driving around the Crozon peninsula. We had also heard of a manor house overlooking the sea which was for sale at a good price.

The unusual shape of this particularly craggy outcrop results from aeons of erosion of the sandstone and shale, and the peninsula is famed for its stunning clifftop walks and sandy beaches; the seabeds as well as the land are heavily protected areas. There is not much to see at the main town of Crozon, but Morgat has a long, crescent-shaped beach and is the departure point for boat trips around the headlands and past the many tidal caves. In summer the main attraction is the Festival of the End of the World (in the geographical rather than time sense) and there are also regular jazz beanos said to attract fans from around Europe. While in the area, another popular tourist spot worth a visit is Le Faou, a medieval fishing port set in its own estuary.

*

The manor house was certainly in a stunning position, but a classic example of how a property can sometimes be too expensive if it is free. The previous owners had been a professional builder and his interior designer wife who had got as far as stripping the house and outbuildings back to the very basics before they went their separate ways. The rift was caused when the woman returned home unexpectedly to find her husband wearing one of her most expensive and extravagant outfits. It is alleged that what really upset her was that he was wearing his cement-covered boots beneath the ensemble. As a result, they split up, Arthur became Martha and the manor house sits looking forlornly out to sea, doubtless pondering on the vagaries of humankind. Having walked around the cavernous rooms, it was obvious that the restoration of the property would cost more than we could hope to earn in total for the rest of our

95

lives, barring a very special best-seller. As we drove away I looked in the mirror at the gaunt silhouette of the topless building and thought about a story an expat Briton told me. Arriving home from school, her ten-year-old son said that his French classmates believed the English to be a very hardy race, as they obviously preferred living in homes with no roofs.

*

On our way back from the roofless *manoir*, we stopped off to investigate the House of Beer and walk around a place which sells itself as The Village That Time Forgot.

Between the coast and prefecture town of Quimper, Locronan made its name as a fifteenth-century centre for supplying the woven linen to make sails for the Spanish, French and English navies. The village is said to have fallen into a sudden economic decline which accounts for the complete lack of modern buildings in or around the place. I do not know how that would account for a complete lack of television aerials, parking spaces, street furniture or any other evidence of modern living, and have my own theory on how Locronan came to be, as the publicity blurb has it, frozen in time.

I suspect that, a century or so ago, a really forward-thinking member of the council came up with a superb example of lateral thinking. Instead of trying to modernise and create new industries and bring work to the town, he proposed, the local authorities should do the opposite and leave things exactly as they were. It might not do the commune much good in the near future, but in a hundred years people would come flocking to see what a typical Breton village once looked like.

His wheeze proved to be a brilliant one, and like Golden Hill in Shaftesbury, the period look attracted a queue of film and tv advert makers. Roman Polanski relocated the setting for Tess of the D'Urbervilles here, and now thousands of visitors arrive daily to walk around the strangely anodyne streets and look at old buildings which are filled with the usual tourist tat.

The most noticeable aspect of our visit was how pushing our way through the crowded streets was like being transported back to a busy town centre in Britain. Eye contact was avoided, and nobody acknowledged anyone else. I found this puzzling until my wife pointed out that nobody was or could be a local here; they like us, were all strangers, so had fallen into the big town habit of pretending not to see each other.

Thursday 24th

Two of our hens have gone off lay, and the response from Breton friends and neighbours has been predictably true-to-type.

When he arrived on his daily visit to check out what madness we have been up to, Alain said this was a signal that it was time to start eating our chickens rather than just their eggs. If we were too squeamish, it would take no more than a minute for him to stretch the selected necks. If we were unfamiliar with the simple but delicious classic country dish *poule au pot* (code for 'As you are British and thus not able to boil an egg properly'), he would be only too pleased to do the cooking and invite us over for dinner.

When my wife huffily explained that she had no wish to have her adopted daughters murdered and would not dream of eating them, our neighbour went into overdrive with his pantomiming of a mixture of shock, bemusement and incredulity, then scurried off to tell Jean-Yves about our latest demonstration of Martian-like behaviour.

Our next visitor was Little Georges, and it came as no surprise that his solution was not to kill and eat our hens, but to get a cock in to sort the females out.

*

Jean-Yves was not wearing his hearing aids when we met at the village rubbish bins, so our conversation was limited to a mixture of me yelling in bad Breton and both of us using universal sign language. As we exchanged pleasantries, Jean saw me watching Milly crouching on the verge and asked if studying the state of their dogs and children's bowels was a common British pastime. He said he had heard of a couple of expatriates living in a nearby village who actually liked to record their Springer spaniel's daily motions. Because the wife suffers with her legs and is unable to walk the dog, her husband takes advantage of the latest digital technology by filming it. When back from the morning walk, he plugs the camera into their wide-screen television so they can study the evidence together over breakfast. Another advantage of transferring the film to the big screen is that they can show the footage to other dog-loving visitors.

Home cooking

Brittany has a coastline to each of its departments, so it is not surprising that the Brets have developed lots of ways of preparing and cooking seafood over the centuries. I usually hold that the best way to eat oysters is, as we did at Bindy Point, straight from the sea and in the nude except for a simple dressing of vinegar, oil and finely chopped shallots. That's the oysters and not me in the oiled nude, of course. However, the following regional speciality could make me change my mind.

Sabayon of Breton Oysters

Ingredients

28 oysters (if you are dining *à deux*, more if not)
200grams (7oz) fresh spinach
Salt and pepper
100 grams butter
Three eggs
120ml (half a cup) of heavy cream

Method

Open the oysters and detach them from their shells. Collect the liquor and strain it through a fine cheesecloth or suitable fine sieve. Put the liquid and oysters into a sauté pan over a low heat. As soon as the liquid begins to bubble, remove the oysters. Remove the stems from the spinach leaves, and wrap each oyster in a leaf before placing it in one of the shells. Place them all on a baking sheet and set aside. Melt the butter in a pan, remove from the heat, skim off the foam and pour off the clarified butter. Set aside in a pan over a bowl of hot water. Place the eggs and cream into a saucepan and whisk until frothy. Put the saucepan over another pan of almost boiling water and whisk until the *sabayon* thickens. Remove from the heat and gradually blend in the clarified butter. Add two tablespoons of the oyster liquid and season to taste. Put the oysters under a grill for three minutes. Spoon some of the *sabayon* over each oyster and re-grill until brown and bubbly. Cover each serving plate with coarse salt and arrange oysters on top.

Magdalene Madeleines

Proust based his autobiography on them, and they are the only type of cake made by my wife that our neighbour Alain will agree to eat. The origins of this simple but ubiquitous cakelet are unknown, but Madeleine is a French form of Magdalene, and it is a tradition for them to be home-made and eaten in the saint's honour on her feast day of July 22nd. The madeleine is said to originate in Commercy in the north-east of France, but is enjoyed across the country and claimed to be best made by many other departments and regions, including Brittany.

Ingredients

5 eggs
180 grams castor sugar
180g butter
200g flour
One sachet vanilla sugar
One small sachet of baking powder

Method

Gently melt the butter in a small saucepan on a cooler part of the range. Whisk the eggs, sugar and vanilla sugar vigorously in a bowl. Add the barely warm, melted butter. Delicately mix in the flour and baking powder with a spatula. Butter the nearest thing you have to a madeleine mould and coat with flour. Three-quarter fill the moulds with the mixture and cook in a hot oven at around

200 degrees C. The cooking process should take about ten minutes. You will know they are ready when a knife pushed in comes out clean.

*

Expat Hits and Misses

I would lay a bet that the first Ancient Brit who buggered off to live elsewhere after the Roman conquest said he was moving abroad because the country was going to the dogs. That is still the single biggest reason or excuse, though I have observed that there are several other significant reasons for quitting Britain. Some departees have an urgent need to be elsewhere, and traditionally chose destinations with cheap plastic surgery options and no extradition treaty with the UK. Others fool themselves into thinking that living permanently somewhere they go for a couple of weeks a year will be like one long holiday. The saddest of all are those who think that moving to a foreign country to start a new life will repair an ailing relationship. Almost invariably, the stresses of the change actually sever rather than strengthen the knot.

Many Britons do settle and remain happily in a foreign country, but all - whether they admit it or not - will miss certain aspects of where they used to live. It is my experience that the most allegedly contented British expats will moan about their host country in exact ratio to the amount of drinks consumed at any gathering. Especially in the local Brit Bar. Of course, there are also aspects of not living in modern Britain which give all expatriates reasons to be cheerful.

Conducted specifically for this book, my survey (see p.102) invited the 40,000 users of an expatriate on-line forum to list what they most and least missed about not living in Blighty. The list reflects the most common recurring items, is clearly highly unscientific but does make interesting reading. A thought-provoking point is that the list of things missed is so much longer than the list of things not missed. This can be explained in part by the items in the 'not missed' column having a narrow bandwidth which focuses on yobbish behaviour and political correctness. There is much more variety in the 'missed' column, which includes some pretty trivial and unlikely items. Would you, for instance, miss cats' eyes, charity shops and frozen peas?

Most Missed

A British sense of humour
All-day shopping
Boots the chemist
British newspapers
BOGOF (buy-one-get-one-free) offers
Cat's eye road studs
Charity shops
Church choirs
Clotted cream
Cornish pasties
Customer service
Drivers and pedestrians acknowledging a
courtesy
English beer
English pubs
English toilet rolls
Family
Fish and chips anywhere anytime
Friends
Guinness
Hard cheese
Libraries
Marks and Spencers
My mum
Night life
Proper bacon
Proper British curry restaurants
Proper garden centres
Proper paint
Proper paint brushes
Proper sausages
Pub grub
Sausage rolls

Most Not Missed

Feeling a stranger in the country of my birth

Gangs of threatening teenagers

Health & Safety regulations

My mother-in-law

Little Chefs

Nosey neighbours

Obsession with property values

Parking meters

Personalised number plates

Political correctness

Restaurants where children are barred or sneered at

Restaurants where other people's children run riot and totally spoil the meal

Vandalism

Road works

Traffic cones

Traffic jams

The X Factor and other rubbish telly

August

Paule, Glomel, Gouarec, Rostrenen, Le Relec,
St-Jean-de-Doigt, Châteauneuf-du-Faou, Roscoff,
Île-de-Batz, Carentec, L' Île Callot , Saint-Pol-de-Léon

The ripening of the year, and mountains and moors are rich in life and death. As we walked up the track this morning, a tiny coal tit burst from the hedgerow with a ferociously screeching sparrowhawk on its tail. The chaser and chased wheeled and turned in perfect formation until disappearing into a hedge along the track. I don't know if the little bird got away, but I hope so.

Later, a deer soared effortlessly over the path as we approached, and I watched a confused-looking bumble bee buzzing erratically around the single remaining flower on a foxglove stalk. The Breton name for the foxglove is Our Lady's Thimbles, and I think it a much better description of the *digitalis purpurea*, as the delicate tubular blooms would fit on the paws of no fox I know. Other unsuitable British folk names include Bloody Fingers and Dead Men's Bells. Curiously, the foxglove is prolific nearly everywhere in Europe, but will not grow in Shetland or some eastern counties of England. The one being harried by the bumble bee was pure white, and though unusual is not rare. When I told Alain about my find, he predictably said it was well known that white foxgloves grow only in Brittany, and especially in our part of Finistère.

Monday 4th

A week of serious house-hunting ahead, starting with a visit to a coastal B&B establishment which is suspiciously cheap. As there seem to be more places for people to stay in France than there are visitors, there is a glut of these money-pits which seem so fatally attractive to British couples who want to earn a living while living in France. I also think many claim they are taking on a B&B to supplement their income, but really it is so they can indulge the modern obsession for having more bathrooms than people who live in a house.

The asking price for the eight-bedroomed property is enticingly low, and on arriving, we saw why. The rooms had clearly been designed for the use of Dobby the house-elf, and the conversion and 'improvements' work was obviously a classic example of Destroy-it-Yourself. This phenomenon occurs surprisingly often, and always when a Briton whose sole experience in building matters is putting up the odd shelf decides he can single-handedly restore and transform a dilapidated property.

A further drawback with this property was that it lay at the bottom of a deeply rutted track, surrounded by rusting farm buildings. The golden rule in France is that gites should be in the countryside, and bed and breakfast establishments in town or on a busy road with lots of passing trade. The only passers-by at this place will come in the form of cows, and the former owner. An invariable rule of French property exchange is that if a farmer sells a house that has been in his family for generations, he and his kin will soon forget it no longer belongs to them and naturally begin to resent what they see as a foreign squatter.

Another recurring feature with this sort of property in this sort of location is that many of the British couples who opt for a bed and breakfast business in the hinterland of France seem to have a taste in décor and furnishings which suggests a marriage of minds between Laura Ashley and Dexie's Midnight Runners. Walls, architraves, clothes, furniture and even somnolent family pets are often rag-rolled to near-death, and darkly coloured drapes, scatter cushions and somehow sinister-looking brass ornaments will add a hint of Turkish brothel. Pink will be adjacent to lime green and tangerine, terra cotta and Bovril as colours of proximity and choice, and every flat vertical surface will boast those curious plastic stick-on crescent moons and stars. Sometimes a display will appear to have been fixed to the ceiling, but will be the real thing, showing through a hole overlooked or even created by the ardent DIY-er.

Tuesday 5th

Another mouth to feed, and it looks as if there could soon be several more. Alain's cat Bisdu has taken to arriving each morning to demand her supplementary breakfast of best tinned fish and a bowl of full-fat cream. Alain sensibly gives her nothing but dried food, but she has discovered that Donella is an easy touch. By the look of the changes to her once-sleek outline, Bisdu is putting on weight because of the luxury diet, or there will soon be a significant addition to the cat population of Lesmenez.

*

I find the canal increasingly beguiling.

Of all the magically magnetic places in Brittany, there is something very special about the meandering waterway connecting Nantes to Brest. The happy confluence of natural rivers and artificial cuts is a living conduit, connecting all the people who live or pass along its length. Although a place of peace and sometimes isolation, there is still always the chance of occasional human contact. Perhaps this is the reason I so enjoy walking the canal, as the connectivity without involvement suits me to perfection. When you live in isolation at the bottom of a mill track you are truly alone, and the only way to see other people and places is to visit a village or town. Lakes and ponds are nice but do not go anywhere. Here, I find it an enchanting thought that, if I wished, I could walk or cycle more than two hundred miles and meet with people and places and experiences without let or hindrance or traffic. This promise of opportunity of escape is perhaps part of the reason people have always liked to live beside water.

Another delight of this particular waterway is how little it is used. In Britain, there are now more vessels and pleasure-seekers using the canal system than in the days when the network was the main highway for commercial traffic. Here, the towpath and water stretch unoccupied for miles. Across the Channel, the logjams mean there will be a raft of regulations for using the waterways and operating the lock gates. Here, the only

106

rule is that the *écluse* must be left as the user finds it, which is invariably empty.

Of all the hours I have walked beside the canal, I have twice seen a boat using one of the hundreds of locks that level off the combination of rivers and artificial channels. The odd kayak will risk the plunge down the piece of oversized guttering alongside the lock gates, but generally the canal is left to its natural inhabitants.

Although or perhaps even because it has such serenity and sometimes haunting beauty, the canal is a favoured spot for suicides. I recently met a British couple who said how they saw a young girl floating towards the weir as she repeatedly ducked her head beneath the water to try and overcome her natural instincts of self-preservation. The couple watching in horror from the bank were not strong swimmers and did not feel they could help as she was swept to her death. I would not like to be put in a similar position and have to find out the truth about myself and what I felt able to do.

Although I enjoy most of my encounters on the towpath, there are exceptions, and they always come on two wheels. In decades of using shared country ways, I have had no more than a handful of confrontations with horse riders. In general, I keep my dog from under their animals' hooves, and they will thank me for it as they pass. Those on smaller saddles usually have a different mindset. Country pathway cyclists on either side of the Channel seem to specialise in either ignoring or terrorising walkers, and the more ludicrously dressed the more offensive they are.

But this is a minor lycra-clad irritation. Another huge attraction for me is the sort of people who choose to live in the lock-keepers cottages which mark the ups and downs of the canal on its way from southern Brittany to the north-west. Until relatively recently, these dwellings were not popular because of the difficulty of getting to the nearest road, the lack of living space and the risk of flooding. Now, so many have been bought and renovated to picture-postcard style by Britons that they have become fashionable with the people who once spurned them. But some are still in unusual hands. One cottage I pass regularly has a commune of retired hippies living in and around it; at another you can hire, sponsor or even sleep with a donkey. Outside another, a Vietnamese pot-bellied pig grazes contentedly alongside a llama, and I already know of two clairvoyants and a water diviner living beside the water course. His claims of mystical divination when seeking out water weaken a little when you point out he is living next to a canal, but he is an entertaining fellow.

Yesterday I met a Scotsman who believes he is a reincarnation of an ancient Breton king with magical powers, though to me he looks more like a reincarnation of Rab C Nesbit on a particularly bad hair and teeth day. Riothamus (or Dougal to his former friends in East Kilbride) lives in an impressively distressed caravan, carefully hidden from official view alongside an as-yet unrestored stretch of canal. We met when I was passing his hideaway and he accosted me to say he recognized me from a past life. Steeling myself for a probable touch, I accepted his invitation to take a cup of dandelion tea, and was fascinated to learn that apart from his other talents, he is a skilled windmaker. With the right incantation and frame of mind, he says he can raise anything from a zephyr to a full-blown hurricane. Unfortunately, when I asked for a demonstration he said it did not work when there were other humans around to interfere with the temporal forces. Riothamus says that the canal was deliberately built along a really strong leyline and always attracted unusual people, and I believe him. After I slipped him a few Euros to keep him going until he secures his next windmaking commission, we parted and promised to look each other up in another thousand years.

*

As small and unremarkable communities go, Paule seems a pleasant place. Some villages appear to take offence when you drive through them, or you may be turned against them for no more reason than a particularly ugly building or surly stare. Others appear at ease with what and where they are, and, like Paule, give off an air of comfortable well-being.

Close to the canal and within easy reach of the ancient Roman habitation of Carhaix-Plouguer, Paule has some interesting and lived-in buildings, a *tabac*, a basic grocery store, and a bar-restaurant run by a Welsh magician. David Owen used to earn his living by entertaining passengers on Brittany Ferry crossings in between appearances by an Abba tribute band. Now he performs tricks for his customers in the bar, and puts his creative cookery magic into a very good value *plat du jour*.

On the day we ate at the Cheval de Fer there was a pleasing mix of local and foreign custom, and I was able to add another amiable eccentric to the day's tally. While I paid the bill, Donella struck up a conversation with an elderly man from Hastings. Showing her his wooden leg, he said he and his wife had picked a cottage close to the canal as it was obviously very flat and easy to walk. He also figured that the leg would help him float if he fell off the tow path on the way home after a long session in the bar.

*

After lunch, we walked eastwards towards Rostrenen and through a stretch holding eight locks in not much more than a mile. The Grande Tranchée was and is a considerable feat of engineering, created to accommodate the point where the canal reaches its greatest height above sea level. There are some interesting chapels, traces of a prehistoric camp and the remains of a Roman bridge along the way, and small towns or large villages along this part of the canal include Glomel and Gouarec. The word 'jewel' comes up a lot in reviews of Gouarec, and it is certainly a small, sparkling gem of a waterside town. Away from the bits which have to put up with the thunder of the N164 (a by-pass is in the process of being built), the old part of Gouarec has some impressive buildings, a couple of good restaurants and a really friendly bar near to the canal.

About as far away from the sea as you can get in Brittany, Glomel has an excellent lake with a beach. All roads in this part of Côtes d'Armor seem to lead to Rostrenen, which appears to be as popular with British settlers as it is unappealing to us. Once an important administrative centre, market town and the eponymous seat of the local baron, Rostrenen dwindled in importance across the centuries. After a dozen visits to try and prove myself wrong, the town still seems to hold an air of resentful defeat, and were it human would, I think, be living on a council estate with a houseful of ungrateful kids and a workshy husband.

Wednesday 6th

This morning I was buzzed by an apparently *kamikaze* house martin as I went into the barn. Then I realised she was deliberately distracting me from her young. High up on the stone wall I found an amazingly intricate, delicate and yet obviously strong nest of mud pellets and straw; peering baldly but unabashedly down from it were four chicks. They will stay there for around three weeks, then take their first flight and continue to roost in the nest and be dependent on their parents for food for another week. House martins are generally a short lived species, though there are records of survival into their teens. We are privileged to be chosen as home territory, but the downside is that I will now be barred from the barn until the birds have flown the nest for good.

Monday 11th

We have discovered a local and undeclared (i.e. non-tax paying) cheese factory.

It is one of many in our region, and they are always in the most remote parts. This is for some good and obvious reasons. You can smell a good goat cheese maturing from miles away, which is why most producers cultivate very large and odiferous muck heaps and silage clamps in their back yards. I don't know if it is the remoteness or even the height above sea level which encourages the setting up of illegal production centres; in America the mountain folk specialised in moonshine whisky, and here it is moonshine cheese. Perhaps this unofficial industry is a reason why Brittany lacks an own-brand cheese.

France famously has a cheese for every day of the year, although virtually all are soft and a lot of them look and taste the same. But every region has its own specific marques. Normandy alone has 27 types of cheese, including the world-famous and stereotypical smelly Camembert. Although hard to believe or swallow, it is said that the bacteria involved in the making of Camembert is identical to that found between the human toes, thus creating the concept of someone having 'cheesy' feet.

But where other regions can boast of their distinctive brands, Brittany has none. In England there is Cheddar and Wensleydale and Double Gloucester, in Wales it is Caerphilly, and even Scotland has Dunlop. Here, there are ten thousand small producers legally and illicitly making their own cheese, but not one cohesive and recognised brand. I find it very hard to believe that over centuries, not a single enterprising Breton dairy or goat farmer woke up with the idea of going regional by giving his cheese some fancy-dan name like Myrrdin and claiming it was a favourite of the first king of Brittany. The mystery deepens when you realise that this absence of a cheese to call its own is in a region with nearly a million cows producing almost five billion litres of milk a year, which is twelve percent of the national total. Eighty thousand tonnes of butter are churned out in Brittany each year, yet the only cheese that a patriotic Breton would claim as home-grown in any great amount is taste-free Emmental. This is because the place of origin forgot to apply for exclusive rights to the name, and now Brittany knocks out more than half of the nation's yearly and inexplicable demand for a cheese which is even more bland and boring than the Dutch variety.

According to some renowned cheeseologists, it is possible that the Black Death in the Middle Ages wiped out all Bretons with the knowledge of how to produce cheese and the secret was lost for eternity. A weak excuse, but, for whatever real reason, though there are many local cheeses produced in Brittany, none have the necessary MOT certificate in the shape of an *appellation d'origine contrôlée*.

Thursday 14th

It is good to be walking across the moors with no more than my dog and a few hundred cows for company. A dramatic and unusual moment in the sky above came when I saw a buzzard struggling with what looked like a length of tubing in its beak. After much flapping and wheeling, the bird screeched in frustration as it let the object fall and I felt a glancing blow on my shoulder. I then saw that it was a viper, and now quite dead. It could have been uncomfortable had it bitten me, but I was still much luckier than the Greek playwright Aeschylus. He was killed when a tortoise was dropped on his head by a passing eagle.

Friday 15th

It is the day of the Assumption of the Blessed Virgin Mary, so another excuse for time off from work. Even the dedicated Pagans in our area will take the national holiday.

I have a French friend who says that the reason so many public holidays are sanctioned by the state is because it confuses strike committees and disguises the true figures of how many working days are lost to industrial action.

Today, though, is an important national fete day, and family members will be travelling from across France to spend the weekend together. There will also be any number of fairs and festivities, and those restaurants whose owners are not themselves on holiday will have a field day.

In the southern Brittany town of Quimper, the big event is the Feast of the Soul, which is a day when young couples ask Mary for her blessing on their future. An image of The Virgin will be placed in church doorways, and at dusk carried to the village or town centre for a night of feasting and fun with bonfires and bagpipes calling the tune.

Nearer home, all the action will centre on the still mostly ruined abbey at Le Relec, which was founded by Cistercian monks in 1132. Alain claims that the name comes from the abbey being built to house the body parts of an ancient Breton leader slain in a great battle at Lesmenez. In fact, there seems as little evidence of any relecs at le Relec as there are of saintly fingers in the church on the northern coast at St-John-de-Doigt.

Wisely, given the prevailing weather patterns in the Arrée Mountains, the monks at Le Relec specialised in making use of the mountain streams and rivers flowing past and often through their front door. Locally they were known as The Brothers of The Water, and some of their technical achievements would do credit to a team of modern and much better equipped hydro-engineers. Next to a lake near the abbey are the remains of a mill which appears to have been run by turbo power, and a very early lock system controlling the flow of water from the lake cunningly irrigated a huge area of what would have been either vegetable gardens or perhaps even paddy fields. If I seem to be unsure about exact historical detail, it is because everyone in our area seems to have their own version of the past, and there is little documented evidence.

What is sure is that the monks had a significant effect on the people and landscape of the Monts d'Arrée area. Owners of great tracts of the countryside, the crafty brotherhood set up a system giving the eldest sons of all local families a house, a yard and an area of land for life. In exchange, the monks would have a seventh of the wheat harvest. This gives the area its distinctive patchwork of small fields, and perhaps explains why three of the five families in our hamlet are farmers or former farmers, owning relatively small areas of land. So history can live.

In the way I so admire about how the French treat and use their ancient monuments, Le Relec is satisfyingly unrestored and obviously not over-maintained. There are no notices warning of the danger from crumbling stonework, collapsing archways and unguarded pits, and visitors are welcome to poke around in the cavernous interior and explore places which would be very strictly off limits in any British place of worship. Where the ancient flagstones are missing, there is trampled earth for flooring. Unforbidden and unguarded staircases lead to nowhere but a sheer drop, and timeworn and obviously fragile wooden statues of saintly figures can be freely handled as the visitor lights a candle of thanks or prayer. The last time I was here, a young man was playing a flute in the pulpit. It was a haunting air, and suited the surroundings exactly. A dog with a scarf around its neck was sitting guard over an old beret at the bottom of the stairs. I dropped a couple of Euros in the beret as we passed, then realised the man might be an eminent flautist, practicing for a performance. I tried to retrieve the coin, but the dog turned nasty and so I had to leave it.

The abbey is also very much a working place of worship, and apart from regular masses there are classical music concerts and readings and dramas throughout the summer months.

But today is one of the really big days of the religious calendar, when all local Catholics can expunge their sins of the past year and start again with a clean slate.

It is the day of the Pardon. After a suitably long service in the morning, the faithful gather at the door to atone for their sins by going on a procession of penitence through the surrounding woods and around the grounds before eating and drinking and dancing a lot for a *fest deiz*, which is the generally much soberer version of the night-time rave-up.

*

The priest stands on the steps of the abbey, and looks a little tetchy as the faithful gather to follow him for a walk in the woods. Perhaps he is unhappy because for once he has been upstaged by his parishioners in the fancy-dress stakes. At least a dozen of the older men and women in the crowd are wearing traditional Breton costumes, and it is interesting to speculate on how and why the styles and design came about. Like morris dancers performing outside a pub in England, the wearers look self-conscious, apologetic, defiant or quite pleased with themselves, but only the padre looks at home in his outfit. Perhaps that is because he is the only one in his working clothes.

There seem to be several styles of male costume, and all look like a collection of national dress from other cultures and countries. One of the men appears particularly embarrassed, and perhaps that is because he looks like the lead character in a very amateur theatrical production of The Mask of Zorro. His outfit is all black, and topped off with a broad brimmed and be-ribboned hat which is a hybrid of a sombrero and the sort of homburg favoured by Sephardic Jews. The heavily embroidered bum-freezer bolero jacket is the sort of thing worn by the support acts at a bullfight, but the trousers are wide and baggy and completely

114

spoil what could have otherwise been a quite dashing appearance.

Another version of traditional Breton Sunday best is worn with obvious bum-clinching embarrassment by a tall young man. He constantly looks across at an older woman who has also dressed up for the day, and the way he glares and she smiles back encouragingly, she has to be his mum. She is also entitled to look relaxed as her costume is relatively unsilly, consisting of a voluminous floor length skirt, a crocheted shawl and sort of skull cap made of fine lace. Her son's outfit has the same sort of waistcoat as the older man, but below the belt he is clearly and deservedly mortified to be wearing a really voluminous pair of what a golfer might call plus sixteens. They are heavily embroidered and swell out hugely from the waist before being pinioned at the knees like a pair of joke jodhpurs as favoured by Eric Morecombe. The outfit is finished off with a pair of red woollen tights and oversized sabots. I see that the young man is holding a mobile phone as if to keep in touch with reality, and when it starts to ring the priest shoots him a venomous look. Having silenced the laughing frog ringtone, the fiery-faced youth joins the procession which has now assembled behind a man with a banner as over-embroidered as the waistcoats, and they set off to atone for their commune's sins across the past year. As the cameras click and flash in the dull light, the young man keeps his chin tucked into his chest and stares straight ahead, and it appears to me at least that he is paying enough penance today to make up for a whole village's misdemeanours.

*

The penitents have disappeared in the direction of the woods surrounding the lake and abbey, and it is time for the fun and feasting to begin. From the sound of it, the chief guest at the pig roast has just realised his place in the scheme of things.

In the corner of the abbey courtyard is a large box-trailer hitched to a vintage tractor, and the noise coming from behind the plastic curtains shrouding the trailer, suggest that someone is slaughtering a pig for the barbecue at the last minute to ensure optimum freshness. It also sounds as if the slaughtering is being done very clumsily. Then the side curtain is pulled back by an unseen stage hand, and I see that the noise is in fact coming from a musical trio, who are tuning up their instruments and seeing who can make the most painful sounds. After a while, I realise that the band is not tuning-up, but has launched into its full performance.

Like the costumes, traditional Breton music seems to owe much of its origins to cultures beyond the boundaries of France. If you think about what it might sound like if a full-on Irish *ceilidh* band joined forces with a square dance caller and a tone-deaf snake charmer, you will get the picture. The group consists of acoustic guitar, violin and the chanter pipe from a Breton bagpipe or *veuze*. This is known as a *bombarde*, and when played directly by mouth requires a prodigious amount of breath. This means it can only be played for short bursts at a time, which, to many peoples' way of thinking, is no bad thing.

Making up the ensemble is a severe-looking lady of indeterminate years, whose job is obviously to punish the audience with her vocals while keeping at least one bar ahead of the boys in the band. Like country and western music, the individual tunes are very similar, although I cannot comment on the words as they are Breton. I suspect that most of what we are hearing are former work songs or land shanties, as they are very rhythmically repetitive, insistent and thankfully short.

While all this is going on upon the stage, a number of older and thus less resistant members of the audience have been pressganged into joining in the fun by the dominatrix on stage. I do not know what type of dance they are performing or if it is a local variation on a theme, but basically the routine looks rather like a hokey cokey as it would be performed in a geriatric care home. The dancers form a circle with hands linked, then spend their time hopping creakily from one foot to another before sweeping inwards and outwards in rough time with the music. To be fair, they seem to be enjoying the exercise, and each time the music stops they raise their hands and clap and call out in Breton. Perhaps they are asking for more, or perhaps they are begging the band to give it a rest, but the result is always the same.

As the lady on the stage calls the band and dancers to order and takes a deep breath before launching into the next number, I look at my wife and we head for the temporary bar, which has been set up by the lake and at least a quarter mile from the musical action. Having heard the entertainment and knowing that it will go on until dark, I can now see why the penitents and priest are hiding in the woods and why the beer tent is so distant and so busy.

Sunday 24th

The very narrow narrowboat glides almost apologetically through the placid water, and the hum of the outboard engine amplifies rather than breaks the silence. All is calm as we pass through verdant countryside which evokes thoughts of a time long gone in Britain; at any moment I expect to see Ratty and Mole sculling by in search of the perfect picnic spot.

It is a glorious day for messing about on the river, or just one of the handful of rivers that were joined up and re-routed to create the Nantes to Brest Canal.

Our hosts and owners of the Jenny Wren are new friends Sally and Richard Moore. They live in a very roomy and characterfully dishevelled farmhouse on the banks of the canal after it has oxbowed its way through Châteauneuf-du-Faou. The shortest distance between any two points is a straight line, but clearly nobody pointed that out to the creators of the canal. The Aulne takes on the form of three giant horseshoes as it sidles past one of our favourite Finistèrean towns, but getting anywhere not very fast is of course what river boating is all about. The Bretons seem fond of naming their rivers after trees or plants, and *Faou* is Breton for beech, *Aulne* is French for Alder, and *Rance* for bramble.

The Jenny Wren is just one of the Moores' several boats; they also have homes in other parts of Brittany and Britain, and a couple in Bulgaria for luck. It is not that they are rich or are building up a buy-to-let property portfolio or boat rental business. None of their other houses is occupied by anyone but themselves, and Richard spends most of his time working on the

117

more distressed ones. The reason they have so many and such big homes, garages, barns and boathouses is that they need them to house all their effects. For the Moores are not covetous, just cheerfully self-confessed disposophobics.

I have often observed that the hoarding instinct in one partner is normally balanced by an inclination to throw things away by the other. In the case of the Moores, both Sally and Richard like to collect and keep things on a grand scale. The mini-narrowboat on which we are cruising towards Châteauneuf is one of a small fleet of vessels to be found at their canalside residence, and the couple attend more street markets then many stallholders. The high-ceilinged rooms at Hirgars are consequently filled with booty from the Breton equivalent of boot and garage sales, and acquisitions include a range of chandeliers which would have made Louis XIV envious, more chairs in various states of repair than room could be found for at the dozens of tables taking their ease in every room, and a boar's head complete with pork pie hat looking amicably down from the kitchen wall.

Presiding contentedly over this gloriously unselfconscious jumble of rare and everyday domestic artefacts, Sally Moore is an accomplished artist and a big woman in size and heart. When she is not collecting collectables or knocking out another canvas in her studio, she acts as a super-discreet confidante and bunny mum to a host of British expatriate wives and girlfriends who are finding the going in Brittany emotionally tough.

Today we are all taking a day off to put the Jenny Wren through her paces on her maiden voyage, and there is a jazz festival at which to arrive in style. It will be the first outing for the pocket-sized narrowboat since the Moores bought her on e-bay.

We approach the first lock between us and Châteauneuf-du-Faou, and I think how hard it would be for any tourist body to come up with a better picture explaining why Brittany is the favourite French destination for holidaying Britons. Beyond the lock gates, the Aulne curves past the stone quay and bar, under an ancient stone bridge and on its wending way to Brest. Above us is the stately church, and over our shoulders the great castle for which the town is named. Everywhere is green and pleasantly undulating. The architect Thomas Owen used to create crescents as he knew how appealing they were to the eye. At Châteauneuf-du-Faou, nature is responsible for the aesthetic appeal.

We putter towards the lock, and an elderly fisherman ambles across to take our mooring rope. He lays out four rods in this spot every day of the year, and has never been known to make a catch. The last time we met he said he had a huge pike on a hook, but lost it when a passing boat sheared the line. In fact we know he never baits his lines and does not want to catch any fish. He comes here to enjoy the tranquility of the spot and an occasional chat with passing sailors and cyclists. When I asked one of his fellow fishermen why Benoît spends so little time at home, the man grunted that I obviously had not met his wife.

A small crowd gathers as I climb on to the bank and prepare to help move the boat from the high to the low side of the river. Little water traffic uses this stretch of the canal, so the movement of any boat through the lock is always of interest. In canal-using circles in Britain, there is a special name for the pastime of civilians who like to watch boats go through locks, often in the hope of an entertaining cock-up. Gongoozling is an old canal workers' term of derision, and is thought to come from gawn and gooze, which are Lancashire dialect for staring and gaping.

I find the audience a tad disconcerting, as, though I am trying to look jauntily confident, this will be my first solo gate opening and closing ceremony. Richard is staying with the boat but has given me a very thorough step-by-step guide to the required sequence. Basically, it seems very straightforward. If the gates ahead are open, the boat is gently steered in, the doors shut behind it and then water either allowed in or drained out so that the vessel floats to the level beyond the lock. If you are approaching a closed gate, the reverse procedure applies.

As I climb the ladder and try to look like a really seasoned river rat, the size of the crowd increases. The word has obviously got around, and this being France, the onlookers probably know who I am and that I am a virgin lock operator. One couple pick up their picnic hamper and move along the bank to get a better view, while a group of cyclists draws up and settles down for the show. On the other side of the river I see a party of hikers pointing across, and several are already watching me through binoculars. All these people and particularly the locals will naturally be interested in seeing how a foreigner gets on with the operation of moving the narrowboat in and out of the lock. It is not that they want me to fail or drown or sink the Jenny Wren, but simply that all French people enjoy a bit of drama. Any minor tragedies will obviously add to the pleasure of the event.

Intent on putting on a good show, I adopt a sailor's roll as I walk up to the capstan winch device which opens one of the two giant metal gates barring our progress. This is not a good idea, as one extreme dip of the shoulder coincides with my foot finding a pothole, and I have to grab a handrail to avoid disappearing into the lock. Trying to look as if this were a deliberate manoeuvre, I grab the handle of the winch and give it a hearty heave. Nothing happens, except I lurch forward, sprain my wrist and my nautical-style cap falls into the canal. Nodding sagely and trying to look as if I was merely limbering up for the task ahead, I spit on my hands and give another even heartier heave. Nothing gives except my back, and I realise I am probably trying to turn the winch the wrong way. As I have as little success while straining in the other direction and feel two shirt buttons pop, I hear a discreet cough and look to where Richard is holding up what looks like an oversized starting handle. Then I remember. Before I can open the gates with the capstan winch I will have to take the external pressure off them on the high side by cranking up a panel at the base of each gate and allowing water to flow into the lock.

As I collect the handle, an appetising odour wafts across the towpath and I see a mobile pizza van has spotted the opportunity and is making an unscheduled stop.

Several members of the crowd are taking photographs, and one man with a camcorder is telling his son in a stage whisper that with a bit of luck I will fall in the lock and he will have a dead cert entry for the French equivalent of You've Been Framed.

With trembling hands, I fit the crank handle on to the spigot and, shutting my eyes, pull down. Still no movement, and I open my eyes to see the son of the man with the camcorder approaching. He turns and smiles at the camera before reaching out and casually flicking off the safety catch which stops the cog wheel beneath the handle from moving. I think about pushing him into the canal and giving his father something special to film, but stand back and invite the lad to take over. The crowd parts and I walk to the pizza van to buy lunch and tell the owner how I am more used to sailing the seven seas than a canal, and that my ancestor was batman and close confidante to the Lord Admiral Nelson.

*

The clever-clogs boy has seen us safely through the lock, and we are chugging towards the distant sounds of someone doing a not half bad job on the Humphrey Lyttleton classic, Bad Penny Blues. I have recovered my composure and am keeping a lookout for other vessels, floating logs and sharks from my position at the bows. On either side of the canal, the crowd keeping pace with the Jenny Wren is still growing. Richard says that they are going to the jazz festival, but I reckon they are tagging along to see what sort of cock-up I will make at the next lock.

The music grows louder, and round a bend in the river comes a phalanx of mismatched vessels. The mini-flotilla is led by a beautifully restored old lugger with classic junk-rig red sail, a couple of open crabbers and motor launches flanked by several kayaks and even a pedalo water bicycle. In their wake is a battered old metal barge which probably worked this stretch of the waterways a century or more ago. It is festooned with pennants and bunting, and on the makeshift deck a selection of musicians as mismatched in appearance as the fleet are strutting their stuff. I count two trumpets, a euphonium, banjo, trombone, set of bongos and washboard as we pass on our way to the landing stage specially set up for the festival.

This being the most prestigious and popular jazz event in the area, the authorities have spared no expense or effort on the venue. A stage has been set up overlooking the canal for the top artistes, and there are at least a dozen other venues where amateur players can sit in and play together. Going by the noise, it seems some of the groups are playing four or five different tunes at the same time. The temporary bar is under siege and a remarkably orderly queue waits at the entrance to the arena to pay their admission fee. Even more remarkably, they are queuing to pay when there is a major gap in the fencing lining the towpath. The riggers had obviously run out of metal panels before fencing off the area completely, and this being rural France, had not bothered to close the gap.

The sun drops behind a row of poplars as the Jenny Wren coasts towards the landing stage, and a murmur of anticipation rises from the crowd which has followed us from the lock. The star turn is about to take to the stage behind them, but they are clearly far more interested in seeing what sort of performance the incompetent Englishman is going to put on with his boat hook and length of mooring rope.

I bow, then wave to the young boy who helped me out of trouble, throw him the rope and myself into the canal as the spectators applaud and the man with the camcorder goes into filming overload. I surface, tread water and think how it has been a wonderful day on the water, and how my only regret is that I did not discover the delights of river cruising long ago. But then, perhaps if I had I would not have found it so enjoyable now.

Monday 25th

If I were thinking of setting up a risk-free business in Brittany, it would certainly not be a bar or even an English teashop and grocery store. Based on the principles of supply and demand and potential business levels, I would launch a mobile wing mirror replacement service.

Whether by coincidence or design, all the country roads in our part of the region work out at the width of two standard-sized cars, plus about a metre breathing space. Maybe that was what it took for two carts to pass, or perhaps the road improvers enjoyed the idea of making it such a tight fit. As the average Breton likes to drive at least a half metre away from the verge and refuses to pull over when meeting an oncoming car, It does not take much of a head for figures to work out that something has to give.

This morning we came down from the mountain road pursued by a car from the Aude as if our bumpers had become entangled. As expected, the driver zoomed by as we pulled up at a junction, sheered across our bonnet and made for the hump-back bridge by the lake as if pursued by demons. Coming the other way was a local car, and it was obviously going to be a race to see who could get there first and take right of passage. Predictably, both arrived at the same time and both refused to give way. The two cars scraped past each other with no more than a coat of paint to spare, but both left wing mirrors as well as curses and interesting hand signals behind as they roared off.

It says much about French attitudes to driving that neither bothered to stop and at least discuss who was in the wrong and therefore who should pay for the damage. They will probably not bother to replace their dead mirrors, so perhaps my business plan is not such a good one.

Wednesday 27th

My wife has reminded me that I have forgotten our wedding anniversary. Again. My argument that she should remind me each year and so avoid being upset does not appeal to her feminine logic.

To make up for my lapse, I am treating us to lunch at what is said to be a very good low-price restaurant in our area. It is not just that I am a cheapskate, but Donella would not appreciate any meal that is charged out at ten times the cost of the ingredients because you are eating it off a posh tablecloth and under the long noses of snotty waiters.

We shall be spoiled for choice as to a venue, as there are hundreds of *relais* and *ouvrier* restaurants in Finistère, and thousands in the region. The word 'restaurant' actually comes from the old French verb 'to restore' and refers to how the customers felt after a restoring visit. This is why you still see the word '*Restoration*' outside the eating houses which specialise in more modest and modern dishes. It is commonly agreed that the first restaurant to bear the name was opened in Paris around 1765. Before that, a 'restaurant' was usually a broth which, quite literally, was meant to restore the drinker. *Relais Routiers* and *Ouvrier* restaurants can be found in any part of France, and are the equivalent of transport cafes in Britain, though not a lot of people either side of the Channel would agree with that comparison. But, like the old lorry drivers' roadside caffs in Britain, these unpretentious pearls exist to supply big portions of no-nonsense regional and traditional food at lunchtime. Of course it is not just blue-collar people who appreciate great food and at a price guaranteed to enhance digestion, and though the *relais* are aimed at truckers and *ouvrier* literally means 'worker', you are just as likely to find bank managers and other high-flyers sharing a plastic tablecloth with the sort of people they would not approve a loan to.

It is a vital part of my research into Brittany's culture and cuisine that we try as many different lunchtime restaurants as we can afford. The problem with the gruelling schedule of eating our way around the region and cooking and trying recipes at home is that I now have trouble fitting in through some restaurant doors.

For the sake of my art I have put on at least two stone since coming here, and I now stand out in any crowd, unless it is a crowd of very heavily-pregnant women. It is a curious fact that, in rural France, men are either slim, sturdy or very fat. But as a woman friend pointed out while surveying the male talent in a local bar, French men are fat in a different way to the typical British male. She did not add 'like you' but I knew what she meant. In France the obese male seems to be evenly larded, as if by an expert Gallic chef; in the UK, we fat blokes like to carry most of our excess weight in front of us. There is, as far as I know, no physiological explanation for this difference. It has nothing to do with what we drink, as I know lifelong tee-totallers who have bigger beer-bellies than me. My lady friend's theory is that it is what and when each race eats, and not how much of it. In general, as she says, French men do not snack, and particularly not on crap food. When, she likes to ask, did you last see a French man of any class noshing a chocolate bar while walking down the road or navigating a steak pie at the wheel?

Regardless of the precise reasons why I now waddle rather than walk, my wife is insisting I go on a diet. I have agreed, but only as long as I eat my slimming meals after our regular blow-outs in the name of research. There are still at least 1346 local luncheon clubs in Brittany we have not tried out, and I am not one to skimp on research.

Friday 29th

In rural England, it is the time of year when many normally sociable types go into hiding. They remain indoors for days on end, making their trips to 24/7 supermarkets in the small hours, and even give up their weekly visits to the local. This is not because they have developed agoraphobia. They are all avoiding the annual festival of embarrassment caused by an overabundance of home-grown vegetables.

It may seem a trifle, but basic social etiquette knows no more challenging an encounter to deal with than a man offering you a basketful of manky potatoes when you already have a mountain hidden in the bathroom. I know people who go on holiday to avoid the annual swap-fest which results from the home-grown vegetable glut. Elsewhere in Europe, I assume a man would tell his neighbour that he had sufficient brussel sprouts to see them through a lifetime of Christmases. Not so in Britain, where, despite the changes in our society, we still do not like to be rude. To refuse any gift is seen as churlish. To refuse a gift of food has all sorts of connotations, not least that the offerer's veg is crap. All over Britain at this moment, people are feigning surprise and delight as they accept yet another bunch of misshapen radishes, then stealing out in the dead of night to dump them far away from the eye of the giver.

I thought things would be different here, but this is the first time we have lived in a Breton hamlet where the rules are obviously even more rigid and labyrinthine. There is also the added complication that we, as foreigners, are considered unable to grow as well as prepare and cook anything edible.

I came out to greet the morning last week and found a basket of courgettes swathed tenderly in a blanket and laying on the step like an abandoned baby. There was no note but I recognised the basket and the way the courgettes were

125

assembled in order of size. Arriving later at Alain's with the empty basket and a box of eggs, I was given a one-hour masterclass on how to make a very basic ratatouille.

Returning across the lane I was waylaid by Mr Vitre, who asked me, in the manner of a man with an overabundance of pornographic photographs, if I liked vegetables. Five minutes later and I was staggering back to Paradise with a basket of even more regimentally ordered courgettes. I also had a sheet of paper telling me how to make courgette cake.

Arriving in the kitchen, I found my wife at the sink cleaning off the first of the hundred courgettes which have been growing contentedly in her vegetable garden. There are only so many ways to prepare and cook any vegetable, and it will be interesting to see how the courgette pickle, jam, relish and cordial turn out.

Saturday 30th

Another scorching day, so we have been to the seaside.

Just along the coast from Morlaix, Carentec is not one of our favourite towns, though I cannot put my finger on exactly why. Perhaps it is because, away from the older quarter, there are too many featureless modern white boxes for our taste. There is no reason that people who can afford to should not live in new-build houses with views of the sea, but for me they clash almost painfully with the natural beauty all around them. No matter how different in colour and size and design, each will look exactly the same, and each will have an even newer and shinier identikit car outside.

In contrast with the conspicuous displays of bourgeois conformity, there are some superb cliff top walks along this part of the coast, with the route passing any number of oyster farms and processing plants. For some reason and in contrast to the nearby houses, we find the rickety old warehouses and rusty machinery a relief to the eye and as if they should be there. Also dotted along the coast are some envy-generating islands with houses on them, the allegedly record-breaking lighthouse and the rugged Château du Taureau.

In Carentec, I feel I get more than a whiff of snobbish disdain when we walk the streets in our country yokel clothing, and our prejudices were not helped when we took Milly for a swim today. There were three dogs in the water at a deserted spot at the far end of the beach, but as soon as we sent ours racing into the surf after a ball, an official-looking head popped up from behind a rock. Looking remarkably like Peter Sellers in his Inspector Clouseau role, the uncivil civil policeman marched over to tell us that dogs were not allowed on the beach. When I pointed out that our dog was in the water with the others and not on the beach, he hurrumphed and said that was not the point. After a bracing debate I saw him reaching for his pad of multi-purpose charge sheets, so called Milly out of the water. As she arrived and we gathered up our clothes under his beady eye, I thought I would see if the town cop knew enough English to understand the word 'shake'. Unlike our dog, he obviously did not, and I got a petty buzz of satisfaction to see the large wet patch on the front of his trousers.

Somewhere nearby where dogs are allowed to roam free and we feel really at home - or would like to feel at home - is the Île Callot. This small island is more of a miniature peninsula and only cut off as the tide rises. The trick that the authorities have managed here has been to spend a lot of money to make the island look as if nothing has been done to it. Phone and electricity lines have been buried, and, unlike Locronan, there are no bars or souvenir shops. Even better, there are no commercial enterprises to puncture the illusion you have been transported back to a slower and quieter age. While there and after checking out that Peter Sellers was not hiding behind or under a rock, we spent a pleasant hour gathering cockles and mussels from either side of the causeway.

*

This part of Brittany is known as Léon, and the town of Saint-Pol-de-Léon is named and famed for the 6th-century cathedral built there by Saint Paul Aurelian. On the site now stands a replacement from the 13th century. There are also some impressive buildings marking its time as an administrative centre, and St-Pol was the scene of a notable English success in the Breton War of Succession. Saint Paul was a much-travelled Welshman, and the town is thus suitably twinned with Penarth.

*

It would be unthinkable to spend any time in this part of Finistère and not visit what has to be the only museum in the world devoted to people who sold onions. Although Brittany is famed for its onions, we have found most of those on offer at all supermarkets do not live up to the PR. They are small and anything but perfectly formed, go off very quickly, and would not live alongside a big, shapely, juicy and much better-tasting Spanish variety. It is true there are always posher Breton onions on sale beside the inferior ones, but their superiority is reflected in the price. They are also heavily hyped in a very French way. I once asked a top chef why it was said that Brittany's onions were so much better than elsewhere. He said it was because they were grown and flourished in good Breton shit, but more so in bull shit.

As the legend goes, Henry Olivier was the first Breton trader to see the potential of shipping onions to Britain, which had presumably managed well enough with the home-grown variety. It was he who started the tradition of the Onion Johnnies, who would take boatloads to England for sale at local markets and door-to-door. Some were reckoned to be able to carry a hundred kilos on their bike. The striped sweater, beret and bike are no longer seen in Southern England, though the tradition of persuading snooty housewives to pay through the nose for a common-or-garden vegetable because it has been plaited on a string still pertains. Last year I was in a swish market town in Hampshire where most of the local ladies wear green wellies and drive top-of-the-range Land Rovers though they rarely step off the pavements. At least a dozen of these county and country ladies were queuing up to buy strings of onions at a really knee-trembling price from a man in beret and striped top, complete with a creatively battered old sit-up-and-beg bicycle. When the bike had been stripped of its cargo, I expected the Onion Johnny to cycle off back to base or the ferryport, and was surprised to see him leave the bike and furtively sneak round the back of a nearby pub. Following, I found him draping himself with strings of onions from a huge pile in the back of his white Transit van as he practiced his Gallic shrugs. When I asked him in French what was afoot, he cheerfully owned up that he was from Dagenham, had never crossed the Channel and bought his supplies from Tesco. Plaiting the onions and putting on the sweater, beret and cod broken English accent with the odd 'Zut Alors' chucked in meant he could increase his mark-up on the Spanish onions by fivefold.

If visiting the Onion Johnny museum at Roscoff is not your idea of a wild time, you might wish to spoil yourself with a Thalasso therapy session involving close contact with allegedly special seaweeds. Or a short boat ride across to the blissfully car-free Île de Batz will give you a real taste of what Brittany (and just about anywhere else) was like before the invention and propagation of the internal combustion engine. A major attraction on the island is the Georges Delaselle gardens, showing off more than 3000 exotic plants from around the world.

Back on the mainland, the curving bay which houses the picturesque old town offers more than enough eateries to keep the most passionate foodie occupied for a long fortnight.

Sunday 31st

The flood of well-intended but unwanted vegetables from our two neighbours has been stemmed. Yesterday I took them each a large courgette cake, cooked (I made sure to point out) to the English recipe. If they had any more spare veg, I said, I would use it to make the classic Scottish dish, deep fried courgettes with a battered Mars bar and Curly-Wurly dressing.

Home cooking

Anyone who has seen the acres of tinned embryo peas for sale in supermarkets will know that the French equate smallness with freshness and thus quality. This rule is countermanded in the case of courgettes, which they like to grow to the size of a small marrow. This example of where size does matter put me in mind of an early encounter with the wife of our local bar owner in Normandy. Proud of the size and sheen of my monster marrows, I had taken one in to present to the shapely young woman. When I whipped it out from beneath my jacket and laid it on the counter expecting gasps of awe, she sniffed and said obviously English marrows were like French courgettes, only smaller.

This is the recipe for Parisian Courgette Cake, as passed on by Mr Vitre. As he said, not many families from the swisher part of the capital would admit to eating vegetables, but they, like the terminally misquoted Marie Antoinette, would think it a very suitable way to let the poor people of Paris eat cake. Another surprise is that the cake neither tastes of courgettes nor is green. A bit like snails and frogs' legs are only a vehicle for the butter and garlic, I believe the courgette appellation is only an excuse to give it an unusual name and bemuse foreigners.

Parisian Courgette Cake

Translatory note: I have anglicised this recipe by taking out the butter mountain and suggesting baking powder and bicarbonate. If you want to be truly gallic with it, you should add 250g of best butter, three or four drops of vanilla extract and use baker's yeast. The French recipe I used (I kid you not) also devotes a hundred words on exactly how to lovingly top, tail and grate your courgettes...

Ingredients

Eight ounces of plain wholemeal flour
Two teaspoons baking powder
Two teaspoons bicarbonate of soda
Eight ounces of soft brown sugar

An ounce of chopped walnuts or pecans
An ounce of sultanas
Two mashed bananas
Three beaten eggs
Five ounces of grated but unpeeled courgette
Some quality cooking oil
Some salt

Method

Sift the flour, baking powder, bicarbonate and salt into a bowl, and add the sugar, nuts and sultanas. Mix well, then add the eggs and bananas. Stir in the grated courgette and the oil. Beat the mixture thoroughly for a moment, but expect it to stay a bit lumpy. Butter and line a nine inch cake or large loaf tin with greaseproof paper, add the mixture and bake for an hour at gas mark 4 (375°F/175°C) until a skewer plunged into the heart of the cake comes out clean.

Onion Johnny Soup

Like so many classic pan-France dishes, the invention of onion soup is claimed by a number of regions. Parisians say it was knocked up as a quick and cheap way of keeping the cold out by porters at the capital's famous Les Halles marketplace. The dish was also said to be the brainchild and soup of choice of poor labourers in Lyons' silk industry, and of course many cuisiniers in this region claim that it should correctly be known as Breton rather than French Onion Soup. Whatever the truth, this dish gets top marks from all perspectives including cost, speed and simplicity of preparation and cooking, and of course, taste:

Ingredients

Six red or yellow onions, peeled and thinly sliced
Loads of best butter
A little sugar
Two cloves of garlic, minced

Eight cups of beef stock (all the experts agree that you cannot make a really good and proper onion soup without top quality beef stock, but I usually use stock cubes to no apparent ill-effects)

A cup of dry white wine

A bay leaf

A little dry thyme

Seasoning

Eight rounds of toasted French bread

Plenty of grated Breton Gruyere-style cheese

NB. Other recipes recommend olive oil as the medium for cooking the onions off, but as you will by now have realised, Bretons will always use butter at the thinnest excuse.

Method

Sauté the onions for as long as it takes to turn them a nice golden colour, adding the sugar about ten minutes into the process to help with the caramelisation. Add the garlic and continue to sauté for another minute or two, taking care that nothing burns. Now add the stock, bay leaf, wine and thyme, partially cover and simmer until all ingredients and tastes are nicely blended. Season to taste and remove the bay leaf. Transfer the soup into individual bowls or one large ovenproof receptacle. Put in your slices of toast, cover liberally with the grated cheese and grill until the gruyere is bubbling and screaming for mercy...

Quick goat's milk cheese

As discussed and unlike any other region of France, Brittany does not have its own cheese. Thousands of small producers make their own distinctive types of cheese, and some of the best are those made with goat rather than cow milk. This recipe will not help you become an instant master or mistress of *fromagerie*, but is a quick, easy and fun way to get started. You can try all sorts of herbs or additives to enhance or change the flavour as your confidence grows, and you may get a taste for home-made cheese production. Your neighbours certainly will.

Ingredients

Four pints of goat's milk
Some lemon juice or vinegar
Seasoning
Buttermilk (optional)
Herbs and spices (ditto)

Method

Heat the milk in a stainless pan and allow to simmer, carefully avoiding boiling or burning. Remove from heat and leave to sit. Add lemon or vinegar and stir briskly till the curds separate from the whey. When done, the mixture should look like large lumps of cottage cheese in a thin liquid. Now line a colander with several layers of cheesecloth and ladle in the curds (lumps). Discard the whey. Allow the curds to cool, squeezing as much moisture from them as possible. Now is the time to season the nascent cheese, and add any herbs, spices or berries you want to try. Press the curds into one block, wrap in a clean piece of cheesecloth and put in the fridge for a couple of days before the great taste test.

September

St-Léonard, Dol-de-Bretagne, Mont St-Michel, Dinard,
Dinan, St-Malo, Callac, St-Nicolas-du-Pélem,
Le Bodéo, Moncontour, Châtelaudren, Quintin,
St-Launeuc, Lanrivain, Guingamp, St-Herbot,
Guérande

Summer finery fades and it is time to make ready for a long mountain winter. Our feathered guests are on the wing and heading south, and the air is filled with the keening sound of hungry chain saws. In this department, pine trees grow like weeds, and most are destined to become furniture, floorboarding and the ghastly tongue-and-groove cladding boards with which the French are so obsessed. Pine is full of resin, burns too fast and spits like a premier division footballer, but is mostly free. Especially if you do your firewood collecting after dark.

Our neighbour Alain is predicting a *quatre-corde* winter, which means we must lay in for a prolonged siege of cold. In firewood terms, a cord/*corde* is the amount of logs which would fit into an imaginary box of three cubic metres in volume. The word comes from the Middle English, which itself comes from old French, so for once we two nations are almost in agreement on meaning and spelling and size.

Although there are agreed and exact dimensions on this side of the Channel, the size of a *corde* can vary considerably dependent on the honesty of the vendor and the cupidity of the buyer. The quality of the wood and its condition can also vary, and generally speaking you get what you pay for. All French countrymen are obsessed by the size and shape of their woodpile, and it is a condition which affects many British males who come to live amongst them. For real anoraks, there are said to be websites devoted to 'log blogs', debates on stacking techniques, and even revealing photographs of stripped pine faggots in provocative poses. For both races, size is everything, though a French countryman's personality and character can also be gauged by the style of his stack. Our obsessively tidy Parisian neighbour Mr Vitre has not gone as far as whitewashing his perfectly formed cube of logs, but each one is uniformly cut to length. Jean-Yves's winter fuel is neatly and modestly stacked behind his house. Surprisingly for a single man who lives mostly in one room, Alain LeGoff's wood pile fills his barn, which is bigger than his house. I think he is making some sort of point, and he definitely enjoys visiting our woodshed to look condescendingly at my pathetic attempt to store up heat for winter.

Wednesday 3rd

I think my neighbours are now assured I am clinically insane. This evening I was chatting to Alain and Jean-Yves as they trimmed their parts of the verge with sickle and scythe when Mr. Goarnisson roared by on route for his moorland fields. In passing, the bucket of his tractor clipped the elderberry tree beside our gate, and while gathering up the fallen berries I explained I would be using them to make wine. When I offered to reserve a couple of bottles of Château Lesmenez elderberry champagne and perhaps put on a tasting with some English cheese, Alain turned as green as the berries, and Jean-Yves had to sit down to recover from the shock.

While no Breton would consider making his own wine, many will be enthusiastically preparing for the start of the domestic cider-brewing season. As well as more small independent breweries than anywhere in France, I should think the density of home-brew cider makers in Brittany is rivalled only in Normandy, some parts of Somerset and the odd prison.

The apple is believed to be the first cultivated tree, and at 7,500 types is certainly the one with the most varieties. Apples and the drinks made from them appear in ancient stories across the world. Adam lost his innocence because of an apple, while Sleeping Beauty was poisoned by one. Hercules stole apples from the orchard of the goddess Hera. In Irish legend, the hero Cormac encounters an apple tree which bestows peace and contentment when a branch is shaken. The Gods in Nordic myth were able to remain young for ever just by eating apples. In more recent times, apples made a fine gift for teachers and kept doctors at bay. They also make a wonderfully refreshing and singularly flavoured alcoholic drink. The Egyptians grew apples but never discovered their secret, while the Romans did. As with so many other traditions and customs, the Norman invasion brought a new appreciation of cider to England, and within a century the drink had become part of the stable economy of the kingdom. Brittany was well ahead of the game, with a record of growing apples for at least two thousand years.

Cider can come in many varieties, dry or sweet, clear or cloudy, weak or double-hammer hangover strength. My cider will taste all the sweeter as it will be made from someone else's apples. On the track up to the moors stands a single apple tree, and I have enjoyed watching it blossom and fruit. The apples are small and misshapen and tart to the taste, but it seems a shame to see them go to waste.

*

The demijohns of elderberry wine and blackberry claret are bubbling away nicely, and my brewing and nuclear-strength chutney-making activities make the kitchen look like Frankenstein's laboratory when the doctor was having a really untidy day. Donella is equally busy with great vats of spluttering jams and jellies, and all the brewing and conserving is having an effect on our nearest neighbour. Each day, Alain is preceded into the kitchen by his cane, and he has taken to doffing his cap as he crosses the threshold. This is not out of politeness, but so he can clamp it over his mouth as a makeshift mask. As he waits for his eggs he eyes the bottles and flasks on the shelf as if they contained liquid anthrax, and I am sure he made the sign of the cross over his skinny breast as he left.

Saturday 6 th

Many Britons like to think that living in a village in France would be rather like living in a village in England, but with some major advantages. In general terms there would be much better weather, a cheese for every day of the year and wine figuratively growing on trees just down the road. Even better, a picture-postcard cottage would cost a fraction of its equivalent across the Channel.

This may be broadly true, but there are some differences which are not as attractive. To begin with, there is the lack of pubs and shops or much feel of 'community' in so many French villages. As in England fifty years ago, the arrival of big low-cost supermarkets killed off tens of thousands of village stores in France. Also, and unlike in England, a village with a bar is a real exception. This is because most working villagers spend their evenings at home, and the older people can't or won't afford to drink in a bar where a glass of wine costs the same as a couple of litres of the same brand in any supermarket. Another factor is that, even in Brittany, rural French people are not as clubbable as country dwellers in Britain. We hear a lot about café society in France, but I have never seen much evidence of it in France *profonde*.

Today, though, we found a worthy candidate for the perfect village, and it has not one but two bars as well as a thriving grocery shop.

Saint-Léonard lies a little south of Dol-de-Bretagne in the department of Ille-et-Vilaine, and even Prince Charles could not make a better job of designing the perfect village. Pupils at the tiny school can look out at cows grazing in the pastureland surrounding the village, and a small but perfectly formed church sits opposite the bar and grocery store. The Bar du Centre is owned by the de la Chésnais family who also happen to own the nearby *château* and holiday village of Les Ormes. This classic example of a good idea kept simple and the key to success being to give people exactly what they want has a capacity of 5000 campers, caravanners, log cabin and tree house residents, and most are British. Although there are a number of bars on site, the pub at St-Léonard is just half a mile away through a peaceful, winding country lane, and is a popular temporary local. Although determinedly French, it has a British feel to it, and this may be because the manager is an amiable Scouser from Bootle who learned his skills juggling cocktail bottles in Ibiza. In spite of barely being big enough to qualify as a village, Saint Léonard runs a regular market which in season continues into the night. There are no sprawling outskirts or workshops, industrial sites or car breaking yards, and the village is on the road to nowhere. All these things combine to make it a corker of a place to visit or live.

Sunday 7th

We found Dol-de-Bretagne an interesting combination of ancient and modern. Traffic whizzes around the newer bits, and the really ancient quarter is not much more than a cobbled street welded on to a more modern-looking shopping area. But Dol wears its long past like a comfy old cardigan and blends the old with the new quite cheerily. The town also has an interesting connection with Scotland as it is said to be the cradle of the House of Stuart. Bonny Prince Charlie and co. were descendants of the seneschal of Dol, who arrived in England with William the Conqueror and was given big bits of the country as a reward for Scot-bashing duties.

Rather than a Charlieburger outlet, another if less plausible historical aspect of the town is celebrated by a pizza house dedicated to King Arthur and the Knights of the Round Table. Outside the town is a great swathe of marshland centred on the town of Vivier-sur-Mer, and the atmospheric tower at Le Mont Dol was once a ritual Druid site.

Monday 8th

Not counting the Eiffel Tower, Mont St-Michel is the most popular tourist attraction in France. It is also not technically in Brittany. Standing on a tidal island in the bay of the same name, the Mont is still the cause of a degree of ill-will between Normans and Bretons with long memories. The Mont was technically Breton and an Armorican focus of Romano-Breton culture and power in the 6th century until it was annexed in 933 by William Long Sword, the first duke of Normandy. After the monks gave their support to the invasion of 1066, the monastery at St-Michel was awarded properties and lands in England, including a small island off Cornwall where the mini-version was to be built. The influence of the Norman abbey waned with the onset of the Reformation, and it became a prison until being declared an historic monument in 1874.

When we arrived, we had to fight our way through throngs of Japanese tourists and touts promoting the tacky wares of the shops lining the ascent. After a lung-bursting, elbow-jostling climb, we pitched up at the main building entrance to find it would cost a small fortune to go further, and our dog would not be allowed in at any price. Unimpressed, we made the long descent and headed for the nearest chippie.

Tuesday 9th

French pronunciation can be a tricky thing for non-Gallic tongues, and I know people who have booked to stay in Dinan and found themselves in Dinard and vice-versa.

Once upon a time, Dinard was a quiet fishing village, minding its own business opposite St-Malo on the western approaches to the giant estuary of the Rance. Nowadays, it is a very superior seaside resort and sailing mecca, mostly made so by British and American patronage from the nineteenth century.

Having absorbed several villages in its progress to becoming one of Ille-et-Vilaine's social hotspots, the town now bestrides a large chunk of the hilly coastal area. The population count varies dramatically through the year, and is swollen each season by more than 40,000 visitors. The main entrance to Dinard is marked somewhat idiosyncratically by a statue of Alfred Hitchcock. The great man is seen standing on a giant egg with a bird on each shoulder, and found himself there when the authorities wished to commemorate the town's annual English-language film festival. Suitably for a centre of culture playing the south of France at its own game, Dinard also hosts a number of upmarket regattas and ballet spectaculars. Further evidence of the town being a major player in the leading resort stakes is that Pablo Picasso painted one of his best known Mediterranean-style canvases here in the 1920s. Other notables with connections to the town were Lawrence of Arabia, who lived here as a child, and Debussy, Winston Churchill and film star Joan Collins were all regular visitors to what has been called the Cannes of the north. Further attractions include a golf course, a museum of the sea, a casino and many dozens of swish restaurants where the price of a meal could set you back the cost of a cottage here when Dinard was a much smaller, humbler and - for some - more attractive place. For those with an interest in jumelage, Dinard is twinned with another similarly sophisticated seaside resort of high culture, Newquay.

*

We have crossed the border and are back within the eastern reaches of the Côtes d'Armor.

Having around the same population and equally as touristy as Dinard, the oldest part of Dinan looks as if it were only recently knocked up by a team of riggers working on the set of a men-in-tights movie. This bit dates back to medieval times, and a number of the impressively magisterial buildings were put up in the 13th century. A fair stretch of the old walls remain and can be walked, and the biennial *Fête des Ramparts* gives hundreds of locals the excuse to dress up in period costume. But there is more to Dinan than old buildings. It is a real town for all its dressing.

The old inland port is an excellent place to walk or eat alongside the Rance river. Up in the old town, the cobbled streets wind between rows of restaurants, and act as a perfect race-track for local drivers wishing to test their tyres to destruction and build up their tally of restaurant tables, sandwich boards and the odd waiter or diner bagged *en passant*. As it was the fag-end of the season, competition was obviously fierce between the dozens of cheek-to-jowl dining houses and led to an interesting price war between two Italian restaurants at which we paused to study their menus. As we noted the cost of the set menu, a waiter emerged from the establishment next door and ostentatiously rubbed out and replaced and reduced the price of their dish of the day. When we wandered over to that blackboard, the owner of the neigbouring establishment marched out and pointedly wiped out and re-chalked a lower price than his rival. Not wishing to upset the proprietor of either establishment or see them come to blows over the pricing policy, we briefly considered splitting up and eating in both places, but settled for an apologetic shrug before retreating to a pizza house further down the road.

*

St-Malo is very much a town of two parts, or perhaps three. For me, it has one of the most pleasing approaches by water in all France, with the ferry boat threading through a series of rugged islands and promontories towards the ancient walled and one-time island town. This is offset by the depressing drive from the ferryport into the dilapidated dockside and modern-day town. But there is another much more sexy St-Malo. Here you can find one of the highest concentrations of sea food restaurants in Europe, and most of them situated in the Old Town, which is literally as well as figuratively a separate entity. Once the haunt of corsairs, privateers and pirates (there is a technical difference) who forced passing English ships to pay tribute or be sunk, the old town now relieves British visitors of money in a pleasanter way. One can overdose on a surfeit of restored and scrupulously maintained ancient buildings, but I think because it is a walled town and standing on its own, St-Malo works for the visitor in a way that some other historical tourist towns do not. But there is a price for tarrying there, whether in or out of season. The night we visited, every hotel was either booked or way beyond our budget, so we took a broom cupboard with a bed in it on the top floor of a liftless boarding house. While neither knitting nor wearing a mob cap, the elderly lady at the counter did a pretty good imitation of Madame Lafarge, and managed to keep a straight face when telling us the price for renting the windowless garret for six hours.

Coming down in the morning and finding Madame absent, I also found the doors to the street locked. We had been given no pass key, and health and safety requirements obviously went out of the window (like, presumably, the guests in the case of a fire) when compared with the risk of anyone leaving without paying. But unintended revenge was at hand. As I tugged frustratedly at the handle, I broke wind very loudly and odiferously just as Madame appeared on the other side of the desk. Rebuking our dog Milly, I paid the bill and walked innocently and quickly out of the building. On the wall of the porchway, I noticed a sign wishing guests a safe journey in several languages. The German for which is, of course, *gute fahrt*.

Saturday 13th

My wife has prepared a flask of coffee and packed lunch, and is airing a sleeping bag. This is not because we are going camping, but because I need to visit our nearest computer shop. Neither are her preparations because I have a long way to go, but because I will certainly have a long time to wait when I get there.

In the United Kingdom, people camp outside stores before sales days to be sure of getting a bargain. In many of the more rural parts of France, people need to set up camp inside some stores to be sure of surviving until they get served. The waiting time is bad enough in computer shops in Britain; it is even more so in France, as the French have a special flair for these things. Young men can become pensioners while waiting to buy a new gadget, which will anyway be severely out of date by the time they get their hands on it.

There is a clue to the level of customer response speed in the name of the shop I am visiting, as it is called Info-Tech-Rapide. In this respect, weasel words tell the tale on both sides of the Channel. In the UK, any bank that claims to be listening is sure to be deaf to your plea that they should not take the umbrella they are charging you to hire away just when it begins to rain in your life. Any public or commercial operation which claims to care about its customers will clearly not give a toss when the chips are down. The irony here is that, in France, the companies with *rapide*, *vite* or *toutes suite* in their names or slogans actually believe they offer a faster-than-usual service.

Checking my rucksack for iron rations, my copy of War and Peace and that I have at least one change of underwear, I kiss my wife and say goodbye to the cat, dog and chickens. If they are not around when I return, I will hopefully be able to get to know their descendants.

Unsurprisingly, there are no sales personnel on show when I enter the store, but at least there are no other customers, or at least ones who are breathing. I see what looks like a mummified corpse in a corner, then realise it is a life-sized manikin advertising a new sort of virtual reality game.

After an unstimulating conversation with the dummy, I hear distant voices and follow the sound. In a recess on the other side of a pair of curtains, the proprietor sits at his desk, facing a customer. Between them is a computer screen, and my heart sinks. Buying a box of screen wipes here can involve a lengthy bureaucratic transaction. From this conversation, I know that the customer is enquiring about buying a new computer; plus a printer and all sorts of other additional gizmos. I sigh theatrically, smile ingratiatingly at the proprietor and withdraw to pitch my tent.

*

An hour later and another dozen would-be customers have joined me at base camp. The most recent arrivals are a couple who are obviously old hands at computer shop shopping. They struggled in with two camping chairs, an ingenious collapsible table, an enormous picnic hamper, and quite a large portable television. I have been sharing a coffee with them and watching an absorbing round-up of the highlights from all the regional magazine programmes. From the south we learn that it has been a hot summer, and in Normandy a mysterious hole has appeared outside the town hall at Hootville. The presenter says words to the effect that the police are looking into it, and an accompanying clip shows a burly gendarme doing just that.

Meanwhile, back in the Morlaix branch of Info-Tech-Rapide, telephone numbers have been exchanged and new friendships forged, and we have all sworn that we will keep in touch if we ever get out of the shop alive.

Just as we start the tenth consecutive game of Charades, the curtains twitch and the proprietor and his first and only customer of the morning emerge. Across the English Channel there would have been at least a verbal punch-up as we struggled to stake our claim to the owner's attention. Here, everyone gathers round to hear which model and accessories the customer is thinking about thinking about not ordering, and he is given much advice on better and more reliable buys.

At last it is my turn to be served, but by now I have forgotten what I came in for. When I manage to recall what I want, the owner smiles apologetically and explains he does not keep digital camera memory cards, but can tell me where to get one. It is of course coming up for mid-day by now so the other shop will be closed by the time I get there, and it being Wednesday, it will not be business as usual until tomorrow morning.

I thank him, shake hands all round and strike camp. Driving home I muse on how differently things can be done in rural France. Some people would say it is annoying to waste so much time not buying something, but there are advantages. Only another half a dozen visits to Info-Tech-Rapide and I will have achieved something that many people spend a life time not doing, and that is reading War and Peace from cover to cover.

Sunday 14th:

To Callac in the western end of the Côtes d'Armor department for a very English event. The Autumn Fayre is staged by a magazine aimed at British expats, and is sure to be awash with people trying to sell each other home-made Cornish pasties, chutney, imported and hand-made furniture and other results of attempting to make some kind of a living out of living in France.

Callac has a high local British expat headcount, but is still very Breton. Many farmers choose to retire here, and at the weekly market the language of the region reigns. Attractions include a Roman bridge, a renowned *boulangerie* and tea rooms and a genuine Basque restaurant.

It is surprising how often I arrive in an innocent and inoffensive town and immediately take against it. Perhaps it is something in the air, or an off-putting juxtaposition of architectural features or street layout. Or It might be because of a bad experience on the road in, or indigestion, or just because I am in a bad mood. Now we have got to know and feel comfortable in Callac, I have apologised for my unfair pre-judgement and we are getting on well.

The grubby and tracked outskirts indicate its railway town history, but the centre is a pleasant place to be. There is an unusual use of red brick on many of the chimney stacks around the town hall, and the church looks like it was built in stages from the Perpendicular through Norman to Victorian Neo-Gothic. If it were human, I think Callac would be a friendly, welcoming and big-hearted mum who was not too fussy about the cleaning.

After the fayre and laden down with pasties and some brands of chutney untried even by my wife, we crossed the square and called in at The Rendezvous, an English-style bar owned by the amiable Gary and Nicole Mull. There is an extra frisson to having a drink at the Rendezvous when you know its former incarnation was an ancient chapel where condemned prisoners were given the Last Rites before their final journey to the gallows in the place of public execution just across the road. Nowadays, the Rendezvous specializes in being a home-from-home for expat Brits and a place of exotic foreign appeal for locals. English real ale is always available, and as a nod to the grisly past of the premises, Nicole has created a drink called Last Orders.

*

On the way home we stopped off at the Forest of Beffou to look for the Fountain of Youth. Disappointingly there are no signs or clues as to where it is. This swathe of excellent woodland walks is said - like every other patch of trees bigger than a copse in central Brittany - to have once been part of the legendary Brocéliande forest. A place of magic and mystery, Brocéliande was the setting for any number of Arthurian adventures, and is said to be the location for the tomb of Merlin. From personal experience, I can vouch that, at weekends, Beffou is the location for one of the best hamburger vans I have come across in all France.

Tuesday 16th

More trouble on the home-grown front. We have staged a mini-harvest festival, and it has been a subdued affair. Apart from the courgette glut of last month, our attempt to live off the land has not been a success. Had we been relying on the fruits of our vegetable patch for survival, we would now be looking down the barrel at a long and very lean winter. Nowadays, the most rural Bretons only have to nip out to the nearest supermarket to stock up on the limited range of vegetables that the French think suitable to put on one's plate, but it would have been almost a life and death affair for the people who lived in Lesmenez a couple of centuries ago.

For us greenhorns, the rainy and mostly sunless summer and the additional factors of living at this height on unfamiliar soil have combined to make my wife look a complete amateur at growing food. It has in the process given our nearest neighbour another reason to set his wizened features into that familiar told-you-so expression.

When Alain LeGoff said it was impossible to grow tomatoes in this bit of Finistère, I thought we had him. For years my wife has been coaxing prize-winning tomatoes from some really unyielding earth and strange situations. To give her a real edge, I spent hours constructing a luxury home for the dozen plants we had specially imported from England. My purpose-built tomato nursery was cunningly built to be not only portable, but on a turning platform to catch every available blink of sun. If Richard Rogers had designed it, I think it would have won a prize for architectural excellence. But it did not work. Last week I sent an e-mail to our closest friends announcing the birth of the singular East tomato; it was accompanied by a photograph to explain why my promised super-strength green tomato chilli chutney would come out in limited edition only this autumn.

Elsewhere, it has been just as feeble a reward for hundreds of hours of work. Our corn on the cob plants are not as high as even a miniature elephant's eye, and the strawberries have completely failed to show. We planted hundreds of seed potatoes, and the earth has given up no more than a plateful.

Meanwhile, Alain has used his local knowledge and experience to grow only the most responsive vegetables in his huge plot, and is now relishing acting like a lady bountiful. For weeks he has been arriving with wheelbarrow-loads of leeks or spring onions to swap for our eggs, and has now gone into overdrive. Giant pumpkins materialise Tardis-like outside our kitchen door alongside monster marrows that our neighbour claims are just Breton-sized courgettes, and it has got to a point that we have had to resort to subterfuge to keep our end up. To prevent our neighbour from seeing how badly the Brits have done, I have been buying in what my wife would normally have grown. So our carrots are actually counterfeit, and the giant and full-blooded beetroots I have been casually showing off come from supermarket shelf and not our soil. My face-saving scheme worked all the time I kept Alain from seeing the true state of our veg garden by telling him that it was off limits due to a nasty case of wire worm in our English strawberries. Unfortunately, I got too carried away with trying to appear the better gardener, and the three coconuts and a pineapple I tried to claim as home-grown gave the game away. Especially because, as he pointed out, they still wore the Super U special offer sticker and price tag.

Wednesday 17th

A strange encounter as I gave the hens breakfast. At first I thought the whole gable end of the barn was on the move, then saw hundreds of what looked like wasps working their way through the thick covering of ivy. When Alain came over for his daily egg and I told him about the invasion, he said my visitors were bees, not wasps. He also said I should feel honoured that our home had been chosen by the best Breton bee dancer in the area.

Sensing another leg-pull, I asked him to explain. Over a glass of wine in the kitchen, he claimed that all swarms of bees regularly send out scouts to look for the best sources of nectar. Each outrider returns to the main party and reports on its findings, performing a little jig to demonstrate the quality and quantity of the place. The bee who performed the most impressive dance would be the winner of the X factor-style vote, and the rest of the swarm would then follow him to the happy hunting ground. I do not know if this is true, but it sounds so unlikely it could be.

*

I spent this afternoon at our local honey farm, and it seems Alain has not been shooting me a line. What he said about the dancing bees is true, and encouraged by my purchase of an eye-wateringly expensive and very small pot of his finest produce, the apiarist filled me in on some further fascinating facts about bees. For a start, they do not actually create honey for us to steal. In the manner of so many supermarkets serving up pre-digested food in the UK, bees repeatedly regurgitate nectar to come up with what we choose to call honey. In the course of a lifetime, a worker bee will produce no more than a tenth of a teaspoonful of the golden gloop, and the end result of just a pound of honey will have taken 50,000 air miles and the tapping of two million flowers.

And there was more. The variety of males who have been working our grounds will sport black moustaches for collecting plant fragrances, and though females are generally faithful to one partner, the randy male Breton bee may put it about with many partners during his shorter but much more active lifespan.

Thursday 18th

An unpleasant moment at a bar I have not used before when I heard a sour-faced individual muttering about foreigners taking the country over.

In all my years of travelling around and living in France, I have been the subject of deliberate anti-British sentiment just twice. In each case, the aggressor was obviously the worse for drink and took exception to me talking English when in his presence, even though I was in the company of non French-speaking Britons. In each case I told the complainant that my friends were merely visiting his beautiful country and spending lots of money in it so the high level of his unemployment benefit could be maintained. I also asked if he would learn to speak Chinese if visiting China. When this did not appeal to the logic of either, I told them that my father had given his life for France in World War II, though I had only given a leg. Neither of these statements was anywhere near true, but it made me feel a lot better to hear the silence as I limped melodramatically from the bar.

*

On second thoughts, the anti-Brit I encountered earlier may have a point.

This evening we called in at a village which seems to have been shanghai'd from the original inhabitants. Even worse were the hypocrisy levels of the incomers.

The bar is owned by a Briton, as are most of the houses which surround it like a wagon train drawn into a circle of defence against the natives. Even if they wanted to move back, the houses are now far too expensive for their previous owners to afford.

The owner, who I shall call Ken Avo, is like a climate campaigner who jets around the world to harangue people about the need to cut down on their personal travel. He was sporting a Breton beret and clogs as he wagged a verbal finger at me during his lecture on the requirement for incomers to integrate with the locals and respect and preserve the region's culture and language. After finishing off his non-Breton beer, he ejected the two Breton customers, closed the bar and invited us to join him and his English clients at the nearby British-owned caravan site for the traditional Thursday evening special of Cottage Pie and Chips.

Friday 19th

Bisdu did not appear at the kitchen door for her breakfast, so it looks as if she has gone into confinement. Donella has assembled a very comfortable and private birthing station in the barn from old curtains, pillows and my favourite dressing gown

149

in case she chooses to have her kittens on our premises. My wife says she will ask Alain if she can take one of the litter, and feels that Toots our now aged werecat will be happy to accept a kitten into the house.

*

An embarrassing encounter at dusk with Mr Vitre when I took my new kilt for a test run in the lane. There is a strong affinity between Bretons and any other Celtic race, so I have decided to cash in on my Scots and Irish ancestry. As a proper kilt in either the Kelly or Young clan tartans would be prohibitively expensive, I have settled for two window-paned checked skirts, sewn together most artfully by my wife. The overall effect when worn with Wellington boots and camouflage jacket is interesting if not particularly Scots in appearance, but I have tried tying a wide distemper paint brush around my waist to resemble a sporran for when I attend official functions.

Our Parisian neighbour is an almost obsessively tidy man, and spends much of his time at Lesmenez clearing up cow dung and repainting the stone blocks guarding his cottage. As I reached his gateway, he looked up from where he was kneeling at the gate, and nearly dropped his trowel. When I explained that I was just trying on something my wife had made, he looked at me thoughtfully for a moment, then said he had heard that many English men like wearing their wife's clothes at the weekend. Being French and a Parisian, he was clearly not disturbed by the thought of living across the lane from a seventeen stone bearded transvestite, and said his wife was about to throw out a lot of her old dresses if I was interested in trying some on.

Saturday 20th

Of the four departments, Côtes d'Armor seems to us to be closest to what has gone before, or what is said to have gone before. The further away from roads and habitations, the more timeless the surroundings become. It is as if the membrane between now and then and ourselves and nature is at its thinnest in the wild places. If Korrigans and other Breton sprites did or do exist, I think they will have set up home here.

We are staying with friends at St-Nicolas-du-Pélem, which is a small, neat and inoffensively anglicised town. It has a high proportion of British residents, an English grocery shop, and a hotel and bar run very capably by a couple from Yorkshire who have managed the rare trick of attracting both local and expatriate trade. In the bar yesterday, I saw a young Breton woman in a stylish business suit tackling an all-day breakfast baguette. As the yolk ran down her chin, I thought that the gallicised egg-and-bacon sarnie was a very suitable example of how cultures can fuse and combine for a positive outcome.

Behind the hotel and bar are the remains of a half-built castle which was started in the late nineteenth century to jazz the town up and impress a pretender to the French throne. He thoughtlessly gave up his claim, so the local aristo building it decided to save some money and stop work on the project.

Beyond the unfinished castle is a great forest, with miles of walks past the remnants of iron age encampments which include the remains of a motte and bailey fort. It may look no more than a small hill with a ditch around it, but to stand at the top as the dying light filters through the forest is really to feel at one with the past. Depending where you are coming from, at the end or beginning of the forest walk there is a magnificently theatrical water mill, where water cascades down to the wheel over the huge rocks and boulders which are one of this department's most striking features. There are also hidden treasures to seek out. This morning, we found and followed a trail of trees inset with carvings of nymphs and elves and other mystical creatures. It led ever deeper into the forest, and then to a tiny cottage in a clearing. There were no television aerials or power or telephone cables, and the place looked unoccupied in spite of the smoke twirling from the satisfyingly crooked chimney stack. After sneaking a look through the window, I touched the wall and was almost disappointed it was not made of gingerbread. As we walked back into the forest I looked back and was half-surprised to see it still there.

A little later we heard the hullabaloo of a hunting party. In other regions of France, the hunters at least try to sneak up on their prey. Here in artistic Brittany, each outing in the forest must be a performance. Horns are sounded, drums beaten, guns fired in the air just for the dramatic potential, and the hunters crash through the brush shouting to each other about a cloud formation or the way the light falls on a tree and the interesting texture of its bark. When the party has exhausted itself and scared off all local wildlife, the members will retire to the local bar to discuss the day's proceedings and bemoan the lack of game.

The last time we were in this part of the forest we found another isolated cottage, and in the front garden was the biggest and closest live boar I had seen. It was contentedly grazing at the vegetable patch, and when we shouted a warning to the householder, a lady came out, scratched its back affectionately and said the huge creature was not an intruder but a pet. Claude had taken shelter from the hunt in her woodshed last year, and stayed on. Her husband (for whom the beast was named) had died just before the boar appeared, and she found its personality and manners far more acceptable.

Just up the road from the great forest is the hamlet of Bothoa, where can be found a school museum. Bothoa was also the birthplace of a particularly bloodthirsty 16th-century bandit called The Wolf, but more of him later.

Our hosts in St-Nic are Californian painter Eric Hendrickson and his wife Kris, a former London policewoman. They have lived in St-Nicolas for five years and had their fair share of adventures while restoring their 18th-century town house. They are on their fifth builder so far, and intend keeping him. They say he is no more reliable than the rest but his excuses for non-arrival are much more creative than the norm and appeal to Eric's artistic sensibilities. The builder has not been near their house for a month, and when they tracked him down to his favourite bar he said he was having to do some urgent restoration work on his own home. Over a drink he told them how a neighbour's cat had got into their house while he and his wife were away on an extended break. The cat had chased a mouse up the chimney and become stuck. It had died there, and the first the owners had known about the small tragedy was when they returned home and lit the fire. The gases from the decomposing corpse had exploded and caused the chimney breast to collapse into the living room just as the couple were settling down for the weekly omnibus of Eastenders. It would take at least a month to repair the damage and find enough pieces of the cat to give back to the neighbours, but as soon as he had done that he would be round to pick up where he had left off on the Hendrickson's roof.

*

As mentioned previously, another curious Celtic link between Brittany and Wales is that the anthem of the region has the same tune as Land of My Fathers. The two were winningly combined during a visit this evening to a cross-culture singalong at a bar in the remote village of Le Bodéo.

Like Tony Blair in his early on-message days, Bretons have a penchant for dropping vowels, and the P'tit Bar is a good example. The combined bar and grocery store is run by a British couple who have made the place a success against all the odds. The freehold came up for sale after the owner had fallen out with the mayor and barred him from the premises. This is not usually a good idea in rural France, especially when the first citizen makes up a tenth of your regular custom. To add to the odds stacked against them, the new owners had never run a pub or any other sort of related business, and spoke no French. Almost unbelievably, they have made a go of it, and the P'tit is now a thriving social centre for local Brits and Brets. It is very much a case of an exception proving a rule, but gives hope to all those who dream usually impossible dreams.

The singalong was a general success, and I found it interesting that the pace and tune of the Breton songs and music evoked more of an Arabian than rural French feel. It also seemed to me that most traditional Breton work songs are the same song. Like sea shanties, they are deliberately repetitive in tune and rhythm for obvious reasons. Our hosts were a group of ladies whose total age must have been close to that of the church opposite, and they seemed to have an inexhaustible supply of songs about gathering in and threshing the wheat or having a high old time picking the scabs off potatoes. Often it seemed that the next song was a repeat of the last song, and the gaps between became shorter and shorter. The guest of honour was the previously banned mayor, and I suspect he would have preferred the exclusion order to have still been in place. A typical politician, he sat with a rictus smile on his face, feigning fascination at each repeat performance. At the conclusion of the song or at any convenient pause, he would stand up and try to get started on a speech thanking the ladies, but each time they would set off again with even more gusto.

Finally, they sat down and chattered excitedly amongst themselves in Breton, probably deciding which hundred airs they were going to perform next. After a short speech from the mayor, it was our turn.

My wife's delivery in her sweet, clear voice of Land of My Fathers in Welsh ended in a rapt silence, followed by a storm of applause. Neither Breton nor English members of the audience would understand the words, but the feeling and theme of deep love of homeland was clear to all. I could not let Wales take all the glory, but my version of Will Ye No Come Back Again brought polite but puzzled rather than enthusiastic applause. After another couple of glasses of strong Breton cider, I attempted to demonstrate some basic steps in Scottish country dancing, but fell over a table. This resulted in the breaking of an ashtray, and, as I was conforming to tradition vis-à-vis underwear beneath my skirt-kilt, due cause for our Breton ladies' choir to break into a fresh bout of birdlike chattering.

Sunday 21st

I am not usually taken with medieval towns which show off their history like a tart in excessive make-up and provocative clothing. Freshly cobbled streets and over-the-top olde-worlde street furniture and shop and street signs and menus in indecipherable gothic-horror type face invariably get up my nose. But for me, there is something cheerily down-to-earth about Moncontour which allows the town to get away with looking like a 1930s Hollywood film set designer's LSD-induced interpretation of what

154

the average English village looked like in the reign of Good King Richard.

Attractions include a biennial medieval fete, and the contrast of the extremely photogenic ancient buildings, hundreds of extras in costume and thousands of visitors snapping away with their digital cameras is an almost surreal sight. Now the season is over, the town has won back its cobbled streets and it is very pleasant to take a coffee in the shadow of buildings which have stood for centuries but look as if they could fall down at any time.

From Moncontour we drove on to Châtelaudren, another pretty place which claims the title of *petite cité de caractère*. I don't know what the exact qualifications are for being awarded the recognition under a scheme which started in 1977, but both towns seem to fit the bill by being full of character in their own way. A historic capital of the Göelo area, Châtelaudren is more quirky than Moncontour, and another magnet for arty folks. It was also once said to be the second most important fashion town in France (presumably after Paris). A clue as to why it was awarded this honour may be found in the presence of the former printing works beside the lake, which produced the country's first magazine aimed solely at women and launched in 1938, an organ rejoicing in the name 'Le Petit Écho de la Mode'. Hundreds of thousands of dressmaking patterns were also churned out here. The lakeside buildings are now a warren of arts and crafts workshops and design studios, and it is the only place on earth I know to have an Association of the Friends of the Mill of the Wig. I do not think this is because the giant mills made hairpieces, but the title is recognition of the value of using available resources for other purposes. At least, that's what I deciphered from the publicity hand-out. On our walk around the friendly, arty-feeling town we stopped off at a stall for the Breton equivalent of a fried egg sandwich, and found it almost an art form to eat one without suffering third-degree burns.

*

On and through Quintin, an ancient fortified town in the sumptuously appealing Gouët river valley. The town made its name and fortune with two hundred years of hemp production.

Oversubscribed with public monuments, it was once a centre of the Marian knighthood cult (more Celtic and Arthurian echoes) but nowadays does a fine line in floral displays. Next month is a big date for all pub and public singers in the region as Quintin hosts the yearly *chanteurs de rue*. Hundreds of locals get into costume and take part in musical processions through the cobbled streets, with buskers and barrel organs and parades aplenty. The event is coupled with the fair of Saint Martin, who is the patron saint of beggars, soldiers, tailors and wine-growers.

*

Brittany is rich in the forests and woodlands which cover 330,000 hectares of the region, and a surprising nine-tenths of all Breton forests are in private hands.

A remnant of the ancient Dark Forest which covered most of central Brittany is Hardouinais, forty miles due west of Rennes. This great wooded place surrounds a lake with beaches, and reaches out towards the village of Saint-Launeuc. The pretty village is home to two hundred souls and sports a very unlikely example of mutual co-existence.

Yew trees are common in ancient churchyards as they deterred visits from marauding goats and other plant species, and also grew the wood with which to make the best longbows. (We allegedly copied the idea and bow from the French, but that is still a matter of dispute between historians on either side of the Channel). At St-Launeuc, the 13th century yew at the centre of the churchyard has a mature cherry tree growing from its trunk, so has for many years been happily defying all the relevant rules of nature and science.

Facing the churchyard is a building with another example of mutual need resulting in strange bedfellows. The former manor house there is a majestic building of granite complete with turret and priest's hole, and was bought as a ruin by Sue and Paul Joyce in 2003. Its particular distinction is that it was a safe house for a strange mix of counter-revolutionaries who supported the church and monarchy during the Terror. Chouan is an old French surname, loosely translated as The Silent One, and was used as a nom-de-geurre by the insurgents. Amongst the chouan band of brothers were Breton high-borns and smugglers who preferred the old ways for their particular purposes. Their secret symbol was a heart surmounted by a cross, and their motto *Dieu et Roi*.

*

We have stopped for afternoon tea at Guingamp, home of my wife's ancestors. The break in the journey will also allow Donella to pose by the statue of a forebear who designed the great church. Other claims to fame are the remains of the town's three castles, burned down by order of Cardinal Richelieu, and there are any number of seasonal outdoor events. Most notably there is the Breton dance festival of Saint Loup, and a massive pardon which pays homage to the Black Virgin in the Basilica-de-Notre-Dame-de-Bon-Secours. If you like clothes, this is the place for you, as every other shop in the high street seems devoted to fashion. Guingamp is also the home of the most expensive ice cream I have bought in France.

*

A pleasant end to a very long day and I am now confirmed as the biggest liar in Brittany.

On the way to St-Nicolas-du-Pélem we stopped off to walk through the gorge of Toul Goulic. The path alongside river and rocks and caves connects the villages of Trémargat and Lanrivain, where can be found an absolutely corking bar. As well as a penchant for placing apostrophes where vowels should live, there is a long-established custom of story-telling in Brittany; the Caf' Conte is one of the venues for a yearly event where raconteurs compete to spin the most beguiling tales. The centre of the far-flung community, the bar-cum-grocery store was run for decades by the present owner's indomitable mother, and mighty figures from past administrations have come here to pay court to Madame Chelin.

The Conte is one of those increasingly rare bars which appears totally unconscious as well as unselfconscious in its glorious eccentricity of structure, design, décor, fixtures, furniture and furnishings. The customers reflect the unusualness of their surroundings, and the patron even more so. Didier Chelin is said to have been a marksman in the French Special Forces, and the first time we met he produced a shotgun from beneath the bar as we walked in. When I raised my arms to the nicotine-coloured ceiling, gulped and asked what was on the menu, he said he did not know until he had shot it. He then pointed out where the beer and bottles were kept, explained how not to work the cash register and set off for the woods. On his return he disappeared into the kitchen while we and the regulars helped ourselves to drinks. It was one of the simplest and best bar meals I have had in any country. I still do not know the exact ingredients of Didier's game soup, but did not like to ask as he still had the shotgun slung over his shoulder as he served us and might have taken my enquiry as a criticism.

In our honour this evening, the bar staged an impromptu story-telling bout with the winner to be the entrant who could come up with the most unlikely or preposterous story. After a selection of the tallest of tales featuring ogres, dragons and other fantastical creatures, I gave a brief talk on how talented and creative many English cooks are nowadays and won the prize of a spoonful of best Guérande salt hands down.

Sunday 28th

Brittany has four hundred saints, though only three are recognised by the Catholic church. The Vatican may find it fishy that the region has more than enough saints for each day of the year, and thus an excuse for non-stop partying. Coincidentally (or perhaps not), the most popular and oft-celebrated Breton saints are those linked with food and drink. One weekend will see due homage being paid to the patron saint of cider-making, the next a festival of the holy individual responsible for fruits of the sea. As far as I could discover, it is all a bit sexist as the only female Breton saint seems to be Anne, the mother of the Virgin Mary.

Today we visited the home turf of the patron saint of all things bovine for a feast of butter. St-Herbot is a tranquil village in mid-Finistère and unusual in that it has a village green and pub alongside the church. With a huddle of well-kept and whitewashed half-beamed cottages looking on, it is very like the idealised version of an English village. The quietly comfortable air of the place may be because Herbot was one of the richest saints in Brittany. Legend suggests he made his pile by running a pretty effective protection racket. The story goes that Herbot's preaching and hectoring so distracted the men from their labours in the field that the women of his home village of Berrien drove him out. In revenge, he set up shop in the village now bearing his name, and cursed the cattle of his home village. To keep on his right side and make sure the cows continued to come up with milk and healthy calves, it became the custom to make offerings and tributes to Saintt Herbot.

Each year, the *Fête du Beurre* begins with an early mass and continues until after dark with music, dancing and a marathon dawn to dusk licence for the bars. When we arrived, at least two hundred cars lined the roads, but the village green was eerily deserted. Alongside the green, lines of vintage tractors had been left in mid-formation dance layout. At the craft stall, a half-finished basket swung creakily in the breeze. Even the temporary bar had been deserted. The only signs of life were a bored bull and cow tied to a tree. Then the church bells marked the middle of the day, and we realised the cause of the abandonment. Beyond the church and screened by a line of ancient oaks, we joined the end of a queue snaking towards a distant tent. Once it was said that everything stopped for tea in England. In rural France, everything still stops for lunch.

Ille-et-Vilaine info

One of the original eighty-three departments created in 1790 after the Revolution, Ille-et-Vilaine occupies the easternmost part of Brittany and is named for its two main rivers. Though elevated and hilly, it is a very watery area with the Rance another major river which lost out when the department was named. Ille-et-Vilaine also boasts Rennes - the capital town of Brittany - and Fougères and Dinard amongst its impressive list of major historical towns.

Ranked 23rd for departmental population at just under a million, it has an uncrowded density of 133 residents per square kilometre. By rights, Bécherel should be twinned with Haye-on-Wye, as it is known as the Village of Books. There are fifteen bookshops operating there at last count, which works out at one for every 51 Bécherellais. Some of the delightful literary events taking place there are the European Festival of Ancient Greek and Latin, the Spring of Poets, the Fêtes du Livre each Easter weekend, and the wonderfully named Night of Books in August.

Home cooking

Breton Apple Pie

As far as I can see, an apple pie is an apple pie. According to aficionados, what makes this one special is the dough.

Ingredients

For the filling:
2lb Golden Delicious apples
Half cup sugar
Three tablespoons of butter
One tablespoon lemon juice
Half a tablespoon of cinnamon
Two tablespoons of home-brew Calvados (failing that, dark rum will do)

For the dough:
Three cups of all-purpose flour
One cup butter
One cup sugar
One teaspoon vanilla extract
One tablespoon Calvados (see above if you can't get hold of any)
Four egg yolks

Method

Peel, core and slice the apples into a large saucepan. Add the remaining ingredients, cover and cook on a low heat until the apples exude their juices. Uncover and allow the juices to evaporate and the apples to cool. For the dough, beat the butter till soft, then beat in the sugar and continue till mixture lightens. Then beat in the Calvados and vanilla, then the yolks, one at a time. Keep beating until the mixture is very soft and light. Then, using a rubber spatula, fold in the flour until the dough is smooth. Preheat the oven to 350°F. Butter a ten inch by 2 inches deep baking dish, then fit a disc of baking paper and butter it. Put half the dough in the dish and smooth it out. Add the filling and then top with the other half of the dough after shaping to fit. Brush with beaten egg, then bake for 40-50 minutes or until well-coloured.

Home brewing

Cider

Basically, cider is cider, wherever it is made. To the Breton enthusiast, the rougher stuff is *chistr*, while to his or her opposite number in Somerset it is scrumpy. Whatever you call it, the recipe varies little, and consists of apples, apples and more apples. Regional finesse and fine preferences may include cowhide or dead meat to add to the flavour, but more of that later.

Cider is created by the most natural process, and like the best discoveries, was probably accidental after an ancient imbiber was so desperate for a snifter that he drank the juice from a tub of rotting apples. It takes around 24 pounds or eleven kilos of apples to make a gallon of cider, and a good pre-pressing pulp should include skin, pips, core, rotten bits and any maggots or other foreign bodies present. In my youth I was a drayman delivering barrels of scrumpy to hundreds of rather rough pubs in Portsmouth. It sold at sixpence in old money a pint, and it was said that no sailor in Her Majesty's Fleet could drink more than four pints at one sitting. And sitting was the operative word. Some pubs would sell hundreds of gallons a week when the fleet was in, and descending into the cellars to rack the scrumpy barrels gave an indication of what the stuff did to the drinker's innards. Inch-thick oaken floorboards had been eaten away by centuries of exposure to the drippings, and a bar whimsy of the time was to leave an old copper coin in a glass overnight. By the morning session it would look newly minted. I know of landlords who swore by leaving their false teeth in a glass of scrumpy overnight, and one renowned male prostitute had a trick of leaving his glass eye in his pint of cider when he went to the toilet on business. It was, he said, one way of keeping an eye on his drink, and the eye socket also provided an interesting additional service for his jaundiced sailor punters.

Technical note/warning: The ABV (Alcohol By Volume) strength of cider can vary from the wimpish three percent of French cidre doux to the head-banging eight or even more percent of true westcountry style scrumpy. As in most things to do with alcoholic beverages, the French do not generally see anything clever in making drinks really strong. The exceptions are, of course, all regional home-made eau de vie specialities magicked up from the most commonly available or chosen preferred fruit. In Normandy and Brittany, that fruit is apples. Though there is a limit as to how strong a long drink can be made before the need to distil it down, the recipe below should give you a brew strong enough to clean the most stained dentures.

Fascinating fact:

The word 'scrumpy' is said to derive from the practice of making cider from windfall apples (scrumps) which was also used as a verb for the practice of stealing them from someone else's tree. So my cider will qualify on either count.

Ingredients

12 lbs apples. As above, 24 pounds (11kilos) of apples to every gallon of cider is the usual yardstick, but this recipe is slightly different

Half pound raisins

Half pound raw meat (said to be for flavour but actually to help break down the apples)

A gallon of water at 70 degrees Fahrenheit

Some baker's yeast

Method

Chop/mash/pulp/grind/blend the apples. A food processor is a good modern shortcut. Put the water in a plastic bucket with a lid and add the apples and chopped raisins and meat. If you want to be posh, get a proper brewing container with an airlock to stop unwanted bacteria getting in. Add the yeast, and stir every day for a week before moving to a secondary fermentation vessel similar to the first one. If you want particularly dry cider, add some more yeast at this point. Leave till the fermentation again slows to the odd bubble, then transfer your scrumpy by siphon to a carboy or demijohn. After another week and when the heavier particles have settled, transfer to bottles and leave for at least three months. Before that, your scrumpy will taste vinegary and have an unpleasant smell. Mind you, some brews I have made have smelled and tasted like vinegar after a year.

Elderberry Port

Despite what my neighbours think, the fruit and flowers of the elder make a tolerable selection of drinks. There are between five and thirty shrubs and small trees in the family, and, like ours, elders were historically planted at the start of a pathway or entrance to a cottage to ward off approaching menace. If a tree was cut down without chanting a rhyme dedicated to the Elder Mother, she would take her revenge. The posh name for the elder is *sambucus*, though no fruit of the tree is used in the production of the Italian drink which bears a similar name.

Ingredients

2lb elderberries
1lb oranges
A gallon of water
Some brewers' yeast
3 lb sugar

Method

Strip the elderberries from the clumps. This is an irritatingly fiddly task, and some people get the job done quicker by using the tines of a fork to detach the berries. I usually get fed up and wrench them off in bunches. Peel the oranges and slice the fruit, using the peel and skin for some other household job. Boil the water and pour over the fruit. Allow to cool to handleable temperature and then strain through a fine sieve or muslin cloth into a demijohn. Dissolve the sugar in a little very hot water and add to the demijohn. Sprinkle some brewers' yeast into the demijohn and agitate. Now add an air lock and watch as it (hopefully) froths madly for a few days. When the madness has subsided, top up with boiled but cold water, and leave for a year for the best results. Or until you cannot resist trying it.

Cider Apple & Blackberry atomic chutney

Generally, the Brets seem as one with the rest of France when it comes to mistrust of unfamiliar (i.e. foreign) foodstuffs and recipes. So on a recent chutney-prepping visit to the local Super U, I was astonished to find a small box of Scotch Bonnet chilli peppers in the fruit and veg department. This was an almost Tutankhamen moment, as the usual idea of what constitutes exotic foreign groceries in a French supermarket is a jar of Marmite in the English section, which will be discreetly located in a rarely visited corner so as not to cause offence to sensitive customers.

For those not in the know, the Scotch Bonnet is the big daddy of chilli peppers, rating more than 100,000 on the Scoville Heat Scale. By comparison, the tongue-scorching jalapeno is set at a relatively wimpish 2000. As it was obviously a mistaken delivery and the Scotch Bonnets were probably destined for Bangladesh rather than Brittany, there was no descriptive notice or price tag on the box. I took a handful to the check-out, and when I showed them to the girl and explained they were named for my ancestors' favoured headgear, she pressed the panic button.

As is usual in these cases, a senior management meeting was convened on the spot, and after a lengthy debate the most junior member of staff was dispatched in suitable protective clothing to remove the box. I was allowed to take my handful of peppers home at no charge, but only after signing a waiver declaring I would not sue Super U or any of its employees for any terminal illnesses caused by eating the product.

We used a sliver of one chilli in the following recipe, and I gave the list of ingredients, mode of operation and the remaining peppers to a young market trader who lives in the next village and is known for his entrepreneurial ambitions and willingness to embrace foreign cultures and traditional Brit shopping preferences. Now my extra-spicy apple and blackberry chutney appears alongside the Hob-Nobs and Pot Noodles on Yannick's stall, and he has inevitably become known to local expats with a sense of history and humour as... Pan Yan, the Breton god of pickles.

Ingredients

2lbs cider apples or windfalls, cored and peeled
2 lbs blackberries
12 fluid ounces of cider vinegar
Half a pound of raw sugar
A teaspoon of sea salt
4 ounces of seedless raisins
4 ounces sultanas
4 chopped onions
2 cloves of crushed garlic
A teaspoon of ground ginger
A seeded and finely diced Scotch Bonnet pepper
A teaspoon of hot chilli oil

Method

Crush the blackberries in a large pan with the vinegar. Simmer for twenty minutes and then rub through a coarse sieve or colander. Add all the other ingredients and cook gently till the mixture thickens, which should take less than an hour. Put the chutney into properly sterilised and warm sealable jars, and add a warning notice with radio-active symbol.

NB. *Even the most fervent or spendthrift purists would not recommend using salt from Guérande for this or any other chutney recipe. The low-lying areas of marshland and mild micro-climate of this south-westerly border town are said to make it ideal territory for producing sea salt of the very finest quality. The revered sel gris de Guérande is harvested by the hand of a specialist paludier. It takes eighty pounds of fine grey salt to provide the gourmet's delight which is Fleur de Sel, and that winnowing down is reflected in the going rate of up to twenty pound per pound. Ironically, the reverse-selling pitch is that the flavour of this posh seasoning is so subtle that you cannot overdo it when adding to a dish in the making.*

October

Summer drags its heels, which is fine by us. Each morning, the mist hangs low across the moors before the sun appears to warm and clear the air. It is like being given a second chance as winter is kept at bay.

For us, the days are long and lazy, and we are no nearer finding a new home. In truth, I think we have not been looking too hard, and nowhere we have seen remotely matches what we have here in Lesmenez and Little Paradise.

But the month has started sadly. Donella took a cake across the lane to Alain this morning and returned in tears. When she asked about Bisdu and if the kittens had arrived, he smiled almost fondly and said she had delivered a litter of six. When Donella asked to see them, he pointed at a bucket in the corner of the kitchen and said he had drowned them. He did not know anyone in the village who wanted and needed a cat, so it was the best and quickest way to get rid of them.

No matter how long we live here I think we will always find it impossible to come to terms with the differences between some aspects of our cultures.

Friday 3rd

Bisdu appeared at the kitchen door early this morning. I would be fanciful to say she looked bereaved, but there seemed to be something subdued about the way she rubbed herself against my wife's leg and mewed rather than yowled for her breakfast. It is a mistake to anthropomorphise animals, if for no other reason than it distorts our perception of what is really going on in the mind of another species. I think the best description of how an animal must feel to lose her young is in Tarka the Otter. When the female's litter is killed, she feels not sorrow, but a sort of emptiness and poignant yearning for something that she does not understand.

167

Saturday 4th

I have persuaded our nearest neighbour that not all Britons who come to live in rural France are eccentric millionaires. Alain shimmered into sight from behind an ash tree as I was harvesting the tenderest leaves from our carefully-cultivated nettle patch with a pair of nail scissors. After the usual blowing out of cheeks, shoving of cap to the back of the head and elaborate brow-scratching performance which would have left mime supremo Marcel Marceau for dead (which he sadly is), he said it would be much quicker to get rid of the *orties* if he went and got a scythe. When I explained that I was collecting leaves to make soup for our evening meal, he disappeared and returned a few moments later with a basket of vegetables. In a first-ever display of any emotion approaching remorse, he said he was sorry he had not believed me when I claimed to be a poor writer, and could not stand by and watch a neighbour have to eat weeds and pretend to enjoy them.

Sunday 5th

Dusk falls slowly over the canal as we break open a bottle and cut into a particularly feisty roll of *saucisson*. Interestingly, this visually unappealing but deliciously spicy dry sausage gets its name from a primitive explosive fuse of the same shape which was used to set off small bombs like the *petards* employed to blow up castle gates during a siege. Sometimes when too much wine had been taken by the bombardier, he would set the fuse wrongly and be blown up together with the fortifications under attack. Thus, he had been hoist by his own petard.

So far today we have covered the best part of ten miles and had several bracing encounters with packs of the sort of cyclists who manage to have their arses and noses in the air at the same time as they whizz disdainfully and dangerously by. In contrast to the bikers, anglers are generally pleased to pass the time of day and talk about what fish they are not going to catch. In my considered opinion, nobody is more courteous than a polite French man or woman, and nobody more pig-ignorant than a rude one. But this may be because the average French person does not use our definition as to what constitutes rudery. Just lately I have been developing a theory that for thirty years I have been confusing simple indifference with rude or arrogant behaviour. It is perhaps not that the cyclists particularly wish to upset us; it is just that they are congenitally unable to put themselves in our walking boots and understand how they would feel to be menaced by a lycra-clad speedster. If my theory holds water, it would account for all that thoughtless and mad behaviour on the roads, a total un-understanding of the concept of the queuing system, and the complete lack of concern shown by any public official when you have been waiting for an audience for two hours and noon arrives.

An interesting challenge today has been to find a former lock-keeper's cottage not owned by a Briton. Though small, these almost painfully quaint properties make perfect second homes. I think the high ratio of British ownership also signifies another disparity between our two races. As the relative price of river, lake, canal and coastal properties in Britain shows, we all love to live near water. Although it is a huge generality, Bretons seem to be broadly divided into two types in this regard. There are those on the coast who love to live by it and will pay a relatively high price to do so. Then there are the inland Bretons of the Argoat (Land of the Trees). They have earth and some would say mud in their genes and are not fussed about living near any sort of expanse or course of water. In extreme cases, they dislike or even fear it.

Like most picture-postcard properties, there are drawbacks to living in any lock cottage, and we have agreed we could not bring ourselves to pay the going rate. Having said that, each time I come around a bend and see a tiny whitewashed and blue-shuttered building nestling beside the canal, I half hope to see a For Sale sign on the door.

Monday 6th

Woken by a fusillade of gunfire this morning, I looked out at an angry red dawn. The coming light revealed a coverlet of mist resting gently on the craggy peaks of the moors above Lesmenez. Another cloud drifted like woodsmoke through the forest far beyond the rooftops of the cottages across the lane.

Leaning from the window, I saw two cars parked by the old stone cross and realised the hunting season has officially begun. From the look of the beaten-up Renault, it seemed as if the owner of one of the vehicles has been keeping a record of his successes in the manner of a wartime fighter pilot. From my observation point, I could see two boars' heads and at least a dozen pheasants had been painted on the driver's side. Dressing quickly, I went down to see who was shooting at what, and to ensure that our dog, chickens, cat and fox were safely out of the line of fire.

Reaching the *calvaire*, I realised that rather than listing all the wild animals the driver has slaughtered, the car was actually a mobile mural depicting the glories of nature. The driver's side displayed skilfully drawn profiles of a host of wild creatures, while the whole of the nearside (including most of the windows) was devoted to the representation of a sylvan glen with the principal animals dancing in joyful harmony to the pipes of the great god Pan. As another fusillade echoed around the moors, I reflected on how this sort of ambivalent attitude could happen only in Brittany.

Thursday 7th

A significant advance in anglo-franco culinary *detente*.

Last week Alain ran out of bread, and actually agreed to accept one of Donella's home-baked loaves. I also told our other neighbour Jean-Yves that I was making some celery soup, and he asked if he could try a bowl. Unlike Alain, Jean is obviously not disturbed by the idea of experimenting with exotic foreign foods.

Friday 8th

Our attempt to bridge the chasm between the attitudes to food and cooking of our two nations has not been a complete success.

When delivering Alain's daily egg, Donella found a pile of familiar-looking breadcrumbs along the top of his garden wall. Even at this time of year they had been left untouched by the hundreds of local wild birds, which proves that the distrust of British cuisine goes beyond even the human population of France.

Saturday 9th

A classic example of the triumph of hope and ambition over logic and any shred of common sense came this morning when we learned someone had bought a redundant bar and restaurant in a nearby village. The locals say it has not been open for a decade, and only a madman or a Briton would try to make it work.

As we drove past I saw a couple standing on a pile of rubble inside the bar. They were holding small paintbrushes and large tins of paint, and had the look of preoccupied concern probably worn by Hansel and Gretel before they found the gingerbread house. When I climbed over the piles of old plaster and wood and stone and asked them in French if and when the bar was re-opening, the faces of both took on that rabbits-in-the-headlights look which meant they had to be Brits. As they seemed happy to tell me, they had no idea of the re-opening date as there had been a dispute with the builders. They were also having a problem doing a deal with any local breweries and suppliers, but their game plan was to create a 'fusion' pub, which would attract British and French customers from far and wide. Apart from not speaking French, neither had a shred of experience in any sort of business, but both said they had gained experience and preparedness for the challenge by having an increased number of friends to dinner back home in Surrey. The menu, they twittered, would be an artful blend of French and British delicacies.

As we drove away, I thought about the irony that in spite of all the doom-laden auguries, the new pub might just be a raging success. The paradoxical thing I have found about British-run businesses in France is that those which seem sound often fail, and those which would seem to stand as much chance of being a hit as a bacon factory in Haifa often survive and even prosper.

171

It may be that the gods look after those who seem most in need of help, or maybe it is the Gallic equivalent of Sodd's Law in action.

Depressing French Fact:

As reported earlier, the failure rate of all types of British-run businesses in France is more than 90 percent, and most fail in the first year. The failure rate of British-run pubs and restaurants is even more horrific….and happens even more quickly.

Sunday 10th

A full moon; it was eerily like daytime when I walked up the track to give the fox its supper. A blackbird was working the ground, and when it took off it almost collided with a bat. High above, a buzzard was circling over a field in which a trio of beef cattle were grazing as if it were mid-day. It is said that the term hunters' moon derived from the clear skies and full moons of October, when migrating birds present an easy target for the men with guns below. As if on cue as I thought about this, a steady flapping signalled the approach of a skein of at least a dozen geese heading south for warmer climes. Earthlocked, I stood and watched in envy as I wondered where they were going and how many would get there.

Sunday 17th

Driving through the mountains this morning we were buzzed by several groups of lunatic motorcyclists, out for what has become a traditional Sunday jaunt to upset other road users. They are an increasing menace, as, if that is possible, the members of these show-off packs have even less road sense and skills than the average French car driver. They delight in roaring past in choreographed phalanxes while weaving in and out of traffic at the most dangerous times. They also have their own sign language and supposedly secret signals for when groups meet, and obviously like to think of themselves as the sort of non-conformist free spirits they have seen in American road movies.

In fact, most will work in call centres and local government offices during the week, and, being French, are actually well mannered and deferential when you meet them off their bikes. We recently stopped off at the picture-postcard town of Josselin, and headed for the restaurant and bar area. On the corner of the square was a 1950s American theme bar with the juke box blaring and huge photo-montages on the wall of Marlon Brando as the rebel biker in The Wild Ones. Although there were a couple of dozen heavily-customised motorbikes lined up in the street outside, the bar was empty and we found all the bikers sitting down for a long lunch in the Michelin-starred restaurant next door. Although they look the business, I think that from a British or American perspective the members of these fastidious coteries would be seen as not so much Hell's Angels as Hell's Nancy Boys.

Josselin is a small canal/riverside town (it is on the Oust) we have visited on several occasions, but find a bit artificially olde-worlde for our liking. What is said to be the grandest *château* in Brittany overlooks the water and is in very good nick despite being another Breton fortification Cardinal Richelieu knocked about a bit. It is very well-kept nowadays and visitors can stroll around the landscaped gardens or visit the doll museum. Though dating back to the 11th century, I have not found it as atmospheric or evocative as some younger but more dishevelled castles, and it does not help that the fairly constant flow of through traffic is routed past the entrance. I think Tolkien got a lot of inspiration for characters and place names from Brittany, and Josselin was a stronghold of the Lords of Rohan. The town is near the site of a formally arranged battle between Franco-Breton and English knights which could well have inspired the planned punch-ups between rival British soccer clubs. The staged fight was known as the Combat of Thirty, and finished when the French side had capture or killed all the English knights.

Monday 18th

A bullying wind practices its winter routine. Branches sway and creak and it is snowing leaves. As always, the acridly rich smell

173

of the bonfire is sublime on the crisp morning air. Bending with the wind, a dense column of smoke rises high into the air, and, this being western Brittany we are half-seriously hoping for a response from any Red Indians living in the vicinity.

This morning Alain appeared to find me counting a pile of maple leaves into the wheelbarrow. When he had finished his cheek-puffing routine, I explained that I wanted to know exactly how many we would collect and burn this year. As I pointed out, the wheel barrow took a little over a thousand leaves, and twenty barrowloads a day over a month would amount to half a million leaves. I understand that to even normal people, my ways of dealing with boring and repetitive jobs might seem anal, but there is a certain logic and history to my fixation.

Of dozens of low-paid, monotonous and unpleasant jobs I have had, the worst by a long way was working in a factory which made cardboard boxes. As a newcomer, I was put on the beginning of a line producing cardboard cartons to hold blocks of ice cream. At the start of every shift, a heavily-laden pallet would be creakingly wheeled to the side of my bench. The pallet carried several thousand sheets of thin card which had been stamped out in the necessary shape to be folded into cartons. The outline was perforated so the unwanted border would not fall into the machine and jam it. My job was to knock the waste bits off with a hammer, throw them into a bin and stack the trimmed cards on to another pallet. A hundred sheets measured an inch, and that was as many as could be dealt with in one go with a high-swung hammer. For eight hours on a rotating shift pattern of mornings, afternoons and nights, I would stand at the bench knocking off the rough edges and stacking the finished sheets on another pallet for later collection. To try and avoid going mad, I would set myself challenges and targets, and would spend the day or night hammering away feverishly to beat my own records. When I got to the last hundred sheets on the pallet, I would hear the creaking of wheels as another load came lumbering down the aisle. Whenever I feel the approach of the black dog of depression, I think of my time in that factory and reflect on how lucky I am to be where I am and doing what I do now.

An early evening visit from Alain, who was with an equally aged friend from another village. Clearly, the word about the Foreign Madman of Lesmenez is spreading, and our neighbour was almost proprietorial in his attitude when introducing me. They arrived in the copse to find me photographing a fine example of a stinkhorn mushroom. I explained that the *phallus impudicus* could shoot up to as much as ten inches in length in just a few hours, and that the country name in my part of England was Old Man's Dick. After looking at the huge erection wistfully for a few moments, Alain's elderly friend said he did not know about England, but in this part of France any old man would be proud to have something of that size and rigidity.

Wednesday 20th

To the capital town of Brittany for a look at what could be our new home.

Having inspected and found wanting more than a hundred cottages, farms, shops and alleged castles, it seems to me we must think about other ways of living in France. Or even all over France.

Perhaps the reason we are not seeing any properties which appeal to us is because in our hearts we do not want to settle in one spot. There is so much of this big and diverse country we need to see before it is too late; paradoxically and as the months flash by, we seem to be becoming less interested in finding somewhere permanent to live. Rather than growing old in one secure setting, I increasingly like the idea of going on the run. I know we can't escape the pale rider by keeping on the move, but the thought of trying to stay one jump ahead is appealing.

What also appeals about a transient lifestyle is having to pay no commune taxes or habitation fees, water rates or electricity bills. I increasingly like the idea of living a life on the water and off the radar, and being able to up anchor and move on when I get bored with the view from the porthole. I come from a long line of seafarers, and 'first turn of the screw pays all debts' was an expression often heard in my family circles.

I know Donella is not so keen as me on the idea of a life afloat, but I have assured her that we can take the cat, dog and hens with us, and the birds of the air and all other freeloaders will be sure to zero in on us wherever we heave-to. Another bonus is that I will never be short of material for future travel books. I know every ex-accountant or schoolteacher who owns a canal boat and obligatory Breton fisherman's smock and cap has written a book about his adventures on the waterways of France, but I am a professional and reckon I could make a much better job of recording my impressions as we saunter down the Loire on our way to overwinter in the sunny south.

Thursday 21st

As is the norm when buying boats or houses, our intended new home does not live up to its photograph and description.

When I spotted the advertisement for the 32-foot riverboat, the asking price of 18,000 Euros appeared a bargain. The photographs showed a gleaming and spacious craft with rakish lines and in apparent mint condition. The owner lives in Spain and seems a nice chap. He told me he was selling the boat as his children had grown up and didn't want to go on family boating holidays anymore. I suppose that should have given me a clue as to the boat's age, as some of the photographs he sent showed young children happily messing around on board. In spite of their severe haircuts, big shorts and lack of tattoos or body piercings, it had not occurred to me that the snaps were souvenirs of a long-ago holiday.

Like the children, the boat has grown older, but, unlike them, has been much neglected. Grass was growing from some of the joints on the deck, and most of the fittings on the superstructure seemed to be held together by gaffer tape. Down below, all the fixtures were of 1970s vintage, and the old newspaper and half-empty Pot Noodle tub on the table gave the vessel an almost Mary Celeste-like air of desolation and abandonment.

Like the boat, Rennes was a disappointment, though, also like the boat, Brittany's first town could hardly have lived up to our expectations.

In spite of all my travelling and a fair understanding of history and the periodic development of major centres of habitation, I irrationally hope that the ancient towns we are to visit will have somehow remained as they were.

When we visited Avignon, I did not expect to see lots of people dancing around on a quaint old bridge; neither did I expect to have to fight our way to the old walled town through miles of sprawling and sometimes obscenely ugly outskirts of tower blocks and tawdry shopping centres and those tragic commercial estates where the businesses have names as tritely jolly as the products they sell are sad.

When we arrived at Arles, I did not really hope to see the odd farm cart rumble slowly by as a man with a straw hat, ginger beard and a big bandage where his right ear should have been strolled to the nearest bar. Then there is the equally irrational disappointment of visiting a town and not immediately encountering the product for which it is famous. I did not see or smell a single wedge of Rochefort cheese when we toured that town, not everyone in Nimes was wearing denim, and Chantilly seemed to have no more than its fair share of lace on show. Though to be fair, most Chantilly lace was made in Bayeux in Normandy.

Because of the tourist brochures and in spite of previous disappointments, I expected to see a goodly display of half-timbered and gaily-coloured medieval buildings as we bumped down quaintly cobbled streets towards the river at the heart of Rennes. As it was, we sat for half an hour in a three-lane traffic jam outside a soaring selection of cathedrals to shopping, with the biggest and most intimidating topped off by a massive C&A logo.

With a population of coming up for a quarter of a million and another half a million living around the town, I suppose we should have expected Rennes to be busy. I am sure it is a nice town to

177

live or work in for the young or business-minded, but not for a couple of ageing travellers looking for a trace of history and the feel of what the town was once like and why and how it came to be the capital of Brittany. Of course, Rennes and any historic and significant French town will be riddled with reminders of its past in the shape of preserved buildings and an adequacy of museums and galleries. But to get to them, you usually have to plough through a reminder of the worst aspects of how we live now.

Perhaps in the future there will be holograms or Disney-like facsimiles near all historic towns and sites so people can get a proper feel of what they were truly like. Until then, I will continue to seek out places which will be as I have fondly and illogically imagined them. And they do exist.

In the Carmargue last year and when we turned our backs on the distant derricks and rusting coasters, we looked across a haunting and unchanging marshland which looked exactly as the tourist brochures would have you believe it would be. There were white horses running free, and the morning sky did turn pink when a thousand flamingoes flapped lazily away as a fisherman poled his punt across the shallow silver waters. The horses and the pink birds and even the aged fisherman may well have been supplied by the regional tourist board, but it seemed the area was at one with itself and how it always had been. Most enchantingly, it also seemed that just by standing there in dumb wonder we had become part of that magical place and its past.

Friday 22nd

On the way home from Rennes we stopped off to explore the area around St-Brieuc. The principal or at least the biggest town in the Côtes d'Armor department, it is named for a Welsh monk who evangelised the region in the sixth century.

Understandably given its origins, St-Brieuc is twinned with Aberystwyth, and, less understandably with Aghia Paraskevi in Greece. The last head count of Briochins arrived at a population of nearly 50,000, which is normally enough to put the town in the stay-away category for us. But St-Brieuc avoids the normal predictability and blandness of a big modern town mostly because of its location. Billed as the city of the hills and vales, it sits overlooking an estuary in which two rivers combine before entering the English Channel. The vast Bay of St-Brieuc is freckled with interesting and secluded villages on cliffs, headlands or abutting sandy beaches, and we spent the night at the confluence of a posh marina and a very not-posh commercial docks.

What we liked about the port of Le Légué (and so many similarly situated marinas in France) was the way the million-Euro yachts bobbed disdainfully alongside unconcerned and very rusty old scows, and the trendy eateries rubbed shoulders with derelict warehouses at the business end of the port. One day those warehouses will become flash apartments, each costing more than the value of the port a couple of hundred years ago, but for the moment they lie empty and unvalued. Mountains of gravel and walls of cement bags line the dockside, and between them and the expensive yachts is our idea of the perfect waterside pub.

Les Mouettes is a PMU/*tabac*, which means you can buy your fags and have a drink while laying a bet on the next race at Longchamp. The comfortably scruffy bar overlooks the water and is staffed by the sort of seen-it-all, no-nonsense but good-hearted barmaids who cannot be bested for crisp service with or without a smile or a cuss. Outside on the quayside, we found the mix of vessels and buildings satisfyingly echoed by the mélange of smart yachties and weatherbeaten deckhands and wharf rats.

As we sat with a drink as dusk fell, snowstorms of terns wheeled and turned overhead, while a solemn line of cormorants pumped through the air on their way home after a day's work. These big and serious-minded birds fly in a very straight line, and I have often wondered why we say 'as the crow flies' rather than 'as the cormorant flies'. Most crows I see do not fly in anything like a straight line for long.

Not ready to retire, we took a late-night drive up the hill and through the old quarter of St-Brieuc. The inviting lights of satisfyingly seedy-looking bars drew us through the empty streets as a police car pulled up to move on Dixie's Midnight

Runners and their assorted dogs. It is only in provincial France that you see this sort of grungy and somehow old-fashioned wanderer, and one who will wear his mismatching assortment of old clothing with such panache. Bib and brace overalls with beret and neckerchief are the permanent fashion, and the hair is braided or cropped or even violently coloured and groomed 1970s punk vintage. The wearers generally cause no harm and add colour to the streetscene, and their dogs always look well fed and amiable. They also have the great appeal of not trying to sell you a copy of the Big Issue, and can generally play the musical instruments with which they solicit your spare change.

As we settled down outside a bar with a coffee-calva nightcap, a sign-written van pulled up and solved a dispute which has been going on for two thousand years between opposing French and British forces. The name of the carpenter owner of the van was writ large on the side panelling, and showed that, contrary to long-held English conviction, (Eric) God is a Frenchman.

Saturday 23rd

An almost surreal experience on the road out of St-Brieuc.

Realising I had taken a cunningly misplaced direction sign at face value and was heading back into town, I pulled into a driveway to make a turn. Too late, I found I was at the end of a queue, and another car entering the drive blocked my escape route. Five minutes later and after three decades of messing around in France, we were sitting at a hatchway and about to undergo our first Drive-In-Bakery Experience. Purists would be outraged, but it was somehow heartening to see France taking an American invention and French-ising rather than, as with MacDonald's, franchising it.

As we watched in fascination, the driver in front stuck his hand out and took delivery of an obviously oven-fresh baguette and sped off. Shuffling up to the window to ask directions to get us back on the road home, we thought it only polite to buy a brace of giant almond croissants.

We are back in the mountains, refreshed and relaxed from our night at an excellent quayside hotel. On my rating system, the Grenier à Sel scores eight or a bit more out of ten.

As a veteran reviewer of and editor of a magazine largely about hotels, my general view is that while basic facilities like glass in the windows and a bed in your room must be a given, the type you like to stay in should be a matter of individual taste and not dependent on some immutable scorecard. As with eating places, you should only compare like with like and price. Some travellers like a modern and anonymous hotel with all the facilities and no character. Others like a more relaxed and even louche establishment, and will put up with minor inconveniences like a non-working lift in return for a feeling of place and presence that marks a hotel that, like an experienced older woman, knows its stuff.

As to facilities, some people will pay through the nose for drinks from a mini-bar, with the Mark IV Corby trouser press and a soft porn channel to hand. We like a hotel with a roomy room and hopefully a pleasant view, a sensibly priced restaurant and a late-serving bar. A comfortable full-sized bed (i.e. not a single masquerading as a double) is a must, but apart from these basics, just about the most important item on my tick list is the shower cubicle rating. Even more so, the shower head manoeuvrability tog ranking.

I have been in - or tried to get into - shower cubicles which would make a coalminer claustrophobic. I have been in shower cubicles that have rat-trap doors which threaten to part a man from his most vital appendages just for the fun of it. But the thing most likely to goad me into a fury is a dodgy shower head. A proper shower head will glide up and down to the right level for any height of guest, or any part of the body or head he or she wishes to focus on. A proper shower head can also be adjusted to spray at any angle. A fixed and non-negotiable shower head is a curse on humanity, and unless you are able to perform a legs-akimbo hand-stand in a very limited space, it is also a threat to health and safety of yourself and those near to you. The

Grenier à Sel was comfortable and clean, with a corking waitress, good food, a decent-sized bed, and a fully rotatable and adjustable shower head, so passed our test with flying colours.

Thursday 28th

I am in Huelgoat to pick up a month's worth of British newspapers from a friend's pub. Apart from a good country hostelry and curry house (and of course our friends and some of our relatives) the thing I miss most from my past life is a daily British newspaper. We can watch and listen to the news from Britain, but it is not the same as being able to read the story behind the headlines. Another benefit is that for some curious reason, English papers make much better firelighters than French journals.

Turning into the square I had to swerve to avoid running into Eddie Izzard. He was emerging from the pork butcher's shop and favoured me with a cool stare before flouncing off in the direction of the post office. It was of course not Eddie Izzard, but a local lady doing an unintentional but impressive impression of the comic with an unusual dress sense.

Brittany certainly seems to be the European capital of lookalikes, and Huelgoat its headquarters. As well as the Clint Eastwood and Rasputin doppelgangers, the owner of the crêperie down the road is a spitting image of Robbie Williams. There is also a woman who strongly resembles Margaret Thatcher - had she become a bag lady instead of one of our greatest Prime Ministers. In one of the bars, there is even a small and particularly repugnant pug dog with a sneer very reminiscent of Elvis Presley. Perhaps because of the number of lookalikes per square kilometre, at least one town in the area stages a regular contest for those who resemble a famous personality. Last month there was a special event at a town near us to find who looked most like the mayor. The contest was won, unsurprisingly, by the mayor.

It is good to have a licensed outlet to suit one's every mood, and today I am definitely in the mood for a visit to the Homme au Chapeau. The pub is named for its owner Roger Jennings, who I have seen in every state of dress and undress except without his cap. Once a dealer in London's Paddington Green, Roger bought the defunct hotel some years ago and set about filling it with his eclectic collection of antiques and bric-a-brac. I think he could be a really successful dealer if it were not for his reluctance to sell anything he has bought. He would put Sally and Richard Moore in the shade as disposophobics, and every room and corner of the hotel is jammed full with his stock. It is difficult to move around the place for fear of barking your shin on a heavily gilded Louis Quinze table, or worse injury from a thoughtlessly placed chain saw.

The premises have become ever more chaotic since the departure of Roger's wife, Cherie. She is an American who ran the bar before they split up, though it is alleged by some regulars that she pretended to be Canadian during the height of the Cheese-Eating-Surrender-Monkeys Franco-American dispute over the invasion of Iraq.

I find the range of customers at the Man with the Hat as interesting as the patron, and it is the only pub I know where so many of the customers are former members of the Special Air Services. One claims to have been a half-Colonel in the SAS, and he is certainly no taller than five feet four inches. If he was a high-ranking and presumably hands-off officer, it could explain why he is so bad at unarmed combat. The last time he tried to demonstrate how he could kill me with one finger, he missed and fell through the door into the street.

It is peculiar how Brittany appears to attract people with a mysterious past, and according to the British landlord of a pub in nearby Carhaix-Plouguer, the majority of his French clients claim to have seen service in either the Foreign Legion or some other elite fighting force. Another extraordinary statistic is that the parents of every single one of his customers were in the Resistance.

Friday 29th

We have been gathering the last of this year's free food from the hedgerows. Walking up the track, Milly sent up a pheasant and chased it into a blackthorn bush I had not noticed before. We have had our first frosts, so the berries are as ripe as they will become and I picked a pocketful.

Superstition surrounds the blackthorn, and it is said to be the traditional wood used by magicians for their wands. In parts of England a wreath of blackthorn would be burned in fields on the first day of the new year to keep the Devil away. In Ireland the Little People were said to live in blackthorn trees, and there were severe penalties for cutting off the branches at certain times of year, though the wood was prized for shillelagh-making. The blackthorn is also said to be an emblem of both life and death as the flowers appear when the tree has no leaves.

Unlikely as it sounds, blackthorn leaves were once used to make what was known as English tea. Medicinally, extracts and compounds of the blackthorn have been used across the centuries for bowel and eye problems, and the paste as a tooth whitener.

Sloe berries are still used to flavour gin and vodka, and country people used to bury them in straw-lined pits till they sweetened. That being said, I have yet to find a way of making the fruit of the blackthorn edible, and that includes the recipe below.

Home Cooking

I could not compile any list of Breton dishes without including *Kig ar Farz*, or *Kig ha Farz* if you come from another part of the region. Whichever dialect you speak, the name seems to translate as 'stuffed meat'. Actually, completely stuffed is how you feel after eating a couple of platefuls. By any other name, this gargantuan meal is basically a beef stew with dumplings. And a pork stew with dumplings. And a lamb stew with dumplings.

In some parts of France the locals cook tiny songbirds and hide their shame by eating them with napkins over their heads. Here, country people like to keep the cold out with a mountainous plate of mixed meats, garnished with what looks like a giant dumpling which has disintegrated on the plate. This is because, if done properly, the buckwheat flour has been cooked inside a cotton bag hanging in the pot; purists say that the bag should be cobbled-up from the sleeve of a shirt belonging to an elderly man. The level of heart-stopping cholesterol produced by the traditional dish can be gauged when you realise this is a very restrained version:

Ingredients

2lb of beef shoulder or leg
A salted pork knuckle
1lb streaky bacon
One uncooked smoked sausage
A small cabbage
Some carrots
Some turnips
Some leeks
Some onions
A stick of celery
Thyme
A bay leaf
1 lb buckwheat flour
Half a pound of wheat flour
8 ounces salted butter
4 ounces sugar
4 ounces raisins
2 eggs
Lots of crème fraiche
Some milk
Seasoning of coarse sea salt and roughly ground black pepper

I have specified raisins as an ingredient in the dumpling mix, but the idea of adding something sweet to add to a savoury dish like this varies from area to area. Some puritanical types prefer their dumplings unsullied, those of a more hedonistic inclination may even pour maple syrup on before adding to the dish.

Method

De-salt the knuckle by bringing it to the boil in a pan, then simmer for 20 minutes. Blanch the cabbage by soaking it in boiling water in another saucepan and cooking for five minutes. Place the de-salted knuckle and other meats - except the smoked sausage - in a large casserole. Add the onion (preferably stuffed with herbs and cloves) and cover with water and bring to the boil. Cook for two hours before adding the other vegetables, sausage and seasoning. For the dumpling, mix the eggs, raisins, milk and butter and cream in a large bowl, then gradually add the flour, sugar and salt, stirring until smooth. Put the mixture into your bag, leaving enough room for expansion, then suspend it in the simmering broth/stew. After hanging around for another couple of hours, remove the bag and work it around until you feel the contents breaking up into large crumbs. Serve with the stew.

Fast Sloe Cheese

A pre-Mrs Beeton educator of middle-class housewives was Elizabeth Raffald. *The Experienced English Housekeeper* came out in 1747, and included instructions on how to lay out a table, make ice cream, orange wine and a sort of sloe cheese. It is of course nothing like cheese, but simple to make and has quite an interesting appearance and texture if virtually no taste.

Ingredients

3lbs washed sloe berries
Some water
Some sugar
Juice of one lemon

Method

Put the sloes and lemon juice in a pot with enough water to make the fruit just float. Boil then simmer till the sloes are very soft and sieve through a colander. For each cup of pulp add one cup of sugar, then bring to the boil and cook slowly until the mixture becomes a thick paste. Place the mixture into a baking tin and allow to cool naturally. If the 'cheese' has not set after a day, put it in the oven on a very low heat until it does.

Pumpkin soup

Generally, we have found no better usage for pumpkin flesh than filling holes in walls or tracks. But it does make a delicious soup if you use the usual accessories of lashings of butter and cream as follows:

Ingredients

Two finely chopped large onions
Some olive oil
Two pounds of pumpkin, peeled and de-seeded and roughly diced
700ml of vegetable or chicken stock
200ml of double cream
A slice or two of granary bread
Some dried pumpkin seeds
Lots of ground black pepper

Method

Put half the oil into a pan and cook the onions off until they are soft but not browned. Add the pumpkin chunks and continue to cook till the pieces become brown (obviously, the time needed will depend on how big or small you have cut the chunks). Pour the stock into the pan and season, then bring to the boil and simmer till the pumpkin is very soft. Add the cream and re-boil for a moment, then purée with a blender. Cut the bread into croutons and fry in the remaining olive oil together with the pumpkin seeds. Garnish the soup and serve, drizzling a little more oil over the croutons if you will.

November

Guerlesquin, Le Rick, St-Goazec, Spézet, Laz

Winter still waits in the wings, but we have had a taste of things to come.

People in towns generally think of wind and rain as inconveniences which can spoil a round of golf or a hair-do. In the countryside, the elements revel in showing what damage they can do.

We have had the mother of all storms, with the mountain weather gods in full-on battle mode. Massive fir trees bent to the fury of the wind or gave up the struggle and came crashing down across the lanes and tracks. Great flashes of light were chased by thunderous peals which rolled and reverberated across the moors and craggy peaks. And then came the rain. At first in giant droplets which a thin dog could move between without getting wet, and then in a sheeting curtain. The normally solid track up to the moors became a morass in moments as a torrent came boiling down from the heights.

Then, as suddenly as it had arrived, it was gone. Content to have reminded us of their presence and powers, the weather gods went back to their rest and the sun appeared.

After the great summer storm we have learned not to ignore our neighbour's understanding of these things, so the acorns were lined up ready on our window sills well before the drama commenced. Almost annoyingly and to Alain's smug satisfaction, all the electrical equipment in our house escaped damage.

Wednesday 3rd

Another reminder of the need to treat the elements and their manifestations with due respect as I walked the moors alone this morning.

I had heard of people getting lost in suddenly-descending fog on moorland, but could not see how that could happen on such familiar terrain and so close to home. There was an almost painful sharpness to the light as I set out, but by the time I reached the moors it looked as if someone had stolen the great ring of crags overlooking our village.

When I looked back, Lesmenez had also disappeared. As the mist closed in and visibility shortened to a handful of yards, the silence was broken only by the scrape of my boots and the increasingly panicky sound of my breathing. I often take short cuts away from the track and cross-country to discover new ways of returning to the hamlet, and had done so today. Now all my familiar points of reference had vanished.

I walked on for half an hour, hoping to come across a familiar track or signpost, but saw nothing but gorse and grass. Though so close to home, I was truly lost. I had no food or drink or phone, and all I could do was head downhill and hope to come across a familiar landmark.

With the route becoming increasingly rocky, I inched my way forward and downward into the white wall. I did not want to even think of the consequences of a fall, and was getting very tired, wet and cold. Finding a gorse bush, I stripped it as best I could and stuffed the spiky fronds in my jacket for extra insulation, then curled up beneath the remains of the bush.

As I thought about how much I would miss my wife and family and dog, I heard a tinkling sound. It sounded like a small bell, so might be a passing goat. Then a swirl of wind lifted the curtain for a moment, and I saw a small child on a toy bicycle. Behind him loomed a strange and monstrous shape. It was the plastic elephant. I had somehow missed Lesmenez and ended up in someone's back garden in Kernelec. As the child burst into tears and ran home, I rose stiffly to my feet and made my way down the track to tell my wife a suitably edited tale of my heroic and epic journey to safety.

Friday 5th

It is often the small and apparently unimportant things which enhance or detract from a life lived abroad. Yob-free town centres and trying to have a fruitful conversation with an Orange France shop assistant are two good examples at either end of the spectrum.

This morning I clocked up Good Reason 985 for us and our animals being in France on and around this date. It is an irony that many people in Britain who send their money up in smoke long before and after the fifth day of November will not have a clue as to who Guy Fawkes was or what he tried to do.

Monday 8th

Another day, another unsuitable property and business to view.

This afternoon we visited what is likely to be the only ostrich *élevage* in Brittany, or at least the only one for sale.

The ostrich is the largest living bird, and consequently lays the largest egg. The meat is similar to lean beef in taste, and low in fat and cholesterol. It is still mostly a novelty food, especially in rural France, and I think the owners may be before their time. They are a French couple who say they are moving to Canada to start a new life, but I think it is really because the husband has run out of creatures to shoot and stuff.

We were disappointed to see no giant birds in the corrals surrounding the isolated farmhouse near Guerlesquin, but found plenty inside. A fully grown ostrich can exceed seven feet in height and run at up to 45mph, but even that speed had obviously not been enough to escape their owner and his taxidermy tools. Inside the house, stuffed ostriches loomed everywhere, and all wearing the same understandably surprised expression. As well as the stuffed birds, there were foxes, badgers, ermine and even what looked suspiciously like a domestic cat, all frozen for eternity, and all with the same bemused expression.

Upstairs in the master bedroom, the owner had established a sniping station, and invited me to handle his well-oiled and telescopic-sighted rifle. I declined, and while my wife went to wait in the car and start making a plasticine effigy of him, we finished the tour at the killing room. When I had also declined his offer of a demonstration of how the electrodes worked, we shook hands and the owner suggested we might like to stay for something to eat. He would, he said, also be happy to show me some examples of his latest taxidermical projects. As he had said earlier, there was no species that could not be preserved, and he was always looking for new challenges. As he ran a casual eye over me, I ducked under the neck of the giant bird guarding the front door and made for the car, blurting out that we had had a heavy lunch and were already stuffed, thanks all the same.

*

There is a very genuine Celtic bar in the high street at Guerlesquin. An unspoiled and unaffected place, the town is also unusual for its weekly musical market. This does not mean that violins, used drum kits and banjos are on sale, but that shoppers at the Monday market are pursued by bands of roving musicians who entertain or irritate them with traditional Breton airs.

Another oddity is a wonderfully over-the-top mini-fortress in the main square, built by a local lord as a gaol. It has all the turrets and monumental twiddly bits one would expect on a full-sized castle, but is not much bigger than the average living room. Another attraction is a large artificial lake just outside the town which is pleasant to walk around in spite of a nearby factory producing something mysteriously odiferous. I have been told that Guerlesquin is also the setting for a same-sex nightclub where all sorts of unexpected (for rural Brittany) things can happen, but saw no evidence of its premises or likely users during our daytime visit.

Monday 15th

It is a prime rule of the Law of Sodd that windscreen wipers only fail to work when it is raining. My wife says it is actually that you only find out they are not working when you switch them on because it is raining. Sometimes I think she takes far too practical a stance on the mysteries of Life.

Middling to high on my list of most annoying things about French road users is their contradictory attitudes to driving in adverse conditions. If a wisp of cloud passes across or close to the sun, as one they switch their lights on. It is another example of the sort of Borg-like conformist mass behaviour I find least pleasing about the Gallic character. On cue and as the first drop of rain falls, they will turn their headlights to full beam and switch on all fog lamps, storm beacons, hazard and searchlights to hand.

Now here's the really infuriating bit: Having totally overreacted to the conditions and now protected by the magic amulet of blazing lights, the typical French driver will proceed to drive even more insanely than before.

Indeed, the lunacy of their actions will relate directly to how bad those conditions are. The wetter the road becomes, the closer the car behind will come to your back bumper, as if seeking comfort and company in the inclement conditions. Also, the faster the driver will take corners and bends awash with more surface water than you will find gushing down the biggest, baddest flume at Alton Towers.

Given that prior knowledge, I suppose it was extremely irresponsible of me to try to drive home without windscreen wipers. Especially on an expressway. It was not until we joined the N147 that I realised that the faster one drives without the wipers on, the more blurred the screen becomes. I also forgot the way the average French driver's mind works in these conditions, and the first giant truck loomed in my rear mirror within seconds of our speed dropping under 90kph.

I do not know how we saw the escape route reserved for lorry drivers whose brakes fail, but we did and took it. A bonnet full of sand was better than a juggernaut in the boot.

Wednesday 17th

The wipers are fixed, and a greater cause for celebration is that we may have found our next home in France. It could be that we will soon be the owners of a very large hole in the ground.

I have learned in life that the longer one seeks perfection, the harder it is to find. This applies particularly to soul mates, homes and home-made Indian curries, and I believe the best attitude to take with all three is to settle for less than you were looking for.

Our problem has been that the more we have looked for the perfect place to live and work, the more boxes we have added to the tick list. This, as any determined and picky house hunter will tell you, is because there is always one feature you will like in every property you view. It might be something as crucial as the location and style and size of the house, or as small as the shape of the staircase or the way the kitchen cabinet doors close with a gentle sigh. The point is that no place on earth will embody all the assets and features you seek and at some time you have to stop looking.

If you think that is a problem when looking for a new home in Britain, consider how much more complex it is on this side of the Channel. If you want to change addresses in the United Kingdom, you will know exactly what your budget is, what sort of house it will buy, and where it needs to be. When you move to France or buy a second home here, you have a country four times the size of England to choose a billet in. Within the limitations of your budget and DIY ability, you also have to decide whether you want an old or new, untouched or completely restored property. You also have to decide whether your new home should be in town or countryside. If not in a large or small town, will it be in a busy village, peaceful hamlet - or truly in the middle of the middle of nowhere?

I know couples who have spent decades looking for the perfect home in France and eventually given up. Some have gone mad and marriages been broken by the continuing and growing obsession of one or both of the partners. I know a couple who became so frustrated and mentally exhausted by their search that they invented an imaginary second home in France. That way, they reasoned, it could be exactly what and where they wanted, the overheads and maintenance costs would be zero, and they would even be able to feel smug when the property boom meant their virtual home became worth twice as much as they did not pay for it.

We are in a more fortunate position than most as we have owned and lived in properties in all situations, locations and states of repair in France, so know in advance what we want rather than what we think we want. But the more we look for

Paradise, the longer and fussier and even unreasonable our wish list becomes.

Our next home and perhaps business in France must be within the budget we have set to allow for improvement and restoration work and our financial survival, although all good intentions will go out of the window if we see something we cannot afford but makes our knees buckle. The perfect setting will be in the countryside and far away from major roads and traffic noise, but very near running water. It will have a characterful small town close to hand, and a characterful big town no more than an hour's drive away. Above all, the place we will spend most of the rest of our lives in must be quirky. By that I mean it must have some form of extra and unusual feature or eccentricity. With the place we have just seen, I think almost all our boxes have been ticked.

Le Rick is the name of both the property and nearest hamlet, which is a good start. The house stands in the midst of thirty acres of thickly wooded terrain and one side is bounded by a half mile stretch of the Nantes to Brest canal. Most importantly, one of our favourite towns is only a couple of miles away by road, and less by water. A friend once described me as a sociable hermit, and I knew what he meant. My wife likes her own company, and I can put up with mine when the surroundings distract me. But I need to know that the nearest centre of civilisation is not far when I need a shot of shoulder-rubbing.

Another very desirable extra is that the views from the property are stunning. The house and two massive barns are in an elevated position as they were built on millions of tons of slate for which the Black Mountain area of Brittany is named. The reason the house sits on a giant spoil heap is because it sits right next door to a deep and ancient slate quarry which belongs with the property.

Commissioned by the exotically-named Lords of Laz, the quarry once employed hundreds of local men who toiled to wrest slate from the subterranean passages and galleries. After being hauled up by a complex series of pulleys, the great slabs would be lowered down the slope to the canal and the waiting barges.

Although long-abandoned, the underground passages leading to the galleries and faces are still open, and in the French way there has been no attempt to prohibit entrance or fence-off the sheer drop from beside the house to the watery depths of the great pit. We have heard that old tools and wagons still lay in the network of passages, as does the remains of a particularly unpopular Gestapo officer.

With the quirky box ticked, the other considerations are equally favourable. With the boundary of the canal on one side, and steep slate-littered slopes on the other, Le Rick could not be more private. As for civilisation, the hilltop village of St-Goazec is just half a mile away; we have already discovered it has a good bar, run by a personable and clearly tolerant landlady. Another couple of miles on is Châteauneuf-du-Faou, and it is approachable by canal or tow-path as well as road.

The only drawback is that Sodd's Law has again come into play and the house alongside the quarry is one of the ugliest and strangely designed we have seen on either side of the Channel. Built relatively recently, it has a massive cellar at ground floor level and the living quarters on the first floor. As if the designer or builder had run out of interest or funds, the building then narrows almost to a chisel point where the four cramped bedrooms were squeezed in. On the first floor, all is 1980s car-dealer chic. Rather than using the good, honest slate lying in huge heaps all around the house, all available surfaces had been tiled with highly polished marble-effect sheeting. The handrails of the similarly-clad winding staircases are made from hugely-overwrought wrought iron. As happened in Britain, in twenty years time it will be fashionable to go rural rustic in house decor style. For the moment, the past is too close for those who want to distance themselves from their rural roots. There is a very rural feature in this strange house, though, which is the highly-varnished bole of a tree growing from the centre of the living room up and through the ceiling. There is a veranda with spectacular views of the canal, surrounding countryside and the great Château de Trévarez, but it has been encased in corrugated plastic. I do not know who had this house built, but I bet he had a tendency towards casual shoes with shiny metal

195

instep adornments, or even tassels. But the overweening vulgarity of the house is redeemable, and we could soon have it looking lived-in and liveable-in from our point of taste.

We found Le Rick this afternoon while indulging my wife's hobby of driving down any unmarked country lane or tractor track for no other reason than seeing where it does not lead to. After coming close to driving over the edge of the quarry pit, we almost literally ran into the elderly owners. When we had apologised for the trespass, they invited us to look around and told us they were regretfully putting their home on the market as the fields, woodland and three kilometres of walkways were becoming too much for them to keep in shape.

Throbbing with barely concealed excitement after exploring the terrain, we told the owners we were seriously interested and drove exultantly off to check out the bars between the property and Châteauneuf-du-Faou as we discussed the pros and cons of becoming the Lord and Lady of Le Rick.

To the jaundiced eye, the Château de Trévarez looks like something that an old-style Hollywood movie star with more money and less restraint than Liberace would have had built. Known understandably as The Pink Castle because of its coloured facade, it was one of the last grand *châteaux* to be built in France, and sits in eighty-five acres of gardens and walkways somewhat at odds with the more down-to-earth surroundings of this part of Brittany. Work on Trévarez started at the end of the 19th-century at the behest of the president of the General Council of Finistère, and incorporated all the then mod cons of hot water, central heating, lifts and even flush toilets. The RAF did its best to destroy Trévarez during the latter years of World War II as it was, somewhat bizarrely, used as a rest-and-recreation centre for Japanese submariners heaving-to in Brest. Nowadays, more than 150,000 people visit the Pink Castle every year.

*

We have been exploring the area around Le Rick. There are several choices for mode of travel to Carhaix-Plouguer or

196

Châteauneuf-du-Faou, including the tow path by foot or bicycle, the *contre-halage* (non-tow path side) by quad or motor bike, and on water by boat. We have also found a classic chicken-run across the canal at the Gwaker lock gate. It is a particularly attractive setting, with the former lock-keepers cottage now a gite and a narrow road bridge or *passerelle* over the weir. The interesting thing about the bridge is that it has raised kerbs, the distance between which is same width as the average car. Going by what we have already seen and the debris beneath it, the local sport seems to be to see how fast you can cross the canal without becoming stuck or leaving your side mirrors, hub caps or even complete chassis behind.

*

We have stopped at another cracking small Breton town to have a drink while considering how Le Rick could be encouraged to pay its way.

Near to the canal and conveniently sited between Châteauneuf-du-Faou and Carhaix-Plouguer, Spézet looks at first viewing to be a standard drive-through town. It is only when you count the number of licensed premises that you realise there is something going on here. There is a usually incontrovertible rule as to how many bars or pubs any normal village will support, and it is simply based on the population. There are exceptions where there is a strong holiday influx, but, as with Huelgoat, there seem to be more pubs and clubs in the main street of Spézet than other businesses. For certain it is the only small Breton town I know with two Irish bars. The decor and interior of the one by the church is a typical example of what people in other parts of the world would think an Irish bar would or should look like. The other one looks and feels more like an Irish village bar than many examples of the real thing. It could be a book or bike repair shop from its external presentation, and is comfortably small, lived-in and nicely smoky and dark inside. The first time we called, the landlord refused to let us leave before treating us to a final glass of Guinness. Our next visit was in the morning hours, but he refused to serve us just coffee.

At the far end of the town is another interesting bar. When we first went in, the only customer was a small, middle-aged man who was quietly weeping at the counter. When he eventually rose and staggered out of the door, I asked the landlord why he was so upset. It was simply, said the owner with a very Gallic shrug as he dried a glass at eye level, because the man could not drink another drop and was thus forced to go home to his wife.

*

One of the pleasures of looking at a property with potential is to intricately plan improvements and other changes with which you would put your own stamp on it. With a potential business premises it is even more fun, especially if you do not buy the place and so do not have to put your schemes to the acid test.

We only saw Le Rick a few hours ago, but I have already devised a full range of ways we can exploit the property's natural assets. Some are, I honestly believe, simply inspired.

The terrain's suitability for a campsite is obvious, and the miles of pathways between dense wooded areas would be a perfect setting for paint-ball, go-karting and moto-cross events. Even better, the sheer drop into the quarry would make an ideal setting for climbing and abseiling fans. We could also provide guided tours of the underground chambers, with the old slate wagons taking visitors on the Quarry Experience. This would include a son et lumière presentation, with me narrating the story of how the black treasure was won from the bowels of the earth. I am sure we could find a villager to dress up as the spectre of the Gestapo officer, jump out on the passengers and give the added excitement of a ghost train ride.

Even more potentially profitable is my scheme to cash in on the many thousands of tons of slate covering the slopes down to the canal. We know it would be impossible to gain permission to re-open the quarry without a huge investment in money and bureaucratic wrangling, but everywhere at Le Rick are tons of casually discarded slate which would total a huge sum if bought from a working quarry. Most are irregularly shaped fragments, but thousands are of considerable size and weight. Some pieces would floor an entire room on their own.

As I say to my wife, with a tractor and chains we could drag the suitable slabs into one of the giant barns, then display them in graded sizes and shapes. We would then invite roofers, builders and British DIYers to come to our cash-and-carry premises. Now that the French are becoming used to the idea with strawberries and spinach, we would be running the first pick-your-own slate farm in all France.

Thursday 18th

Back in Lesmenez, and our aged neighbour has come up with another Ancient Breton folk remedy.

I heard an indignant squawking from the henhouse this morning, and found Alain emerging with a handful of tail feathers. When I asked him if he had been trying to catch one of the birds, he said he had actually caught a cold, and knew we would not mind if he helped himself to the remedy. The certain cure for a rheum, he said, was to wear a chicken's tail feather around your neck for a week and a day. I looked at him for a long moment, opened my mouth to scoff, then closed it and kept my silence.

Remembering how a line of acorns on the window sill protected our home from the last great storm, it seems almost logical that a feather could distract and lure away a ticklish cough.

Saturday 23rd

We have had news of Le Rick, and it is not good. Our house detective friend has been doing some in-depth research on the property, and the results could indicate why it is such an apparent bargain.

In all civilised countries, sites of special historical interest attract all sorts of restraints and requirements of the owner, and ancient monuments more so. Le Rick is both, and is also in France.

The long list of terms and conditions include a codicil that the quarry may not be worked, but that it be kept open and available for regular visits by local history groups. There is also a risk of subsidence as it is not known how far and in what direction the subterranean passages stretch, and the house which may or may not be sitting on them was built without planning permission. Our researcher has also discovered that the property was bought in the mid-Seventies by an entrepreneurial Parisian (probably with a liking for tasselled shoes). He not only built the house without bothering to ask for planning permission, but also forgot to tell anyone when he re-opened the quarry and brought in a handful of men to work it. The business and quarry were shut down and he was made bankrupt, and Le Rick was bought by the present owners. The house has been there long enough to have gained retrospective planning permission, said our house detective, but we should remember that this is France.

*

We spent the afternoon sitting by the big pond, talking about what might have been at Le Rick. We also had a last-ditch debate as to whether we should go ahead, take a huge gamble and hope that all will turn out for the best.

In Normandy, we bought and restored a house just inches from what was to become a busy by-pass then moved to a manor house next door to a thriving dog kennels, so are veterans at buying attractive properties which seem to be a very attractive price. As I said to my wife, this could be third time lucky and it could be that we would be allowed to set up the PYO slate farm. It might also be that the house is not sitting on a void, and that we would not be ordered to tear it down. As my wife replied, if it did all go wrong with the house, we would be left with nowhere to live and nothing but a very expensive hole in the ground to maintain so that other people could visit it.

As dusk fell, we agreed we would not be making an offer for the ancient slate quarry. Perhaps we are becoming more fearful with age, or perhaps we are becoming more sensible. Whichever it is, our search for a new home in France will continue, and I cannot help thinking that I will remember Le Rick as the one that got away.

200

Home Cooking

Cotriade

As *bouillabaisse* is to Marseilles and fish chowder is to New England, *cotriade* is to Brittany, and particularly southern Brittany. In fact, an interesting factoid is that it is believed that the word 'chowder' comes from the old French for a cooking pot, and was introduced to the New world by Breton fishermen who were following the tradition of chucking off-cuts and any odd bits of the day's catch in to a *chaudière*. Another possible derivation is from the old English word for a fishmonger specialising in peddling scraps, which is 'jowter'. But let us not get carried away with the etymology. This is the important bit:

Ingredients

3 lb of any fish to hand, with as many varieties as you fancy (eel, mackerel, coley etc.)
1lb of potatoes
4 ounces of butter
3 onions
3 cloves of garlic
A bouquet garni
Some parsley
Some coarse bread
Seasoning
About two litres of water

Method

Clean the fish well and reserve the heads. Boil the water in a big pan. Peel and chop the potatoes and onion and peel the garlic. Fry the onion in another pan until golden, then add the potatoes and mix well. Pour the boiling water over, then add the garlic and bouquet garni and parsley and season. Boil for twenty minutes before adding the fish pieces and simmering for a further quarter of an hour. Taste and adjust seasoning if necessary before sieving and pouring into a pot. Remove the bouquet garni, parsley and fish heads, put the potato and fish pieces into the individual soup bowls and pour the broth over before adding the buttered bread.

Gâteau Breton

Apart from an inordinate number of bars, Spézet has another claim to distinction. Every Trinity Sunday, the chapel of Notre Dame du Crann is the setting for a Butter Pardon, which is similar in origin but not the same as the *Fête du Beurre* at St-Herbot. After the procession of banners, relics and statues, the penitents leave a richly sculpted block of butter in the chapel, where it will remain on display presumably until it becomes rancid. In past times there were three blocks, each weighing in at sixty kilograms. The town's non dairy-producers would keep their end up by presenting the chapel with banknotes arranged to represent garlands of flowers. More than perhaps any other symbol, butter embodied fertility and contentment in Brittany, which is presumably why they use so much of it in their cooking and recipes. The following is a pretty good example, using as it does almost as much butter as flour:

Ingredients

300 grams self-raising flour
250 grams butter
200 grams sugar
6 egg yolks

Method

Preheat the oven to 190°F. Mix the flour and sugar in a big bowl, then make a well and incorporate five of the egg yolks. Mix well and roll the mixture between your fingertips. Now put the butter in to the mixture in small pieces and rub in till fully absorbed. Press the mixture in a shallow, buttered cake tin and use a fork to pattern the top. Now use the final yolk to glaze the cake. Put in the oven and cook for an hour, then test with a knife blade.

December

Le Faouët, Quimperlé, Fôret de Carnoët, Le Pouldu, Moëlan-sur-Mer, Pont-Aven, Concarneau, Essé, Janzé, Pont L'Abbe

The mood of the weather darkens as the winter solstice nears. There is a threat of snow in the keening wind from the moors, and old Alain has doubled the number of chicken feathers on his anti-influenza necklace.

It was inevitable that he would appear just as the extending ladder collapsed and left me stranded high in the giant oak next to the stone cross. For months I have been coveting the voluptuous sprays of mistletoe attached to its upper branches, and could resist them no longer. At a Christmas market in Britain, the going rate is a fiver for a couple of sprigs tied with a ribbon, and I reckon there must be a hundred bunches in this one tree. Although it is so highly valued across the Channel at this time of year, mistletoe is thought of as no more than an infestation by French farmers. Though generally unpoliced, it is still technically an offence in Normandy to allow it to flourish in your apple orchard and threaten the cider and calva crop.

Mistletoe is a curious plant, and has engendered almost as many myths as the Holy Grail. The Druids believed mistletoe growing on oak trees offered protection from evil. We also know the plant was linked with fertility and thought to be an aphrodisiac, which may have led to the British excuse for stealing a kiss at Christmas.

In the early years, the custom was to claim a kiss and then remove a berry from the bunch. When the berries were gone, the kissing would have to stop. A truly mysterious fact about the plant is that though birds and wind and other carriers recognise no artificial borders, mistletoe will often flourish in one part of a region and yet not grow in another.

After he had propped the ladder back up and I had joined him on the ground, Alain screwed his face up into the usual expression of pained bemusement as I told him of the history and origins of mistletoe. But he did show real interest when I got to the kissing custom, and I noticed he slipped a sprig in his pocket before continuing his walk. He is due to call tomorrow morning for his daily egg, and I suspect he will be offering Donella more than a leek in exchange.

Thursday 9th

It is a curiosity of human nature that not being able to have something makes it so much more attractive, regardless of blemishes.

Last year while here to find a place to rent, we were sent the details of a presbytery for sale. We knew the picture-postcard village, and we made an appointment to see it the next day. When we arrived, the agent met us with an apology for wasting our time. An offer for the property had been accepted that morning. Even though we would not have been able to buy it at that time, we felt we had found and lost our next home in France in one day. Walking round the outside we realised what a buy it was, and the more we looked the better the house and surroundings became. The no-nonsense granite building had three proper floors and had obviously been well maintained. A river ran by it, the grounds backed on to a forest, and the village even had its own pub. We went home to sulk, and the more we thought of what we had missed, the more desirable it became.

Some time later, the same agent phoned to say another house in the village had come up for sale. Rushing there before it too was snapped up, we found the environs had changed quite dramatically. On our previous visit I had not noticed the tumbledown agricultural buildings and corrugated iron-roofed wrecks amongst the twee cottages. Nor had I noticed that the road leading through the village joined two noisy and very fast highways, and was obviously a handy short-cut for drivers in a real hurry. I had also not been aware of the family of noisy dogs living opposite the bar.

Since then we have seen a hundred homes and businesses and found them all wanting. I do not know if we will ever find the perfect home and setting, but this evening I sat in our local bar and drew up a complete specification.

My fantasy village sits at the end of a lane which leads to nowhere but itself. Our house is the furthest from the road, and behind it is a wide canal with a landing stage which we own. Boats may pass our domain, but crews attempting to land who are not approved by the Access Committee (me) will be repelled, and in extreme cases have their boats boarded and sunk.

The population of Paradise is a hundred or so, and nobody under the age of forty lives there. Adults from outside the village are allowed to visit their parents and relatives, but any small children and (especially) adolescents must remain in the secure detention centre outside the village.

Although small, the population is mostly made up of writers and artists and sculptors, so able to maintain a bar. Most importantly, the Rideau Cramoisi is modelled on a left-bank Parisian bar of the 1950s, has a classic zinc-covered counter; and it is busy each night with customers arguing passionately about which are the greatest works of art, what is the meaning of Life, and whose round it is. Smoking is actively encouraged if not compulsory, and the speciality of the house is absinthe dribbled into the glass over a lump of sugar. The dribbling will be done by Mimi, the barmaid. She will be forever 39 and single, but obliging, be especially sympathetic and fond of older men, and have a truly enormous pair of tits.

I realise that it is not likely that we will ever find such a place, and indeed my wife does not agree with me on some of the qualifications, especially the one about the barmaid with the big tits.

Saturday 11th

Any town with some interesting old buildings around a proper market square has something going for it. Le Faouët has the bonus of an ancient and largely untouched covered market, complete with mud floor. The Ancient Bretons did these buildings very well, with sometimes quite intricately carved stone or wooden pillars holding up a wide-spanned slate roof which may be garnished by a contrastingly delicate mini-tower or other embellishment. The covered market at Le Faouët has not been messed around with, and it is easy to half-close one's eyes and block out the cars and modern surroundings and imagine what it must have been like here a couple of hundred years ago.

Another interesting building in the square is the Celtic bar, holding up what is left of an ancient chapel. The Breton landlord was a little grumpy on the day we called in, but that was understandable as it was raining and cold, he had just been delivered of a stack of bills, and he said the poor exchange rate had totally buggered his summer tourist trade. His lack of warmth was overcome by my discovery of a classic period French 'footprints' stand-and-deliver bowl-less toilet, shared (though not usually at the same time) by men and women customers.

We are on a tour of the south, and called in at Le Faouët because it is near a special hamlet and chapel. Saint Fiacre is the patron of all gardeners and cab-drivers, and the hamlet named for him sits just outside the town. The significance of the elaborate chapel and huddle of houses for me is that this is where Pierre Jakez Hélias grew up and wrote about in The Horse of Pride. This excellently written record of day-to-day life in a Breton village is set between the wars, but would have changed little in the preceding hundred years. For anyone who wants to know what real life was like in rural Brittany away from funny hats, clogs and quaint customs, it is a compelling read.

*

Quimperlé sets out its stall to visitors even before they arrive, as there is a pleasant wood and water-lined descent into the outskirts. Any town with a wide and busy river running through it which is flanked by imposing buildings will obviously have a well-heeled history, and the local authorities have seen the value of cashing in on the eye-appeal with expensively re-cobbled streets running between the often medieval shops and houses. This is another town with an interesting and old covered market, though this one is clad in coloured brick. But Quimperlé is much more than a well-preserved or reconstructed tourist trap. Apart from the tourist inflow, the population of 10,000 means it is a busy, living town, with lots always going on. Kayakers enjoy the fast-flowing waters where the confluence of the Isole and Ellé rivers become the Laita, and Quimperlois are also big on culture and the arts. There is a well-known and respected school of dance and music and a purpose-built cultural centre bursting with books, DVDs and CDs. In the centre of the pleasing muddle of medieval streets and half-timbered housing is the abbey of St-Croix, which owes its unusual shape to being copied from a plan of the Holy Sepulchre in Jerusalem, with the idea brought back by Crusaders.

*

Heading for the coast, we pass through yet another great forest as well-stocked with myths and legends as with trees. The Fôret de Carnouët covers 1875 acres, and was once plagued by wolves. Step forward Saint Maurice, the then abbot of Langonnet. Though refusing to excommunicate the marauding wolves, he used his Heavenly powers to drive them out, and further ambitious miracles attributed to him include raising the dead.

*

I grew up by the sea and have rarely lived more than a mile from the coast in Britain. Perhaps this is why I find it peculiar that so many French people who do not sail or fish or even swim or sunbathe will pay so much to live as close as they can to the coast.

Le Pouldu is an unremarkable and mostly new-build seaside town, and looks like so many of the hundreds of other seaside towns which, as recently as a generation ago, were wilder and much more scarcely populated places. Now, new houses on identikit estates jostle for a glimpse of the sea, and their owners jostle in their cars to get away from the coast and to work. On the plus side, it is a bracing place to be on a blowy winter's day, and there is a nice rocky and sandy-beached cove to enjoy when you have passed through the looming apartment blocks which are sprouting all along the coast. A reminder of a less uniform past comes in the shape of a couple of old cottages high on the headland, looking out to sea and with their backs resolutely turned to the approaching menace.

*

When we first drove through Pont-Aven on a summer Sunday we thought there was a mass protest going on. The streets were completely clogged with people, but they turned out to be visitors and not protesters.

The appeal of this small town lies not just in its quaint old buildings, fast-flowing river, collection of water mills and attractive estuary marina. Pont-Aven was discovered and settled in the last quarter of the mid-19th century by a group of American painters. They were attracted by the light and colours and scenery, and their desire to get close to and capture nature was made easier by the recent invention of paint in a tube. One of the collective wrote to the impressionist Paul Gauguin in 1886 about the delights of Pont-Aven. He was broke, his marriage in ruins and the movement he had helped found was falling apart, so needed little encouragement to join them. Here he revelled in the company of fellow avant-garde thinkers, and came up with a new style of painting called Synthetism. Its credo was that the artist should 'paint what he saw and not what was'.

The nearby Love Forest got its name from the freewheeling lifestyles of the modernists and the admirers who flocked to see them, and it was here that Gauguin gave Paul Sérusier a famous painting lesson in 1888. The result was a masterpiece on a cigar box panel, and *Le Talisman* is now on permanent exhibition at the Musée d'Orsay in Paris.

Nowadays, Pont-Aven makes no bones about cashing in on the Gauguin connection, and there is a determinedly arty feel about the town. We find it a pleasant place to visit, but that is not always the same as a good place to live.

*

Concarneau is Breton for Bay of Cornwall, and if I could afford to live by the sea in France it would be in a place just like this.

I like ports and dockland cities where a living is or has been made from the sea. 'Bustling' should be a red-card word for travel

208

writers, but it suits this town of 19,000 so well. There is an air of things going on, deals being done and people getting on with their lives, which is because that is what has been happening on this part of the coast for centuries.

Adding to the interest is that, like St-Malo, Concarneau is a town of two halves. The modern part is on the mainland, while the medieval bit sits nicely cut off from the present on an island in the harbour. As with St-Malo, this separating of very old and not-so new has helped the old avoid unedifying clashes, and there is a wonderfully theatrical drawbridge helping to keep modern times at bay. Though shipbuilding is at the core of Concarneau's economy, the town's wealth was originally based on fishing, particularly tuna.

Once a year the Festival of Blue Nets has a thousand costumed townspeople strutting their stuff and reminding visitors of what it was probably not like in the old days. It might have been the weather or a rush of serotonin after a very good lunch, but for me there was something special about Concarneau.

I think it may have been the juxtaposition of the sea and ancient buildings and boatyards and real life and touristy fantasy. Whatever the reason I am in good company, as Inspector Maigret creator Georges Simenon set his best-selling novel The Yellow Dog in Concarneau.

Saturday 18th

We have arrived at the border dividing southern Brittany from the rest of France, and Christmas really is in the air. Santa Claus is arriving shortly, but by helicopter rather than traditional sleigh. He is coming to the neat, clean and prosperous town of Janzé, in the extremities of the department of Ille-et-Vilaine. While in this part of the region, we have made a detour to look in on a well-known haunt of elves and fairies, so Father Christmas may not have had too far to travel.

Near Essé, the Roches-aux-Fées is what megalith fans would call a covered alley. Traces of animal blood from sacrifices have been found at the entrance to the massive tunnel of stone, which points towards the winter solstice sunrise. Even if the website goes a bit over the top in calling it a mini-Stonehenge, the Fairies' Rock is one of the largest sites of its type still in existence, and acknowledged by experts as one of the leading prehistoric sites in Europe. On a cold and clear December day and far away from modern places and times, it is certainly a place of thought-provoking atmosphere.

*

For us, there are few places better to be at this time of year than a French Christmas market. Except perhaps the nearest bar to a French Christmas market, when the shopping has been done and it is time to relax before a long Saturday lunch.

The tavern in which we sit is not only the nearest to the action in the square, it is also a classic of its genre. The décor appears to have been modelled on or left untouched since the early 70s. Adverts on original enamel posters promote cigarettes that may now not be smoked on the premises, while on the shelving behind the counter sit dusty bottles of drinks elsewhere unavailable or even unheard of. Most satisfyingly, some of the older customers' clothing and hairstyles seem to match the vintage of their surroundings.

To make even a modest profit from a small-town bar requires steady and safe hands, and those hands are usually female. This is usually because her husband is out at work to supplement the family income, or that Madame is a widow. This status can be an advantage, as she will know how to deal with men when they are in drink or out of order, and her male customers will be made to feel at home if they transgress the rules.

In fact, the lady of this bar has a husband, but he has obviously been relegated to back-of-house or at least back-of-counter duties. Madame floats effortlessly around the bar topping up glasses and taking orders and relaying them to her spouse, and is clearly in charge. But in no more a way than the wives of the exclusively male clientele would be in charge of domestic matters in their homes.

At the moment, Madame's attention is devoted to a large table surrounded by farmers. Janzé is big on chicken-growing, and the men will be here to celebrate or complain about the day,

210

month and year's business. As well as several of the older members looking as if they have grown to resemble their stock, the group represents a complete range of age and size. This is another pleasing thing about French bars, where young and old can drink together with not a trace of the awkwardness and alienation that extreme age gaps usually bring in Britain. There are eight members of the agri-group, and they range in years from a downy-cheeked youngster to a frail old man. All wear the standard farming uniform of peaked cap and overalls under a well-worn jacket. One of the men is the biggest Breton I have ever seen. Like so many very big and fat men, he is almost painfully precise and delicate in his movements, and lifts his thimble-sized glass to his lips with just two sausage-sized fingers then pats his mouth dry with a serviette as if he were attending an old-time vicarage tea-party.

Madame is circling the table, topping up glasses from the half-dozen bottles she casually totes. As she reaches the end of the *tournée*, a middle-aged member of the syndicate reaches for a small purse. He seems reluctant to unzip it, but counts out some change and looks at the coins as if parting from a lover before handing them to Madame. The men hold their glasses up for a toast to the day and their friendship, and it is good to see how the youngest man helps the oldest to steady his hand and raise his glass. There is of course a pragmatic origin to this circle of compassion which seems to have mainly disappeared elsewhere. As well as comforting for the oldest member, it will be reassuring for the youngest to know that in the unimaginably distant future he too will be cared for.

Nodding at the circle as I pass, I find the toilet immaculately clean and as comfortingly dated as the rest of the premises. On return, I look through the plastic stripped curtain between passageway and kitchen, and see the table is set for lunch. There are two plates skirted at identically precise distances by knife and fork, a basket of bread, and a bottle opened and ready. It somehow reminds me of an altar setting, and all is clearly ready for the holy sacrament of lunch.

Back in the bar, the tables and chairs are emptying as customers take themselves off for their lunches. In Britain there would have been a call for last orders or a meaningful shuffling of chairs and clearing of tables, but here there has not been a word spoken. Everyone knows that Madame and her husband will be eating on the dot of noon, and that they should be too.

As we pay our bill, I point to where the giant farmer is gently escorting the old man from the premises, and wonder aloud if he is taking the old man home for lunch. My wife watches as the frail figure is helped into a battered van, then speculates that the little old man is the huge man's lunch...

Tuesday 21st

An early Christmas present with the arrival of some courtesy copies of a book I wrote ten years ago. It has been re-published but I don't know how well it has been edited, as my Czech goes no further than 'Hello' and 'Can you tell me the way to the nearest bar?' *(halo! nazdar! Pocínovat yu oznámit mne člen určitý cesta až k člen určitý nejblížší píščina?)*

The rights were bought last year by a Prague-based company founded in Paris in the last century to specialise in erotic literature. As the title of one of the books is French Letters, I think they may have thought the contents are spicier than they are.

But to a whole new readership I am Georgy Eastovi, and I wonder how well the translation into Czech has been done and how my humour travels beyond what was once known as the iron curtain. It would be ironic if the book is a best seller and we become famous there. As one koruna is worth only 0.3 of a pound even in the current hard times for Sterling, we could even be millionaires in Czechoslovakia by this time next year.

Friday 24th

The day before Christmas, and all is still. This is no different from any other day in Lesmenez, but the carols on the radio create a suitably seasonal atmosphere. A soft rain falls, but Alain has promised us snow before the day is out. Given his track record, we may well be in for a White Christmas.

My wife is surrounded by wrapping paper, sealing wax and string, and I am standing on a chair to deck the oak beams in the living room with fern, mistletoe and holly. This is not so much because I want to re-enact the traditions of the distant past, but because I am not allowed to put up the paper chains and baubles which have travelled around France with us for the past decade. A family of mice has set up home in the box of decorations in the loft, and my wife will not permit their eviction at this special time of year. When he arrives for his morning inspection, Alain will think that nailing plants to the ceiling beams is more evidence of British eccentricity, but I find the overall effect quite pleasing.

As I drape the last sprig of holly above the fireplace, an irritated tapping at the window reminds me I have not laid the bird table for breakfast. The impatient diner is our resident robin. Earlier this year we managed to untangle a robin from a length of netting in the barn just before our cat arrived, and Donella believes it is the same bird who arrives each morning. She says he knows her and comes when she calls, and though I laugh at her fancifulness, she has science on her side.

It is true that, of all races, the English have long enjoyed a special relationship with the robin, and even emotionally by-passed ornithologists agree the bird is attracted to human company. It is also true that the robin is very territorial and does not get on well with others of its own species. Insecurity is a trait, which is why they can be so aggressive to their own kind and why you will only see one robin in your garden.

Much more than most other garden birds and perhaps because of our mutual tendency towards insecurity, the robin also displays a curiosity about and perhaps an affinity with humans. Robins appear in Chaucer's works, and are said to be the only bird which will enter a church. They are also harbingers of approaching life and death depending which country lore you choose, and were said to cover the face of dead people with leaves as a sign or respect and compassion. The red breast was believed to come from scorching when the brave bird tried to quench the fires of Hell out of mercy for Man. The penalty for killing a robin is that your cows will give milk laced with blood. Though seen as a very seasonal bird, they are around all year, but we notice them more at Christmas, and see more of them as they are hungry. As with other small birds, the robin seems to hold little interest for the French, unless cooked and served properly.

*

Late afternoon finds us at Châteauneuf-du-Faou. We are here to pick up a Christmas tree which is a gift from Sally and Richard Moore. Hirgars is surrounded by hundreds of thousands of yearling plants which are grown commercially and exported all over France. The Moores have a field of their own, and it is very satisfying to cut down the tree of our choice. Their mini-narrowboat is moored at the bottom of the track leading to the canal, and Sally has festooned the neat little craft with Christmas lights. It would take the most unboaty of hearts not to lurch to see her bobbing gently in the wine-dark waters. We go on board with a couple of bottles of good wine, and it is the deepest of pleasures to sit and talk of the year gone and plans for the next while watching the watery sun turn the surface of the canal into liquid gold.

*

Back on home territory and reluctant to let the special day finish, we have taken a late walk on the moors. This is a very special time for Breton mythology, and so we want to see if the giant standing stones at the top of the track will uproot themselves and amble over to the stream for a drink. We shall also be tasting the water at exactly midnight, when legend claims it will turn to the sweetest of wine for a fleeting moment.

As we stop by the stream, my wife gives a little cry of delight and points up at the vast ocean of stars. The moon is at its leanest, and I see what she has seen. Beneath the tip of the waning moon two stars appear to hang like Christmas baubles. I know that the brighter one is Venus and that it is a little more than twenty five million miles from the moon, but the appearance that a heavenly hand has been putting up the Christmas decorations is a pleasing conceit on this special night.

Saturday 25th

Alain was of course right. Despite all the modern and scientific auguries predicting otherwise, we had a heavy fall of snow during the night.

Early morning finds us foraging in the forest surrounding the ruined abbey at Le Relec. I have stripped the hedgerows at Lesmenez of holly and need more to completely dress the house, and it is a delight to walk through a living Christmas card.

Reaching the top of a slope, I see through a break in the trees towards the old abbey, and, in the far distance, Lesmenez. It is a view I have not seen before and the newness of it delights me. I am a traveller who dislikes travelling, and always looking for new routes through the woods and across the moors so that I can come upon our home as if for the first time. I think that is why I like towns with many roads to and from them, and feel trapped when living on the coast with only one way to go to escape and see new things.

Last week we heard from our distant landlady, who said she is missing Little Paradise and wishes she could have rolled it up and taken it with her to the Midi. I know what she means, but would prefer the ability to change the places I hold dear without losing or moving them too far. While out walking, I often award myself the power to shift the houses of our hamlet around as easily as properties on a Monopoly board. I can also create new lakes and forests and even change the undulation of the landscape as easily as rucking up a counterpane. This way I can continually sculpt unfamiliar and aesthetically pleasing sights and sites, though all in the same well-known place. The familiar is comforting, but can become over-familiar, and I still long to see something new around every corner. When I told a friend about my fantasy, he said that I must have gypsy blood and should buy a caravan and go on the road. That way there would be a new view out of my window each morning.

I know what he meant, but a caravan is not a home. I want it both ways, and perhaps I am just in search of a place of belonging which I will never feel the urge to leave.

As I was struggling to plant our Christmas tree in an old wine carton, Alain appeared on cue to ask why I would try and grow a rootless fir in a box, when we lived in a place surrounded by giant pines. I know he knew what I was at, but it has now become a routine between us. When we arrived here he was genuinely agog at the weird ways of foreign townies; now he enjoys the badinage, and actively looks for things to rag me about. I got my own back by inviting him in for coffee and whisky, then presenting him with a Sainsbury's supasaver Christmas pudding. He hobbled stiff-legged off through the snow, holding the pudding at arm's length as if terrified that the contents would explode if he fell.

*

I have been on a tour of the neighbourhood, which did not take long. The purpose of the goodwill circuit was to demonstrate the English Christmas Day tradition of turning up at the homes of friends and accepting their hospitality before arriving home late for dinner but in good time for a row.

My first call was at the top end of the hamlet to the first people I met when we arrived at Lesmenez. Despite their protests, I presented Mr Goarnisson and Madame Messager with miniature Christmas puddings and mince pies and accepted their offer of a glass or two of moonshine apple brandy. The porridge slab cake was also on offer, but I turned it down on the grounds of the Scottish tradition which forbids me to eat grain on Christmas day.

I and my kilt and musical Father Christmas hat next arrived at the holiday home of Mr and Mrs Vitre, where I demanded a kiss under my mobile mistletoe spray from the lady of the house. I noticed that her husband did not object, but that he made sure he was well out of the line of fire when I came up for air. No doubt the memory of our meeting when I was trying out my skirt-kilt is still fresh in his mind. Madame Vitre remarked that the mistletoe tradition would go down well in Paris, though she had never noticed her friends needing an excuse to get to grips with other people's wives or husbands.

Having sampled some very fine old Napoleon brandy *chez* Vitre, it was on to our nearest neighbour. Alain was not in, and I found him next door at Jean-Yves' home. I was surprised that the femme de ménage who helps look after both their households answered the door, and when I asked if it was normal for her to work on Christmas Day she shrugged and said that every day was the same for old and sick people. She was anyway not officially working, but had dropped in to see that Jean-Yves' wife was comfortable. One of the very best things about France is how it treats its old people, and the way the elderly are looked after in their own homes. Two care visitors arrive every day to see Madame Jean-Yves is comfortable, and the same middle-aged lady comes twice a week to ensure Alain and his home are tidy and clean, the larder full, and a good hot meal on the stove. As Alain says, the relationship has all the advantages of a marriage and none of the drawbacks.

Accepting her warning not to frighten Madame, I followed Josiane through to the bedroom, where Jean-Yves sat, holding his wife's hand and talking softly of past Christmases. They have been together for more than sixty years, but she has not known him for the past ten. Taking off my musical Father Christmas hat, I whispered a goodbye and went home to my own wife, feeling very lucky and not a little guilty at my good fortune.

*

An unexpected Christmas box. Weaving through the short-cut from the lane, I found a plastic cage on the kitchen doorstep. Something large and furry was moving inside. In the kitchen I removed the grille, reached in, then took my bloody finger quickly out. After a moment, a large multi-coloured creature bounced out and on to the table and engaged me in a staring match. Although twice the normal size and of a strange multi-coloured hue, it was clearly a rabbit. I do not know what it had been fed on, but it was grossly obese and had obviously not read the manual about how rabbits are supposed to behave.

Unlike hares, rabbits are born blind and underground. Normally a byword for timidity, they are right at the bottom of the food chain. As herbivores, they predate on no other creature, but are predated upon by large birds, foxes, stoats, dogs and man. This is probably why they breed so prolifically, and are able to produce young just three months after their own birth.

As well as spoiling for a fight, our mystery guest obviously resents the confines of the cage. After it had been fed, watered, groomed and cuddled by my wife, I returned it to its cage on the grounds that it otherwise might attack and savage the dog, cat or even us in our sleep. Within an hour it had picked the lock and rejoined us in the sitting room. Donning my gardening gloves, I put it back in its comfortable lodgings and propped a pile of heavy books in front of the grille. Ten minutes later the creature was back on my wife's lap.

Wherever it came from, I have no doubt the new arrival will become another privileged member of our menagerie. If the word has got around about the levels of hospitality to be had here, it would not surprise me if the giant rabbit had not put himself in the cage and had it posted to our home. In acknowledgement of its unfeasible size I may call it Harvey. Or perhaps because of its ability to break free from any restraints, it should be Hilts, in honour of Steve McQueen's cooler king in The Great Escape. As tradition demands, the film was on TV this evening, and I noticed our new inmate watching with particular interest.

Sunday 26th

The mystery of the rabid rabbit is solved.

Alain arrived this morning to ask if we had cooked the *lapin* he had left outside. It had been a gift from a cousin, but far too much for him. If I liked he would show me how to kill, skin, paunch and cook it. All he would want in return would be a modest portion from the rump. I told him Donella was out shopping for herbs to go with his thoughtful gift. I will obviously not pass his message on to my wife, but will pick up a ready-cooked rabbit from a friend's restaurant and take it across to Alain under cover of darkness. Donella has called our new lodger Peter, but for me he will always be known as Lunch.

218

Monday 27th

Another mouth to feed.

As we walked down the hill from Kernelec and a drink with Morley and Sue Friend, something like a weasel on steroids shot across the track. I investigated and found myself engaged in another staring match. Wherever it came from, we now have a ferret as a permanent boarder.

A close relative of the polecat, the ferret has been domesticated for several thousand years. Originally used for hunting rabbits, they are increasingly being kept as pets in urban areas. They generally get a bad press, and though ferocious in the chase, can be surprisingly affectionate with humans. The old Yorkshire sport of seeing how long contestants can keep a ferret down their trouser front has no basis in fact, though life has followed fiction and there are now regular pub competitions based on that risky activity. There is even a ferret appreciation society which issues regular bulletins on the adventures of their mascot, Huckleberry Finn Ferret. According to the latest reports, Huck has been introduced to the comely Ophelia Ferret but there are no plans or proposals of marriage as yet.

I spent this afternoon making an annexe to the roomy quarters I built for Lunch, and the new resident was moved in by dusk. It may seem thoughtless putting a ferret and rabbit in close proximity, but the wire between the two cages is double-strength and should save Freddie from becoming Lunch's dinner guest.

Friday 31st

My kilt has had its first mass audience airing, as we have been attending a New Year's Eve party at Pont L'Abbe. The Hogmanay bash has become a tradition for a Scots couple who have lived here for many years; they say they stage the event so they can watch their expatriate English guests telling lies about how much they are enjoying themselves in their adopted country. Our hosts come from Glasgow and spent their working lives in England, so say they know what it is really like to be foreigners in a strange land.

The self-appointed capital of the old Bigouden area of Brittany, Pont l'Abbe was founded by an anonymous but clearly industrious monk, who also built or had built the castle and bridge across the estuary for which the town is named. There is a Bigouden museum in the castle (which is now the town hall) and visitors can thrill to the display of local head-dresses made as far back as the 14th century. There are also miles of long but level walks alongside the estuary to a huge and very sheltered bay inhabited by a number of large islands.

It was a well-attended party, with the tribal divisions on red alert. In one corner was a group of long-serving British expats of the sort who think the drawbridge should have been pulled up immediately after they arrived in Brittany. These peculiar creatures get a strange satisfaction from looking down their noses at new settlers, holiday home-owning or even visiting Britons.

In another corner and predictably ignored by the drawbridge tribe was a group of locals, huddled together and looking at the other guests like a group of gazelles sharing a watering hole with a family of peckish lions. I have found it a general truism that no matter how anglophilic they may be, exposure to groups of Britons will make most French people nervous, even on home territory. Another cause for their unease was that they were standing within contamination range of the buffet and its heavily-laden plates of veal and ham pie and pickled onions. The centre piece was a display of ironic deep-fried Mars bars that our mischievous hosts have told their Breton guests is the chief national delicacy of Scotland. I also knew that several Gallic guests would leave the party thinking that the Scotch eggs emerged fully-formed with their sausage meat and breadcrumb coating from the rear end of an ancient species of Hibernian hen.

The third group was also standing close to the buffet table, but that was because they find the proximity of a sausage roll and a cube of cheddar on a cocktail stick somehow comforting. Their expressions and the set of their shoulders indicated that, however much they may deny it, they are reluctant settlers. For whatever reason they made the move to live in France, they now deeply regret it but cannot admit the mistake to anyone else, and sometimes not even to themselves.

Finally, I moved happily on to a larger and far more boisterous group. These were the British couples who have made their lives in Brittany, and by and large made a go of the move. They come in various ages, sizes, political shades and classes, but all have something in common. They have decided that, all things considered, living here is better than living in Britain. Or they have accepted that they have made their choice and must now make the best of things. Like the reluctant settlers, the members of this group will be unhappy with some aspects of the way things are done in France; the difference is that they will openly admit to missing some aspects of life in Britain, even when sober.

This is the group amongst whom we feel most at home. We love the French countryside and have many French friends, but know we can never be like them or part of their culture. We are content to be and to be seen to be friendly foreigners.

As an experiment in cultural comparisons, I then toured the room and told all the groups the story about the rabbit which turned up on our doorstep on Christmas Day. Without exception, the expat women imitated excited pigeons before asking me how the little chap was settling in. All the French women showed immediate interest, and asked how we cooked it and what it tasted like.

*

Midnight has come and gone and we are taking a stroll through the deserted streets of Pont l'Abbe. We caused a few curtains to twitch when we piled outside for the traditional rendering of Auld Lang Syne, but the evening ended without tears, harsh words or a punch-up. It has been an interesting eight months in Brittany, and I feel the best is yet to come. Whatever happens and whether we find our next home here, it has been a small adventure well worth the taking.

Morbihan low-down

Meaning 'Little Sea', this is, for some reason that escapes me beyond snobbery and perhaps a little better weather, the most desirable place to live in Brittany. When I told a Breton property agent who operated solely in Morbihan that we liked the look of the Côtes d'Armor, she was horrified and literally took a step back as if she were afraid of catching something. 'You cannot possibly buy a home in that department', she said with an elegant shudder, 'there are so many flies because of the pigs and chickens and cows that you cannot even put your washing out on the line...'

The funny thing was that she was in deadly earnest, and showed once again that the European country which most often accuses the British of being class-conscious is a stunning example of the pot calling the *bouilloire* black.

Actually, we know lots of French and British people who choose to live in Morbihan, and like quite a few of them. It is true to say that there is a micro-climate in the lower half of Brittany, and the Gulf of Morbihan is a lovely place to live and keep a boat if you can afford it. Generally speaking, house prices in Brittany are, like for like, between a third and a half of what you would expect to pay in England; directly on the coast of Brittany and especially along the Morbihan coast, property prices can be even higher than you would expect to pay in England.

The department has more than eight hundred kilometres of sandy beaches, which are popular with divers as well as sailors due to the clarity of the waters. Inland is awash with wooded valleys, including the legendary Forest of Broceliande.

There are 264 towns in Morbihan, and a permanent population of around 700, 000, which at 94 people per square kilometre is surprisingly thin on the ground when compared to the other departments in the region. Perhaps the property prices keep that figure low.

Home cooking

I do not think the Bretons differ much from the inhabitants of the rest of France in their choice of festive fare at Christmas. Although or perhaps because they are surrounded by them throughout the year, the display of a Christmas tree in garden or window is not common. In ultra-traditionalist families, the main Christmas meal was called *Le Réveillon*, and taken after midnight mass on Christmas Eve. Nowadays, French families tend to eat at less indigestible times over the holiday, and the favoured dish varies from region to region. In Alsace, it will be goose, while in Paris they will enjoy fresh oysters with dinner. Predictably in Brittany, buckwheat *gallettes* with sour cream top the bill. On the coast, top-end seafood like lobster is now particularly popular, but further inland and south, many families opt for this Breton version of our own traditional table bird:

Lower Brittany Christmas Turkey

A large turkey
2 cooked pigs' trotters
2 lbs of sweet apples
I small celeriac root
A pint of chicken stock
10 unpeeled cloves of garlic (yes, really)
20 shallots
1 lb of lamb's lettuce*
A small bunch of marjoram
Some butter
Seasoning

Also known as corn salad, field salad, mache and even rapunzel. It grows wild in parts of Europe and is often seen as a common weed.

Method

Remove flesh from trotters and dice. Peel the apples, cut into chunks and sauté. Peel the celeriac and cut into chunks before cooking in the chicken stock. Mix the trotter meat, apples, celeriac and marjoram leaves and season. Stuff the turkey with mixture and sew up. Butter the turkey generously, then roast in a large casserole, surrounded by the unpeeled garlic cloves and peeled, whole shallots. Roast for an hour on each side and an hour on its back, moistening every fifteen minutes with a small glass of water. Serve the meat with a portion of stuffing and garnished with the lamb's lettuce, and grated truffle if you really want to go to town.

Bûche de Noël

The French are traditionally not so keen on Christmas trees, which is understandable when you look at the price tags. I recently saw one outside a shop which was shorter than me and on special offer at the bargain-buy, last-in-stock price of 65 Euros. But nearly every traditional French household will have a Yule log, and this one is remorseless in its use of chocolate and other rich delights.

Ingredients

2 cups of heavy cream
Half cup confectioner's sugar
Half cup unsweetened cocoa powder
1 teaspoon vanilla extract
Six egg yolks
Half a cup white sugar
Third of a cup unsweetened cocoa powder
One-and-a-half teaspoons of vanilla extract
Some salt
Six egg whites
Quarter cup white sugar
Confectioner's sugar for dusting

Method

Preheat your oven to 375°Fahrenheit and prepare a 10x15-inch shallow baking tray by lining it with parchment paper. In a large bowl, whip the cream and first lot of confectioner's sugar, cocoa powder and vanilla extract until thickly stiff. Refrigerate while you beat the egg yolks with the half cup of sugar (using a blender) until thick and pale. Now blend in the second amounts of cocoa and vanilla, and add a pinch of salt. In a glass bowl, whip egg whites to stiff peaks then gradually add the final amount of white sugar and immediately fold into the yolks. Spread the batter into baking tray and cook in oven for ten to fifteen minutes, or till mixture 'springs back' when lightly prodded. Now comes the tricky bit. Dust a clean teatowel with the confectioner's sugar, run a palette knife around the edge of the tray and turn the warm cake out onto the towel. Discard the paper. Starting at the shorter edge, roll the cake up with the towel and leave to cool for thirty minutes. Unroll the cake and spread the filling to within an inch of the edge. Re-roll and put seam-side down on the serving plate and refrigerate. Dust with confectioner's sugar before serving. Variations on the theme include the use of coffee buttercream and a garnish of marzipan mushrooms.

Mulled cider

This makes a bit of a change from mulled ale:

Ingredients

2 litres of dry cider
80g brown sugar
120ml dark rum
500ml of ginger tea*
4 clementines or small oranges
4 cinnamon sticks
16 cloves

*To make the ginger tea, use three jasmine teabags and a thumb-sized piece of well-pounded fresh ginger. Infuse the mixture and then drain your ginger tea off.

Method

Combine the cider, rum and tea and sugar in a large saucepan and put on a low heat. Quarter the clementines and stud each with a clove. Add to the pan with the cinnamon sticks, and heat until near-boiling (but do not boil!). Then turn down the heat and keep your mulled cider warm until serving.

(My thanks to Hetty's Kitchen and the Central Brittany Journal for the recipe)

January

Virgin snow caps distant crags and blankets the moors, and we have an enchanting new vista. The familiar rutted and muddy tracks have disappeared and all is serenely white and even more silent. The change will not be much fun for farmers and animals still out in the fields, but it makes a wonderful tableau.

It has been snowing just as heavily across the Channel, and I find it irritating to be told by the British media that the nation has come to a full stop and is the laughing stock of the rest of Europe. Contrary to common perception, the authorities in France are no better or quicker at salting and gritting roads. Those who use them are certainly no better than Brits at coping with the adverse conditions.

Yesterday we took the main route to the ferry port at Roscoff, and it was often at a standstill. Finding the road conditions not suited to their style of nose-to-tail brinkmanship, the drivers of at least fifty giant Euro-lorries had decided to pull up where they were. I suppose it is second nature to the average French lorry driver to park in the most awkward place and form a blockade.

As we threaded our way through the static traffic to a chorus of hooting disapproval, three police cars arrived with blue light-flashing and siren-sounding kit on maximum setting. As the cops adjusted their gun belts, lit up their fags with cool and practiced menace and started their arm-waving and whistling routine to ensure a complete snarl-up, I slipped our four-wheel-drive vehicle through a handy gate, across a field and onto a lane which would take us home.

As a disgruntled Brit expat said to me recently, the French are pants at anything to do with roads except maintaining them, but what can you expect from a nation of drivers who call the rear window of a car a toilet seat?

227

Imagine the scene in a dusty book-filled office in Oxford in the last quarter of the Nineteenth century. This little-known bureau is where new words are officially invented and introduced to the English Language. Two men in tweed suits even dustier than the rows of books lining the walls are looking at a small object on the desk between them. After a while, the older man pushes his wire-repaired spectacles to the top of his head, pinches the bridge of his nose, then says 'Right, Blenkinsop; you say this plug thingy is screwed into a hole in the engine of one of these new-fangled motor cars, and provides a spark for some reason. So, what are we going to call it?'

Faced with such a responsibility, the young man gulps nervously and causes his bow tie to bobble, then takes a deep breath and ventures: 'Erm, actually, I rather thought we might call it a 'sparking plug', sir..?'

'Excellent,' responds his boss after a reflective pull on his pipe, '...make it so. Time for tiffin, I think?'

Now let us cross to Paris and the grandly ornate building which houses the Societé Francaise. The French, unsurprisingly, have an official society for everything, including the Society for Appointing and Controlling Societies. For a century or more, this one has been in charge of making sure that when something new has to be named, no new words are coined and that the chosen definition will be as long and cumbersome or unsuitable as possible. Fresh from his recent triumph in decreeing that the typewriter should be known forever as The Machine That Writes, the Society's Head Obfuscationalist is also looking at a small object on the ornate Louis XVI marble desk between him and his assistant.

Leaning back in his even more ornate chair, Monsieur Pompeux strokes his goatee beard, sighs with a deep satisfaction and finally speaks:

'Well, now, Aristide. I have listened to all the submissions from other members as to the most suitable name for this plug which sparks. After much deliberation and thought, I have decided that the most suitable name for the sparking plug shall be.... a candle. Time for *diner*, I think?'

Sunday 2nd

A bracing encounter with a couple of hopeless hunters. I think I know about the true nature of Nature and how red it is in tooth and claw. I also know that meat does not come pre-packed from a supermarket shelf, but from living, sentient creatures. But I cannot understand why sometimes perfectly rational and decent men want to kill for the sake of killing. A friend recently lost a goat which had strayed from the garden and was seen, set upon, shot, skinned and jointed by a pack of hunters. They hid the collar which showed it was a pet. As my friend said, it was pointless complaining to the police, as many of them are also hunters.

This morning I saw something very large lumbering across the track and thought our monster rabbit had escaped. Then I realised it was a hare on the run. In the distance I could hear a regular tinkling which explained why the animal was on the move. Hunters hang bells from the necks of their dogs so they will know where they are, but seem too dim to realise this will also tell the game where their pursuers are. The hare did not seem to be panicking, just loping determinedly but quite calmly across our land and away from the copse. It either sensed it was in no danger from us, or knew from experience how rubbish French hunters are.

The bells also signalled a far greater danger to the hunters than I or a wild boar could pose. The posse of vertically challenged men dressed to kill came blundering through our copse to find Donella waiting, and I felt almost sorry for them. Normally my wife is not one to criticise or judge others for their tastes or hobbies, but she makes an exception for hunters and can be very inventive with her language when meeting them. Especially on her own land.

Having been suitably humiliated, the men were sent off in the opposite direction to the hare, and my only worry now is that it will instinctively return to our land and be invited to join Lunch as an official resident.

Thursday 6th

According to at least one of the seventeen goodwill calendars given us by local grocers, chemists, chain saw repairers and (mostly) bar owners, it is Epiphany, and we have been invited to attend a *Gallettes des Rois* party.

These popular get-togethers are held to mark the Feast of Epiphany, which in itself is a bit of a moveable feast. For western Christians, the epiphany (which is Ancient Greek for 'manifestation') of Christ took place when the three kings arrived to see the baby Jesus on what was to become Twelfth Night. In France, the event is marked in millions of homes as a fair enough reason to get together with a few friends for a nice meal with a glass of wine and a bit of fun for the children.

Every cake shop and supermarket in France will have the special cakes on offer throughout December and January, and inside each will be a tiny trinket. In harder times, the prize would have been a broad bean (*fève*), but is now usually a porcelain figurine. Whoever discovers it and does not choke to death is declared King or Queen and duly crowned with a cardboard crown supplied with the cake. Being a French tradition, a further excuse to make merry at the table is that the person who finds the *fève* is traditionally obliged to stage their own hunt-the-bean party and invite the same guests... and so on. Thus the celebration can last throughout the month of January, and in extreme cases has been known to go right through the year.

Saturday 8th

Waking and instinctively reaching for my baccy pouch this morning, I panicked before remembering I no longer smoke. It is two years since I quit, which means I have not rolled and smoked something like 32,239 cigarettes. When I fleetingly miss having a fag with my coffee, it helps to imagine a thousand ashtrays overflowing with the dog-ends I would have got through had I not packed it in.

To be honest, I think that smoking packed me in rather than the other way round. When we arrived in Normandy twenty years ago, smoking in public was almost compulsory. Not lighting up in any bar could be regarded as anti-social, and non-smoking men were often regarded as slightly untrustworthy. Not many people know that smoking in restaurants and bars in France was first barred fifteen years ago, but nobody took any notice.

This time it was clear that the French government would at least have to be seen to be following the rules as agreed with the rest of Europe. An amnesty was given for the first day of 2008, as it would be understandably difficult for bar owners to whip the Disque Bleu from their clients' mouths as the last stroke of New Year chimes faded. After the day of indulgence, it would be hefty fines and even loss of licence for those patrons who allowed smoking on the premises, or even displayed ashtrays.

To the astonishment of observers throughout Europe, the law was broadly obeyed, and the sight of disgruntled customers sullenly smoking in the rain seemed somehow very un-French. But the application of French logic to get round an inconvenient law has come into play. This is a perfect example of the Gallic thought process in action. In some bars, coffee cup saucers have replaced ashtrays, so the proprietors are, in their view, obeying the law. Elsewhere, smokers are encouraged to group around the fireplace. The golden thread of reasoning has it that the smoke from the fire goes up the chimney, so no law is being broken if it is joined by smoke from other sources. This approach has worked well except in the case where other customers have objected to the smokers hogging the fire, and in some cases has resulted in non-smokers taking up the habit to ensure their fair share of free warmth.

A clue that any bar is breaking the law will be the level of fuss outside as to how strictly they are observing it. Yesterday we stopped at a bar with four non-smoking signs on the door and a huge cider barrel in use as a fag disposal point. Inside, we stumbled through a thick pall of smoke to where a group of locals were standing beneath a large no-smoking sign and trying to blow smoke rings through a hole someone had burned in the placard.

Surprisingly, I had no problem in quitting, but still miss the idea rather than the practice of smoking. I do, though, appreciate the benefits. Apart from being able to walk up the track to the moors without an oxygen mask, I now no longer pat my pockets nervously every five minutes to ensure I have not forgotten the makings. I have also saved a lot of money, though the saving has not been noticeable. As a reward for breaking the habit of the best part of a lifetime, I proposed that we should go out to lunch once a month and spend the money I had saved by giving up smoking. This has not worked, as not only am I spending more than I would have saved on cigarettes, I have put my health into other dangers by piling on weight.

Monday 10th

A bizarre evening when we attended our first pantomime in France. Jack and the Beanstalk is being staged by a group of elderly male expats under the direction of a very theatrical former actor who lives with his boyfriend in a village not far from Morlaix. According to his admirers, Boofy Ashton was very big in the West End after the War, and ended his career on a high with the starring role as the walking fingers in a series of television advertisements for Yellow Pages. He still has, his friend and long-time partner tells me, very expressive and supple hands.

All members of the local commune had been invited to bring their family to the opening night, but the invitations must have either been translated badly or the villagers did not wish to expose their children to Boofy and his bunch. Consequently, the audience of adults-only sat stony-faced through the performance, with me trying to explain the plot and traditions of English pantomime to my Breton neighbours. It was easy enough for them to understand the idea of men playing the part of the dames, but as Boofy had sequestered the role of Principal Boy, it was beyond their reasoning to see why a man should play a woman pretending to be a man.

The buffet afterwards was a joint project, and that was the cause of more embarrassment as the Breton guests attacked their provisions and ignored Boofy's partner's rather camp offerings with names like Suggestive Sausages and Fairy Cakes. The evening ended in a near punch-up when a giant farmer got

232

carried away with constantly sampling his own home-brew cider and goosed Jack's widowed mother.

Wednesday 12th

A day out in Finistère's main town, and allegedly Brittany's most ancient. When I get too old for messing around in the countryside, I would like to go and spend my dotage somewhere very much like Quimper. I would enjoy shuffling across the square and reminding all those fresh-faced young students of the horrors to come by sitting dribbling outside a cafe while accosting passers-by with coarse remarks safe in the knowledge that they are unlikely to attack me.

Quimper is in the trendier and generally more upmarket southern part of the department, and is an *arrondissement* or administrative division as well as a big town by Breton standards. Made up of seventeen cantons and eighty two communes, the university town looks and feels the centre of culture it is, with the bonus of some very nice old buildings. All these things combine to give the centre of Quimper a civilised ambience and that easy air of a town which knows its worth. Even the seedier part of the town near the station has its own louche style, and there is a piano bar belting out real music each lunchtime.

The name comes from the Breton *kemper*, which means confluence, as the town sits on three major rivers. It is famous for its keenly-collected faïence pottery, and also for leather and woollen goods. Quimper is also regionally famous as a centre of excellence for macaroon-making, and we saw at least three premises owned by *artisan artistes* claiming to be the best *macaroniers* in all Brittany, if not all France.

The town also has another claim to fame as far as expats living in the area are concerned. One of the few things I and a few hundred thousand Britons miss when in France is a good anglicised curry. Just the mention of a Chicken Tikka on any expat forum will result in a torrent of drooling reminiscences. Regular postings vote for their favourite curry house in Britain, with exchanges getting heated about the comparative merits of a Bhuna or Phal. There are many on-line services for buying packets and spices, but everyone knows it is impossible to recreate a proper British curry at home. There is an elusive Briton known as the Curry Wallah who promises the best British Indian Restaurant dishes, but he has not replied to my repeated requests for further information. According to rumour, he delivers your order to key points around the region, where you meet him in a car park for the exchange of goods and money like a heavy drug deal going down. With their colonial history, the French are more used to eating couscous in L'Agadir than a chicken tikka in the Star of India. Quimper, though, has two very good Indian-style restaurants.

Another sign of the changing times in France and not, in my opinion, any cause for celebration is the Quimper branch of the Flunch cafeteria chain. As with the ubiquitous Buffalo Grill steak houses, the play on words should not work in French, but Flunch (a contraction of French Lunch) has actually become a verb in slang favoured by young people ('Let's Flunch, man'). The 200 outlets claim to serve sixty million customers a year, and I find that worrying evidence of the McDonaldisation of French eating habits.

I am very much not a food snob, but thought that the Flunch at Quimper combined all the worst aspects of French fast food preparation and service without the slickness of American outlets skilled at dealing with a lot of people eating not very special food at the same time.

The system basically works by customers queuing up at the cash register, then choosing and paying for their main course, which they collect from a short-order chef before helping themselves to vegetables. I chose a Texan Special, which turned out to be a pale imitation of a bacon and eggburger, and the only indication I was in a French eating establishment came when cook asked me how I wanted the meat cooked. Or rather he asked if I wanted it bloody, and posed it as a statement rather than a question. He used the same technique on those waiting in line behind me, and I think there would have been fireworks had anyone asked for their Texan Special well done.

Shuffling on, I was confronted by a huge vat of French chips at their skinniest and soggiest worst, and a selection of vegetables which had been perversely overcooked and then underheated. Least attractive of all was how the dozens of French diners around me ate their food quickly and efficiently as if disposing of a duty rather than relishing a sacred daily occasion. I understand about progress and change and how some people like or need to eat on the run, but I can't help feeling that Flunch is a sign of things to come, and France will be the worse because of it.

Another unwelcome change to French traditions we found in Quimper is the growing urban hostility to dogs. Once upon a time in the not so distant past it was almost compulsory to have a dog with you when eating out. Some supermarkets even provided doggy seats in trolleys for pampered pets to be wheeled around the aisles. Then came the signs telling customers in the most mealy mouthed of terminology that 'our friends' were not allowed entry. Nowadays it seems that the parks, beaches and establishments which allow dogs are the exception rather than the norm. Having said that, the complete disregard for these embargos displayed by most French owners is one example of a Gallic trait I greatly admire.

As evidenced by the no-smoking laws and the wane of high-visibility male peeing in public, the disappearance of the ubiquitous Mobylette moped, corrugated-roofed delivery vans and classic Citroën Deau Chevaux, things could not be expected to stay the same in France. Life has changed elsewhere in Europe, and I suppose it is no more than unreasoning and unreasonable sentimentality which makes me nostalgic for how things used to be here. But I do miss the old France.

Sunday 16th

Another engaging aspect of Brittany is the number and variety of artificial lakes and barrages where those in charge have taken the trouble to make them a delight to visit. Many ban motorised vessels except those small enough to be driven by silent-running electrical outboards which look like oversized hand-held food blenders. Because of the law, nearly all our favourite lakes are free of the curse of speedboats and jet-skis. This is just as well for the safety of all swimmers, fishermen and sailors when you think how the French drive their cars.

Not far from the busy market town of Sizun, Lake Drennec is a classic example of what can be done to create a recreational facility for people who want to do no more than walk themselves or their dogs in a pleasant setting. Covering more than a hundred hectares, the lake is surrounded by pine woods and far enough away from major roads to make it a place of peace. The circuit around the lake measures five miles of well maintained pathways, and even bicycles are banned, making walkers feel special.

Unfortunately, a relatively new craze is sweeping the region which endangers those out for a stroll. Not so long ago, any self-respecting rural Frenchman would never walk when he could drive, and an intake of cigarettes and full-fat milk was generally regarded as healthy living. Now, many younger French people have fallen for the idea that it is their daily regime and not their genes which will determine how long and healthily they will live. This has led to a worrying mass outbreak of jogging.

For some reason, the French shape is not made to jog. Of all races, the French run like big girls. To see a group plodding by, knock-kneed, limp wristed and gasping for breath is not a pleasant sight. Especially when, because they are French, they have to have all the latest kit to make the Sunday run more of a fashion parade. Advanced joggers wear the same sort of luridly-hued lycra outfits as cyclists, and some even sport the same sort of crash helmets. A new and much-favoured accessory is a bandolier holding miniature water bottles, which are removed and sucked on at regular intervals. Very dark glasses are also de rigueur, which is why there are so many collisions with trees, and why the wearers are such a menace to walkers.

*

Cadou was an early Breton martyr and pacifist, so was the obvious choice to be the patron saint of wrestlers. The village named for him is close to Lake Drennec, and if Walt Disney's idea of what an Irish hamlet should look like were made real, it would be just like St-Cadou. The church sits amongst a huddle of sturdy cottages, and there is a bakery in the front room of a nearby cottage, complete with an almost runic hand-made sign over the door.

Close by is an Irish bar which, for once, lives up to its billing. Inside is a satisfying jumble of old school desks and benches around a huge fireplace, and the flock-wallpapered atmosphere really does evoke a village pub in Ballykissangel rather than Brittany. One difference is the type of food to be found in the Saint Hubert. The name of the owner-chef is Christophe Bon, and he really is as good as his name. Highly recommended is this Norman magician's Côte de Boeuf for two, which is cooked to perfect pitch over the pub fire and served where you and your companion want to eat it.

Monday 24th

We have an opportunity to buy a home near the Nantes-Brest canal, and a business on it. An English couple are selling their hire-boat concern at La Gacilly, and the reason given is retirement. This is more reassuring than when the owners claim to have urgent business matters in the UK, which is usually the equivalent of an MP saying he is resigning to spend more time with his family. Another common euphemism for going bust or wanting to escape a wonky business here is illness of one sort or another, and I once saw the continuing sickness of the owners claimed as the reason for selling a health spa.

Tuesday 25th

Bretons do enjoy replacing vowels with apostrophes; in the case of the town formerly known as L'Orient, the signwriters have become increasingly sloppy or the Apostrophe Placement committee have decided to do away with it. In Breton the poshest town in this part of Brittany is An Oriant, yet the inhabitants nowadays are known as Lorientais, so there has obviously been some dispute. Or perhaps in the way that For Him magazine became FH, the trendy townspeople wanted to distance themselves from the past with a bit of contractual contracting.

237

The first and last time we visited Lorient, the bridge across the estuary was under repair and the Department for Road-Blocking had carefully chosen to do the heavy stuff at rush hour. It took us three hours to get in and out of the town, and the waitress at the marina bar was really grumpy. Sticking to our fair trading agreement to give every review town a second chance, we had another look this morning. If anything we found the place even less attractive. It is a classic cubist town, ringed with apartment blocks. The long drive into the centre is also littered with big and ugly commercial centres. The French version of Sofa World contrives to be even more garish and offensive to the eye. As with our first visit, we found the approach to the town centre intimidating, but without being able to say why. When we got there, we found it somehow cold and aloof. I do not know how one can say this about a whole town, but that is how we felt. Perhaps it is because we are yokels, and a big town has to have something pretty special going for it to overcome our trepidation. But we have been in bigger towns and felt much more at ease. (*Subsequent research revealed that the town grew prosperous in the early 17th century after merchants trading with India established warehouses at nearby Port Louis. They built additional warehouses across the bay in 1628, and that area became known as L'Orient. The French East India Company moved in later, thus confirming the oriental connection. The town was heavily bombed by the Allies to destroy its submarine base and supply lines, which explains the mainly 1950s architecture. As we were to a degree responsible for the modernity of the buildings we so disliked, perhaps an apology is due*).

*

Another repeat disappointment. When we first arrived to view the megalith alignment at Carnac, I said I would have asked for my money back had we paid to see it. As with Stonehenge, a busy road runs by the site of the largest collection of standing stones in the world. The roar of passing motors does not help with the ambience, but you get the feeling that Stonehenge was erected at huge effort for some mystic but very significant reason. Standing here and looking at the hundreds of big stones sticking up from the ground like headstones in a giant's graveyard, I got no such frisson of linkage with those prehistoric times.

Apart from the display of menhirs and dolmens, Carnac also offers five user-friendly beaches.

*

On the curving road around the Bay of Angels which leads to the Quiberon peninsula is a museum devoted to the monarchist Chouan movement.

The peninsula is at times no more than a few hundred yards across, and the permanently windy and choppy conditions on both sides make it a windsurfers' paradise. Formerly known as the foremost sardine canning centre in the country, Quiberon is now known mostly as a holiday resort. I have for some time wondered why Finistère's Belle-Isle-en-Terre was so named, and this is because there is one in the water off Quiberon. Belle-Île-en-Mer is Brittany's largest island, and said to be the most beautiful, hence the name. There are regular ferry crossings, and cars or bikes can be hired to explore its nine by seventeen kilometre land area. The island inspired Monet and Matisse, and was the setting for the death of one of the Three Musketeers. Famous visitors and probably non-windsurfers to Quiberon include writer Gustave Flaubert, poet and novelist Anatole France and stage and early film actress Sarah Bernhardt. For me, the rugged naturalness of the rest of the peninsula makes the occupied areas seem overbuilt, and Quiberon must have more traffic lights per head of population than anywhere else in the region, and perhaps all France.

*

I recently read a savage attack on the medieval show-town of Carcassonne. The snooty reviewer said it was a mainly 19th-century reconstruction and now a Disneyesque horror full of restaurants and tacky souvenir shops. His final and most damning evidence was that the town was so vulgar it had a board and video game devoted to it. What he did not understand is that a vulgar, Disneyesque Carcassonne is exactly what is wanted by the millions of tourists who flock there each year.

239

In our region, the former fishing port of the small town of Auray doesn't come close to Carcassonne for Disneyesqueness, but is similarly in-your-face, self-assured and unapologetic about milking its attractive olde-worlde features. Starting from scratch, it would be very hard to create a film set which would look more quaint than Port St-Goustan. Recently re-cobbled lanes wind down through half-timbered houses which look as mouth-wateringly quaint as they must have been uncomfortable in which to live. Shoulder-to-shoulder on the quayside is what would be an overkill of bars and restaurants elsewhere, but all will struggle to cope with the seasonal invasion of sightseers. Further evidence of the no-nonsense statement of intent here is the cashpoint machine set conveniently into the wall of the public toilets.

On the frontage of a really old bar on the quay is more evidence of how more distant countries understand and get on better with France than we do. A distinguished visitor to Auray was Benjamin Franklin, who arrived in the December of 1776 to discuss an alliance between his country and France during the American War of Independence. This, if one were needed, is just another example of just how long we and the French have been thumbing our noses at each other.

*

I am continuing to develop my theory that this land of Celtic myth and legend inspired JR Tolkien to adapt many of the place names here for his Lord of the Rings trilogy. In the books, Rohan was a kingdom of Men; in Brittany it is a canalside town in Morbihan, named for the lords who ruled there. Tolkien's Legolas is an elfin prince, while Daoulas is a coastal resort in Finistère and near the strawberry capital of all France. South-west of Vannes is the pretty little port of Arradon, which at a stretch could be argued to sound a bit like the name of the future king of Gondor. Also close by the Gulf of Morbihan is a place called Elven. I haven't found a soundalike for the dread realm of Mordor yet, but will continue the search.

Accessible from Arradon, Île-aux-Moines is one of the larger and closer islands in the Gulf of Morbihan. The road to Arradon also passes my contender for the most unusual name for an Irish theme pub. Demonstrating its impeccable multi-culturalist credentials by serving a good lunchtime tapas with Guinness (and this after two p.m.), it reflects its location by being called 'The O'Riverside'.

*

Going on our first inspection, Vannes has all the virtues I found missing at Lorient.

Founded by the Romans, it is satisfyingly ancient, which is always a good start. The old centre has also not been mucked about with. It has a proper working inland port, and the surrounding area is nicely ungentrified. From at least one direction, the town is easy and quick to get in and out of. A nice touch and further echo of an old English university town is the cycle scheme, with ranks of bikes for borrowing at strategic points. There is also a nice wrought-iron bandstand near the river, and, like a bike scheme which survives without them all being nicked, I always find that a good indicator of sophistication levels.

Like many towns we find attractive, Vannes looks a bit like several smaller dwelling places joined at the edges, which means you can go to the area which matches your mood. There are some beautifully landscaped gardens alongside the castle, and some interesting road layout patterns. I had heard that the rules of the roads surrounding the old quarter were unusual ('insane' was the exact term) and we twice found ourselves following street marking which led to nowhere but a sheer wall. On the third occasion, we did what we thought we were told, and ended up in the ancient pedestrianised area of old Vannes. Being France, none of the walkers we came close to running down seemed to mind, and I was even asked for an autograph by someone who thought I was the mayor on the way to open a new lingerie shop.

Another real curiosity is why, together with Barouéli in Mali, this beautiful and historic town is twinned with Fareham, a small town near Southampton in Hampshire. Anyone who knows Fareham as well as I do must conclude that, at best, the jumelage panel made the proposal after a very, very good dinner, or were just having a laugh.

*

We shall not be buying the boat-hire business at La Gacilly, as the owners and our idea of what the assets and goodwill are worth are too far apart. But it would be a pleasant place to live and work.

As Pont-Aven is the town of artists, La Gacilly claims to be the town of artisans. There are any number of craft workshops, and a genuine bohemian feel about the commune, which sits around a bridge over a fast-flowing stretch of the Oust. The town is also known for a botanical garden which is maintained by the giant cosmetic company based there. Apart from art, craft and beauty concerns, La Gacilly is also the setting for an unusual competition. Each year sees a number of festivals and many art and craft related events, not least of which is the annual soup-making contest.

Home cooking

This is my submission for a suitably exotic entrant for the next La Gacilly soup concourse. It combines curry and cockles and is thus unusual even by Breton standards:

Curried Cockle Broth

Ingredients

2kg cockles
100g butter
3 shallots
300 ml white wine
300 ml crème fraiche
A teaspoon of curry powder
2 small apples

242

Method

Put the cockles in cold water for at least two hours. Wash in plenty of water and drain. Peel the shallots and chop finely. Put the shallots and white wine into a saucepan, bring to the boil and add the cockles before covering. When steam escapes, take lid off and stir. Re-cover and cook for five minutes before taking the saucepan off the heat. Remove the cockle flesh from shells and place in six soup bowls. Pass the cockle juice through a very fine sieve so any grains of sand are unable to pass through. Add the cream and the curry powder and boil for five minutes. Peel the apples and dice and divide them amongst the soup bowls. Add the butter to the cockle broth and emulsify in a mixer. Check the seasoning, share the broth amongst the bowls and serve.

The King's pancake

This is the standard recipe and procedure for a *Galette du Roi*, which is actually not a galette except in its flat, round shape. The cake also had a movie named for it, released in 1986 and starring Jean Rochefort and Roger Hanin. You will note that this recipe takes the easy way as it suggests you buy-in the puff pastry. You may wish to make your own and get the righteous glow of hard work in pursuit of perfection, but the commercially produced stuff is so good now I think you would have a job improving on it. The same applies to the almond paste filling, which can be bought ready-made by the packet and is usually labeled as frangipane, or *franchipane* if you are shopping in France.

Historical note: According to legend, franchipane was brought as a final treat to Saint Francis of Assisi as he lay dying in 1226.

Ingredients

Quarter cup raw almonds
Quarter cup almond paste
Quarter cup of white sugar
3 tablespoons of unsalted softened butter
2 eggs

Quarter teaspoon vanilla extract
Quarter teaspoon almond extract
2 tablespoons all-purpose flour
A pack of thawed frozen puff pastry
Glaze of one part water and two parts sugar
A pinch or two of salt

Optional extras

One dry kidney bean (for the *fève*) or gold trinket
One silly gold cardboard crown for the finder of the hidden geegaw

Method

Preheat the oven to 450°F. Butter 2 large baking sheets. Purée with a blender the almond paste, sugar and butter and salt until smooth. Add one of the eggs and the vanilla and almond extract, then blend till incorporated. Add flour and mix again. On a lightly-floured surface, roll out one sheet of the pastry to make a 12 inch square. Cut out a circle from the pastry using a pie dish or ring as a guide. Place the round on to the buttered baking dish and chill in the fridge. Repeat the process and leave this round of pastry on the floured surface. Beat the remaining egg and brush some of it on the top of the second round. Score the top decoratively and make some steam vents in the pastry. Take the first round from the fridge and brush some beaten egg in a one inch border round the edge of the pastry. Make a mound of the almond cream in the centre, spreading out slightly, and add your bean or trinket. Place the scored round of pastry on top and press the two together at the edges. Bake for around a quarter of an hour in the lower third of the oven until the pastry is puffed and golden. Remove from the oven and brush with egg again. Return to the top half of the oven and bake again for around fifteen minutes or until the edge is deeply golden. While still on the baking rack, brush the gallete with the glaze mixture.

NB. Do not forget to warn any children or guests with dodgy teeth, expensive crowns or fragile dentures about the presence of the hidden trinket - unless you really do not like them.

Hunter's Return Rabbit

This traditional recipe specifies that the rabbit should be freshly killed and definitely wild. As the old gag has it, I should not think any rabbit would be pleased to be killed, skinned, jointed, cooked and eaten, no matter how classic the dish. Purists say you should skin and paunch the rabbit personally, but unless you have a strong stomach and sure hand, I would earnestly recommend buying it already undressed (as in naked) and dressed (as in having the guts removed). The purists also say you should pick the apples for the recipe during the hunting trip to shoot the rabbit. That is all very well, but what if it is not the right time of year for apples on trees?

Ingredients

One wild (or not) rabbit
Four apples
200g breast of pork
50g butter
2 glasses of cider
6 small shallots
One clove of garlic
One sage leaf

Method

Joint the rabbit by cutting off the legs and the saddle in half. Cut the breast of pork into pieces and brown in the butter with the crushed garlic clove. Add the peeled shallots and sage leaf. When the pork fat is nicely browned, add the rabbit and brown the pieces well without burning the butter. Add the apple, peeled and chopped into rough pieces. Check the seasoning, then add one glass of cider and drink the other whilst you cover the dish and put in a hot oven for around ten minutes.

Milk jam

Here's an unusual and easily made spread which is said to be peculiar to Brittany or Normandy, depending on who is doing the saying. It may seem strange to spread something that tastes exactly like melted toffee on your bread, but who are we Marmite and peanut butter eaters to take issue with the practice?

Ingredients

Two litres full fat milk
One kg sugar
One vanilla pod.

Method

Put the ingredients into a thick-bottomed saucepan and bring to the boil while stirring continuously with a wooden spatula. Cook gently on a low heat for around two hours, by which time the jam should be a light caramel colour. Remove the pod and put the jam into a jar.

February

Plancoët, Saint-Jacut-de-la-Mer, Lannion,
Ste-Anne-la-Palud, Douarnenez, Pointe du Raz, Île de
Ys, Île de Sein, Audierne, Penmarc'h, Landivisiau,
Lampaul-Guimiliau, Guimaëc, Locquirec,

I don't know which old Breton said it, but it is an old Breton saying that you have to like grey if you live in Finistère. Certainly in this lofty area of the department, many older country people prefer to look at the colours of winter through their windows. Some will observe the traditions of the past and get up and go to bed with the light. As dawn does not fully break till around eight o' clock at this time of year and dusk sets in around six, they will be spending more time in bed than out of it. This also saves on heating and food bills, and in a nearby hamlet, Guy the Very Mean and Lazy is said to take to his bed in November and not leave it till May except for obvious necessities. We have not seen Jean-Yves since Christmas, and Alain only leaves home to pick up his daily egg and catch me in compromising situations.

Thursday 3rd

With so many varied geographical features in such a small corner of Planet Earth I am developing a theory that God used Brittany as a practice range. We are heading for the north-eastern coastline, and our journey will take us across moors and mini-mountains, past giant lakes, through vast pine forests and alongside undulating pocket-handkerchief fields ringed with ancient *bocage*. After travelling up hills and down dales we will suddenly arrive at a place of towering cliffs and miniature fjords, sweeping sandy bays and estuaries peppered with islands. And we will still be home in time for tea.

Having the longest coastline in France, the Bretons had to come up with ways of upsetting all less privileged regions, so the Committee for Inventing Exotic Names for Bits of Coastline was formed. Although it looks to me to be the same rock-like colour as the rest, we shall be travelling along what they decided would be called the Pink Granite Coast, and then on to the Emerald, Cornouaille and Megalith coasts. In its spare time, the committee also came up with some pretty nifty legends and metaphors, and most of them are inevitably to do with sex. Along the Goëlo coastline, it is said (by the committee) that back in the dawn of time, the sea signed a love pact with the land, which is why the waves penetrate the coastline so deeply and rhythmically, crashing on the rocks in a climax of....well, you get the picture.

Having set the standard, the possibilities for purple descriptive prose and clunkingly obvious metaphor in the tourist literature were pretty near endless. So, when it is a bit blowy along the coast, the lovers have had a spat; when there is a wild storm there has obviously been a really passionate falling-out over whose turn it was to clean the bath.

What we particularly like about the Brittany coastline is the number of small bays and inlets which lay largely untouched by the usual requirements and impositions of tourism. In other words, the places where the residents do not welcome or want people like us poking around. The major coastal towns and designated beauty spots are increasingly littered with caravan sites and formulaic hotels and places to eat, but there are still hundreds of commercially unexploited places where sea meets shore.

Sometimes it is made very obvious that the locals want to keep a good thing to themselves and have taken steps to do so. Lanes which appear to lead towards the coast will come to a dead end; signs which might have indicated where the sea is to be found will have been removed or point back to where you came from. In extreme cases, I have even seen hand-written signs which would lead the unwary traveller into areas of quicksand or marsh, or even over an unguarded cliff edge.

We have been working our way along this stretch of the ultra-crinkly coastline, and on our last visit found an apparently un-named inlet and community of less than a dozen houses. The residents are obviously not keen on visitors, and make no bones about it.

On the beach is a very large sign strictly forbidding the use of motors of any form on any boats which wish to use the bay. Sailing boats or any craft of more than three metres in length are also banned. On another notice, visitors are warned how treacherous the tides can be. Nearby there is a long list of other potential dangers, including stubbing your toe on underwater obstacles, or as they are known more usually, rocks. This apparent concern for health and safety issues is so un-French that I think it must be another device to deter the few strangers who have managed to get to the water's edge.

*

On the banks of the River Arguenon and no more than a handful of miles inland from the sweeping majesty of the Emerald Coast, Plancoët is the sort of place which effortlessly pleases the eye. It is remarkable for having two significant churches, being mentioned in passing by Châteaubriand in *Memoires d'outre Tombe*, and being the only town in all Brittany to bottle and purvey its own mineral water. It is bottled from the source at Sassay, but I have no idea what it tastes like as I only found out about the water after our visit.

*

It being winter and lunch time, we passed no vehicles or saw any other signs of life on the curving peninsula road to one of the most all-round attractive coastal towns in Brittany.

Snugly bounded by two inlets, St-Jacut-de-la-Mer is another coastal place which looks as if it can take or leave visitors. It is a solid and clearly respectable burgh, with solid and respectable stone buildings and the sort of church designed by a time-travelling architect who whizzed back to make sure it would be a tourist magnet in the future. Other satisfying touches are the lack of pavements and unapologetically low speed limit of 30kph, and a very sensible one-way system taking drivers out to the point. Here are acres of parking space with cracking views, and whoever dreamed up the name for the Emerald Coast must have been looking at the colour and texture of the sea on a day just like today. There are eleven beaches and the town is famous for the quality of its shellfish and fishing opportunities. The island of Ebihens is accessible at low tide, and has an interesting Vauban tower.

For those interested in real and alleged historical figures, Vauban was a 17th-century Marshal of France and the country's leading military designer, responsible for some very well-thought-out and apparently impregnable fortifications on the north coast of France. Saint Jacut was a disciple of Saint Budoc, with whom he probably travelled to Brittany after being turfed out of England by invading Saxons in the fifth century. The hermit saint Budoc had a high standing in the religious community, as he was also a bishop and said to be the result of a union between a king of Brittany and Azenor, daughter of the then ruler of Brest. In the way of these things and to make a story of it, Azenor was exiled in a cask and Budoc born at sea.

*

Further westwards and wedged between the Pink Granite Coast and the Côtes des Bruyères, Lannion is a high-ranking entry on the growing list of our favourite Breton towns. This is because there seem any number of attractive and individualistic towns in this region, which we have not always found to be as true elsewhere in France.

As a small but significant plus, Lannion has a refreshingly low graffiti count. This is a blight which increasingly affects many large-ish French towns. I find it curious that the authorities tolerate the defacing of their fine buildings, but, being French, perhaps regard the visual vandalism as a creative pastime.

An ancient dwelling place with a genuine Templar's church, Lannion is a *sous-préfecture* (lesser administrative town) of Côtes d'Armor and the capital of the Trégor part of the region. Sixty thousand people live around the town, and eighteen thousand of them in the direct urban area. This makes it quite a big and busy place by Breton standards. Lannion is also a classic example of how twinning committees go out of their way to find the most unsuitable match, as it is paired with Caerphilly.

Arranged around the Léguer river a few miles from the stunningly beautiful estuary at Le Yaudet, the oldest part of the town has a high headcount of half-timbered buildings, some with an even higher improbability factor of how they have managed to stay fairly upright for so many centuries. Probably the only town in the region with a shop dedicated to Hungarian goods, Lannion's relaxed mixture of established history and sometimes quirky modernity reminds me of Brighton without the sea, and, as far as I know, the large gay community.

Our last visit to Lannion was unexpectedly expensive, and this is a good time to post a caution to all new travellers in France. Whatever the standard of any toilet, be sure to check the paper dispenser. In my experience, France comes second only to The Pink Leopard pub in Darby for never having any bog paper to hand. Nowadays in France, spotting the problem is harder as the lack of *papier hygiénique* is usually disguised by a large metal dispenser. Perhaps worse than total emptiness is when the last inch of paper on the roll is emerging from the container, promising much but in fact giving far too little for the job in hand.

Lulled by a good lunch, I neglected to check the dispenser before sitting down and doing my business, and was left holding a piece of paper the size of a postage stamp. This was a real dilemma, as the toilet was two flights of stairs up from the bar so I was not able to call for help or beat out the international Morse code distress signal on the soil pipe. My notepad was on the table in the bar, and a quick self-frisk revealed the only paper in my pockets came in the form of three ten-Euro notes.

Faced with the choice of a long and uncomfortable ride home or using the paper money, I completed what was my most expensive visit to a toilet anywhere in the world.

Traveller's tip: When moving around France, always take a sufficient supply of tissue paper, or an old newspaper or suitable number of low denomination notes.

Saturday 5th

Today I had what was, to my knowledge, my closest brush with death. At a rough estimate, the closeness was about five feet six inches.

As I stood by the big pond thinking how pleasant was the day and my surroundings, I heard the sort of groaning I imagine would come from a giant with a very bad toothache. Then came a great tearing, rending sound, and I looked up to see that one of the seventy-foot pine trees which line the far side of the pond was on the move. At first and as we are in Brittany, I thought it might be a distant relation of Tolkien's Ent Treebeard, uprooting itself for a morning stroll. Then I realised that the apparently healthy tree was toppling over. More importantly, it was toppling my way. It did not take me long to work out that I was probably less than seventy feet from its base, and as soon as my legs could be persuaded to move I turned and started to clamber up the bank. Then I slipped on the wet grass and fell, slithering down to nearer the water than when I had started. Rolling on to my back, I saw that I and the tree were still on a collision course, and I had managed to place myself in exactly the spot where it would land.

I had heard that life goes into slow motion at times of high drama, and now know that to be true. There seemed an awful inevitability to what was happening, and with a gesture more futile even than asking a Parisian taxi driver for directions, I held up my hands and shut my eyes.

After a while, I became aware that the rending and groaning and swooshing had stopped. Opening my eyes, I saw that the top of the fallen pine was suspended a couple of metres directly above me, swaying hypnotically up and down and from side to side. Eventually getting up, I tottered around to the far side of the pond. There, I saw that the tree had uprooted from the eroded bank of the river running past the pond, but snagged itself in a conifer standing between it and the pond and me. Had the conifer been less sturdy or not been there, I would certainly be dead.

Thinking about the incident later, I wondered if the event was an act of malicious intent by the tree in revenge for my cutting down so many of its dead relations, or a gift from the Breton gods of firewood. The corpse of the fallen pine will provide at least a month's worth of warmth, and I will certainly never be rude to a conifer again.

Monday 7th

Ste-Anne-la-Palud is no more than half a village on the western coast of Finistère. The sweeping bays and sandy beaches and rolling dunes can be heart-achingly beautiful, and the area is suitably remote and offers little off-season for anyone who wants more than a picnic or long walk by the sea. Typical of much of Brittany, this part of the coast is a paradise for hikers but not much fun if you are after a cup of tea or a bag of chips.

Ste-Anne is a special place for those with an interest in religious buildings, and the eponymous chapel sits in the dunes a little way beyond the village of a dozen mostly holiday homes. There are regular pilgrimages to the chapel and the lady even has a song dedicated to her, asking for protection for Bretons on land or sea. She is also or should be a saint of choice for salt makers and sellers.

The house we had come to view was, as advertised, no more than a couple of minutes walk to the start of the dunes, but stood alone in a large area of uncultivated ground which would not belong to the new owners. This apartness might seem like an attractive feature if you missed the signs for building plots for sale in the immediate area. We know from those who have suffered in this way that there is little more galling than having to put up with years of mess and noise so that lots of other people can come and live next door.

As mentioned earlier, a paludier was and is a specialist sea salt gatherer and/or seller. Brittany has a long history of farming, selling and smuggling salt, and the travelling salt merchant was a feature of Breton life until a century ago. The typical paludier would work on his patch of marshland through the summer, then go on his rounds between All Saints' Day and Christmas. Usually, very little money changed hands as the paludier travelled from village to village, as barter was the most common system. Because of the itinerant nature of his job, most paludiers also acted as messengers, picking up and passing on news and gossip as they went.

For some reason, Douarnenez puts me in mind of Torquay. I can think of no good reason, except that both are on a bay and have a natural harbour. There is something built-up and almost English about the way the houses and hotels look down on the sandy beaches from their elevated positions, though the old quarter of Douarnenez is not at all what you would expect to find on the English Riviera. The twinning committees on either side of the Channel seem to agree with me to some geographical degree, as Douarnenez is matched with Falmouth.

The town's wealth was built on railway services and canning mackerel and sardine, and nowadays the mild climate and pleasant location attracts many seasonal visitors. Just off the mainland is the island of Tristan, linked mysteriously with the legend of Tristan and Iseult. It is also linked with one of the bloodiest villains in Brittany's history, as we will discover shortly.

*

Somewhere in the bay of Douarnenez is said to lay another island with a mysterious past, but in this case it rests below the waves. The legendary island city of Ys has several great stories associated with it, the most common and popular telling how it was built for the princess Dahut by her father Gradlon, king of the Cornouaille region.

As well as suffering from a shortage of letters, Ys was below sea level and protected by a gated dyke for which the king held the only key. The settlement was to become the most impressive and beautiful city in the world, but soon became a byword for sin and corruption. Dahut had a penchant for organizing orgies then killing her lovers when day broke. One fateful evening, a knight in red arrived and was invited to join in the fun. During the night, he suggested that Dahut steal the key from her sleeping father. She did, and the Devil (for it was he) threw open the gates and allowed the sea to swallow Ys. Enraged, the king threw Dahut into the oncoming torrent, where she became a mermaid, doomed to swim the seas alone for all eternity. As with all drowned cities, it is said that on stormy nights you can hear the bells of the church at Ys ring out, and even the mournful cries of the lonely mermaid.

*

An island much easier to locate but with almost as colourful a history as Ys is the Île-de-Sein. Eight kilometres off the Pointe du Raz, this apparently innocuous island is on the sea routes going south from the English Channel and was once the lair of a whole community of wreckers. With a land area of less than a quarter of a square mile and fewer than 250 residents, the island and surrounding treacherous rocks now bristles with lighthouses.

Distinguishing Île-de-Sein from all other islands off Brittany is the fact that during WWII, every male inhabitant fled to London to join the Free French forces. After the war and in recognition of this act, all inhabitants of the island were exempted from paying income tax in perpetuity.

*

Pointing somewhat rudely at the Île-de-Seine, the Pointe du Raz (Raz means tidal race) promontory can be a wild, windy and remote place on a winter's day, and a good place to take a walk through the heather to the cliff's edge at any time. Once upon a time, Audierne was a fishing port, but is now a yachtie heaven and stuffed with crêperies and bars and pricey second homes. From here you can take a boat to the Île-de-Seine, and there's an oyster farm where you can sample the goods.

*

To be found just before the most south-westerly point turns the corner and becomes the south coast of Brittany, Penmarc'h dates back to before the 14th century, and owed its early prosperity to the fecund cod banks there. The discovery of the vast sea riches of Newfoundland and the attentions of a single but truly ferocious bandit in the late 16th century combined to bring about the decline of the town. The aggressor was an aristocratic thug known as The Wolf, who with his gang of four hundred followers enjoyed sacking, looting and pillaging this part of Brittany. After having his way with Penmarc'h in 1595, The Wolf moved on to the isle of Tristan to set up his HQ. In the process he forced the inhabitants to destroy their own homes, and killed fifteen hundred protestors in one day. His vast hoard of booty was said to be secreted on the isle, and may still be there.

Altogether a very interesting part of a fascinating region, and well worth visiting with bucket and spade, particularly if you fancy a crack at the Lost Treasure of The Wolf.

Tuesday 8th

Paradoxically, the longer I live in France, the more foreign the French seem. In theory it should be the other way around, and all the books on the subject say the most important consideration if you want to feel at home in a foreign country is to learn the language. In practice, I find the opposite is true. As my French has improved, so has my understanding and recognition of how different we two races are.

Earlier today, I walked past two men digging a hole in the road, and asked if they were looking for treasure. After a long pause, one man rested on his pick axe and said they were actually looking for a broken drain, but finding some treasure would be nice. As I walked away, I heard the man with the shovel telling his mate how *drôle* I was, especially for a foreigner. It is these little moments when I am clearly on a wavelength with my hosts that emphasise the normal gulf between us. It seems to me that despite all the calls for integration and stressing of the desirability of embracing a gloriously multi-cultural society, we are who we are and cannot be otherwise. I assume it would be the same for a Briton living anywhere else in the world, or for that matter a French person living in Britain. It therefore has to be more than a language which divides and makes us different. I truly believe that any expatriate who says he feels more at home in a foreign country is either lying or, like Lawrence of Arabia, a complete nutter.

Friday 11th

A small tragedy in Paradise.

Yesterday we returned from market to find the grounds around the house strangely silent. There was no birdsong, the ducks had flown from the big pond, and the hens did not come running to meet us. At first we were not concerned as they are truly free to range and like to wander off up the lane. Then we heard a low keening in the barn and found Griselda, Brunhilde and Whitney cowering in a corner. Of Blanche there was no sign.

We spent the next hour walking around the hamlet, across the surrounding fields, through the forest and even up to the moors. When we told Alain that Blanche was missing, he said the fox had obviously broken our verbal agreement that it would leave our hens alone if I fed it. Seeing how upset Donella was, he joined the search and came back minutes later with a handful of white feathers. He had found them by the roots of the big tree that had tried to kill me. But he had changed his mind about who or what might have taken Blanche. Even a fully-grown dog fox would not have been able to drag such a big bird across two streams and through the swamplands and thicket to its den. There would also have been blood or some other signs of an earthbound struggle. When I suggested a human predator, he shook his head and said there were no foot prints in the muddy ground around the uprooted tree. When I asked what else could have taken Blanche, he scratched his chin, then pointed to the sky with his cane. When I asked if he was seriously saying a buzzard could have carried Blanche off, he said that there were other even bigger birds on the moors. In the old days it was said that they took lambs and even babies from the moorland villages, though he thought this to be unlikely, even in the mountains of Finistère.

After Alain left, we went to the barn and sat with Griselda, Brunhilde and Whitney. They were obviously badly traumatised, and must have seen whatever happened to Blanche. As dusk fell, I went and sat at the spot where Alain had found the feathers, and thought about our lost hen. Because we eat them, it suits us to believe chickens are stupid and have no character or personalities. Anyone who has kept hens will know this not to be true. Blanche was the biggest and best layer, but also the softest and furthest down the pecking order. As Donella said, she was like the big, soppy schoolgirl who is bullied by her smaller classmates.

I suppose that made me feel more protective towards her, and she was my favourite hen. I am aware that Brittany is one of the biggest chicken-rearing regions of France, and that millions of birds are efficiently despatched and prepared for supermarket shelves every week. I am also aware of the irony that we eat and enjoy chicken, but this is different as we do not know and love the ones we see on supermarket shelves. She may not have been particularly bright and just a good laying hen, but Blanche was also one of the family.

Sunday 13th

Alain may have been right about Blanche's abductor. Driving on the mountain road this morning, I saw what I thought was an unusually big short-eared owl trawling for breakfast. It was cruising no more than a yard above the moorland, and as I came closer, it gave an indignant shriek and flapped lugubriously away. I could see then that it was far too big and the wrong shape for an owl, and its great white and raked wings looked as if the ends had been dipped in a pot of black paint. I looked the mystery bird up when I got home and realised I had made a rare sighting of a hen harrier. I also realised for the first time why the bird had been given that name.

Tuesday 15th

Sounding like a made-up place name in a novel about sex in the Welsh suburbs, Landivisiau is the sort of town that generally sympathetic tourist guides describe as sturdy. This is usually the default description when somewhere has few or no obvious selling points or is, frankly, pug-ugly.

Lacking a coastline, lake or forest, historic building, a river running through it, famous son or daughter or even borrowed legend, Landivisiau struggles to make any claim to visitorability, or even visibility. Inserting the name in any of the gastronomic websites for the region or area comes up with not a single recommended eating house in or around the town, and the most interesting statistic Wikipedia can summon up is that nearly nine percent of local primary school children attended bilingual schools in 2007.

But this would be a narrow-band assessment, based on conventional tourist appeal ideas. Generally, I find a better reflection of a town's character and local esteem is the size and type of market it can sustain. Each Saturday at cool and trendy Morlaix, stalls selling hand-milled spices in tiny bags at more than the cost of gold dust are under siege. In Huelgoat every Thursday, the British-run enterprises offering lardy cakes and fish and chips give a clue to the expat density level. Landivisiau is a serious country dweller's market, and where you go for lengths of barbed wire, rabbits on the hoof, and, most of all, laying hens.

The Brittany Bird Man's stall is always busy, and one of the few places you will see an orderly queue in France. But not all the people in line are waiting to buy a hen at point of lay or a handful of day-old chicks, turkeys or quail. Some part of the soul of the most urbanised Breton is still steeped in peasantry, and it is revealing to see elegantly dressed women queuing up simply for the pleasure of stroking a farmyard bird.

Unlike the window shoppers, we are here on business, and being veteran hen owners are familiar with the sometimes complex rules of behavioural etiquette when buying a chicken at market in rural France. Having waited for nearly half an hour we have had plenty of time to spot the two birds we want, but it is important that, when we get to the head of the queue, we at least appear to examine and compare the merits and defects of the fifty *pondeuse* (point-of-lay) hens on offer. In truth, we and any other civilians around the stall would not have a clue as to how to identify the better layers, but the customers like to give the impression they can judge the fecundity of a bird on sight. Sensibly, the Bird Man joins in the game, and gives anything from

259

an approving nod to a whistle or even gasp of admiration as he grabs and boxes up the buyer's choice.

When we have spent enough time pointing out imaginary pros and cons of the selection, I indicate the two birds we have chosen. There are at least a dozen hens milling around in the plastic cage, so I point between the bars to identify them, and am immediately assaulted by a small but obviously feisty Rhode Island Red. As I suck my finger and try to look as if the injury was part of the testing and selection process, my wife asks the Bird Man to add my attacker to our takeaway box. Some of the crowd will think my wife picked the bird because it showed spirit, others because it struck a blow for the sisterhood.

What occurs to me as I wrap a carrier bag around my wound is how right my father was when he said that, in life, good luck is more important than good looks or even a good brain. He knew what he was talking about as he was a greyhound bookmaker. The three hens in the box in the back of our car could have gone to an uncaring owner. By being chosen to join my wife's menagerie, they have won first prize in the lottery of avian life.

*

On the way home we stop at a small town which has all the touristic appeal that Landivisiau lacks. Lampaul-Guimiliau has a number of well-reputed restaurants and bars and some interesting old buildings, but is most famous amongst religious building fans for its parish close, ossuary and very baroque baptistery. The church was also renowned for having one of the tallest bell towers in Finistère, but lost the distinction when it was truncated by a lightning strike and fire in 1809.

Though the fact will not be found in many tourist guides, Lampaul-Guimiliau is also the site of one of my favourite bars. In the shadow of the church, the combined pub, tobacconist and paper shop is remarkable for its unremarkableness. The decor has remained obstinately in the 1980s, and the furniture is as eclectic and characterful and time-worn as the clientele. On the wall is a selection of home-made posters, some of which appear to date back to the lightning strike on the belfry. In general, I find Bretons are very good at putting posters up but reluctant to take them down. I think it is their artistic side and the desire to exhibit their creative talent for as long as possible. When I asked the bar owner why she had so many out-of-date posters on the wall, she asked if I would take a favourite painting off my wall because it had been there for a certain time. One of the more recent creations has been translated into English for the benefit of potential British customers, and shows a head and shoulders photograph of a pleasantly round-faced man surrounded by what looks like the European Union circle of stars. Beneath it is the suggestion that readers might like to hire Yvon Fravel and his accordion to play with their balls.

Other permanent features include three classic Breton barflies. I have never been in the pub when they have not been there, and we have dropped in at all hours from breakfast to chucking-out time. The three men dress similarly with a spectacular unconcern for sartorial elegance, are short and stocky and look as if they have been standing in the same place at the bar since before it was built. Like all the best regulars, they cause no trouble, take an active interest in passers-by and visitors, and are always ready to hand out a piece of advice or a comment on the state of the region, France or any other part of the world.

They have also achieved that tricky feat of being more or less permanently on the cusp of total intoxication. But no matter how long they continue drinking, they never get any drunker than their constant cruising level. Being more than three sheets to the wind is part of their persona and overall presentation package, and you get the feeling that if one of the bibulous trio were ever to appear at the bar sober, the landlady and even perhaps his mates would not recognise or like him.

As we arrive, I see that the day's chairman is trawling the local paper for debatable subjects, and when I point out that he is holding it upside down he shrugs and says it reads better that way. Craning my neck, I attempt to make sense of the headline, which appears to concern sausages, crime and cosmetics. As Jan explains and illustrates by running a finger across his throat, *un crime maquillé en saucissonage* actually refers to a grisly murder, with the victim chopped up like the contents of a sausage. On a lighter note, he shows me a story detailing how the French navy has managed to lose a guided missile off the coast of Brittany. As the report uncritically explains, the missile was supposed to float but did not, and there are now several submarines looking for it on the ocean floor.

Wednesday 16th

I take breakfast in the barn as I have been appointed minder to the new hens till they settle in. Rain is pattering on the roof, and I am enjoying the intoxicating aroma of Marmite toast, strong coffee, damp straw and chicken pooh.

As the inmates go about the complex business of sorting out who is to be in charge of whom, I am counting the dressed stones in the far wall, and thinking about the owners of the hands which set them in place. I find that just taking a moment to look closely and quietly at old buildings can reel back time in a most satisfactory manner, and help me try and understand what it was like to be alive all that time ago.

This wall may not be a work of great craft, but like all old buildings, it tells a story. Where there is a badly-laid line of the roughly dressed stones, I wonder if it were put there by someone with a hangover, or by a youngster learning the knack of this part of 18th-century country life. Where the great oak beams straddle the wall, I wonder how many family members it took to hoist each one up, from where the wood came, and how it got from forest or woodland to its final billet. Above all, I marvel at the simplicity and effectiveness of old farm buildings. The door is as old as the stable block, and a perfect example of the application of logic, experience and inspiration. It is made of planks, with the end one extending beyond the others by a few inches at top and bottom. These extensions have been trimmed down to a point and are braced with strips of beaten iron. The protrusions fit into holes in the threshold and lintel, and act as basic but very efficient pivots. By this simple method, the need for vulnerable hinges and all the expense and work of buying and fitting them has been excised. If one of the pivots broke, you would simply have to replace the end plank with another. And a plank of wood would have been

262

much, much cheaper than the most basic hinge. At some time, someone must have looked at a hole in a wall and had the big idea for making and fitting a maintenance-free door. Three hundred or more years ago and with no help from architects, specialist craftsmen or special tools or transport, a group of uneducated farm hands raised this building. It has stood against the centuries, and will be here when I am dust, while the ghosts of those people will remain as long as the barn stands. Whether they knew it at the time, these unknown country people were leaving their mark on history as clearly as any famous leader, warrior or politician.

Friday 18th

We have been walking the cliffs to the north of Morlaix, then stopped near the picture-postcard village of Guimaëc to look at a redundant bar which is up for sale. The inexplicably failed business is on a key road not a mile from the coast and surrounded by campsites and B&Bs. In a coastal holiday area of Britain and especially Cornwall, it would have a price beyond rubies. Here, it cannot pay its way. This may or may not be because the owners of the bar have upset the neighbour, who has then invoked divine powers of retribution. The bar is literally in the shadow of a chapel being restored at obviously huge cost by the commune, and the sign above the door of the scruffy pub identifies it as The Bar of Christ. This alone makes me want to put an offer in on the spot.

Actually, the bar is named for the hamlet in which it stands, but I much prefer to think of it being Our Saviour's local. In rural England, public houses were always built close to the village church and there would often be a tunnel linking them. This was said to be so the faithful could travel from one spiritually uplifting place to the other regardless of the weather, and perhaps more importantly, without being seen by the teetotal members of the community. It was also said that these unsecret passages were used by the curate, and in coastal areas were a ratrun for the parson's contraband brandy. One thing I do miss here is a bar which has the same sort of appeal as a characterful English country pub. This is of course a totally unreasonable expectation, but there are some rural French bars which have that magic.

Down the road from the failed bar is one which the owners have got exactly right, even down to the name. Caplin & Co sits contentedly above a cove at Locquirec, and has an artfully formed lookout balcony. Inside, the walls are lined with books and there are chessboards which are used on a regular basis, and good music is to be heard here on most nights in the summer. A sign of the level of confidence of the patron is that he does not bother to open until well into the afternoon. If I had a seaside bar I would want it to be just like this, and to be able to take myself and my dog for a swim when the weather warranted it. I would also relish being able to sit on the balcony and look out to sea when the fancy took me, and to be successful enough to tell those visitors I did not like to bugger off.

Arriving at Guimaëc, my wife makes straight for the combined cake shop and bar, while I cross the road to check if the village's public facilities are worthy of entry into my collection of Great Public Toilets of France. They are, and then some. It is an increasingly rare treat to discover a vintage installation which consists of not much more than a pair of porcelain footprints with a hole between them. It has obviously been much used, repaired and modified over the decades, and the council artisan responsible for its upkeep has either unknowingly or deliberately replaced the tray with the footprints pointing towards the wall rather than away. As the all-too obvious evidence reveals, this has caused all sorts of problems for those visitors unfamiliar with the procedure, and clearly some who do not know their bums from a hole in the ground...

*

In the bakery shop adjoining the bar in the square, I am treated to another example of how so many French people refuse to believe that anything worth eating was not invented and named by them.

Pointing at a wonderfully fragile-pastried yet thick custard slice, I ask Madame if the topping is, as it appears, *crème anglaise*. Even though it is a French term, just the juxtaposition of the two words is enough to cause her to pale beneath her artfully applied make-up. *Non*, she says crisply, and actually steps back in affront as if I had asked if she used bought-in pastry. When I query what the delicacy is, Madame looks to see if I am being stupid or insolent or both, then says it is (obviously) a flan. Determined not to be put off, I say I understand that it is a flan, but if not a custard flan, what sort of flan might it be? After a long silence, Madame draws herself up to her full height of Gallic superiority and announces that it is a flan flan…

Home cooking

In French, *Matelote d'Anguille* sounds a lot more exotic than eel stew with prunes, but tastes just as well in either language.

Ingredients

4 eels of approx 500g each
10 small onions
200g brown mushrooms
100g butter
100g lean pork cut into small lardon cubes
A bunch of thyme
A bay leaf
12 prunes
A bottle of Chinon red wine

Method

Peel the onions and remove the gritty parts of the mushrooms, then wash them thoroughly and quarter. Clean and skin the eels and cut into round portions. Brown the eel in very hot butter, then remove from heat. Fry the lardons quickly with the small onions, dust with flour and moisten with some of the red wine. Add the thyme and bay leaves and season. Put the eels into the sauce and add the prunes. Fry the mushrooms in oil and add to the stew before cooking at the top of the oven for half an hour.

Oat Cream

If ever there was an example of a sweet dish to keep the cold out and pack the calories in, this is it:

Ingredients

1.5 litres of milk
Half litre of double cream
200g oats
12 egg yolks
180g sugar

Method

Put the oats on a baking tray and roast in the oven on Mark 7 for 20 minutes. They should be roasted like coffee beans. Boil the milk and pour over the oats. Leave to stand for three hours, then drain the oats and keep the milk. Mix the sugar with the egg yolks and add the oated milk after passing through a fine sieve. Now add the double cream. Put the mixture into a porcelain dish and cook at Mark 4 for an hour (the mixture should be no deeper than a little over one inch). Watch carefully and take your oat cream out of the oven when it looks set but is still a little wobbly. Leave to cool, then sprinkle with brown sugar and put at the top of the oven for a minute.

Tasty Toast

I could not complete my selection of favourite Breton dishes without including this familiar snack, which the French call *pain perdu* (lost bread) and they think we call French toast. In fact, where I come from French toast was simply a slice of bread which had only been toasted on one side. Perhaps we were being insulting by alleging that they were too miserly or stupid to toast both sides, but the real thing is much more advanced.

Ingredients

Three eggs
A half litre of milk
100g demerara sugar
50g vanilla sugar
A soup spoon of apple brandy
100g butter
A stale loaf of square bread

Method

Cut the loaf into fairly thick slices and warm the milk to blood heat. Break the eggs into a bowl and beat in the vanilla sugar and brandy. Arrange the slices of bread in a baking dish, pour the milk over and leave to soak for half an hour. Drain the slices and dip into the egg mixture. Fry both sides in really hot and frothy butter, then sprinkle with the demerara sugar before serving. If you want to really make a *cochon* of yourself, you could spread the toast with some of your home-made milk jam.

NB. You can make vanilla sugar at home by putting a single pod into a pickling jar which you then fill with castor sugar. Leave it for a month and eh voila, you have normally expensive vanilla sugar.

March

Day grows longer than night, so the journey through spring and towards summer is truly under way.

There are other early signs of the good times to come. In Paradise, an evening primrose has appeared on the compost heap. Apart from being wildly before its time, its delicately glowing presence amongst the surrounding ordure makes an interesting contrast.

Hosts of miniature daffodils line the driveway, and with the winter aconites and dandelions, yellow is the floral colour of choice. Not many people seem to know that the proper name for the daffodil is narcissus, though I do not think they look particularly self-obsessed.

The feathered population of Lesmenez is obviously preparing for future responsibilities, and this morning I watched a greenfinch struggling to take off with a piece of bread almost bigger than itself. Each time it laboured upwards, it would open its beak as if gasping for breath and the bread would fall back to earth. After a dozen Sisyphusian attempts, the finch sat glumly on the ground as a jay swooped down and effortlessly picked up and flew off with the booty. Thinking how the big and powerful always seem to get the most bread, I went to find a more manageable breakfast for the smaller bird.

Wednesday 2nd

We arrive at Huelgoat to find the former owner of the Man in the Hat pub still wearing the hat, though the pub for which he and it is named no longer exists.

Roger tells us the pub has been sold and all monies frozen by the courts, and he has moved into the large house next door. His estranged wife has only moved just up the road, and this is allegedly so she could be near enough to come and beat him up at regular intervals. The exhibitions are keeping the gendarmerie busy and the locals entertained, and I was recently summonsed to make a statement concerning one bout I witnessed.

It is sad to see the pub closed and in the process of becoming an upmarket restaurant, but our friend says he would not have enough local expats to fill it since so many have packed up and gone home. For many it is the end of the affair, and a small but perhaps significant exodus has begun. There is, Roger thinks, no single cause for the retreat of the Brits after the six-year boom that saw property prices almost double.

For some older expats it will be a death of a spouse; for younger couples it is sometimes the death of a marriage. For others the spur has been the decline of the Pound against the Euro. Other factors will be a failed business, running out of money and not being able to find a job, or simply finding that living in rural France did not live up to the bucolic idyll the misty-eyed immigrants had expected.

For whatever reason, the British population in and around Huelgoat is on the wane. Some locals may be pleased to think what has been called *l'invasion* is over, but many who made money from the Brits will miss them. Every Briton who buys a property in France represents a boost to the local and national economy, but as with their general attitude to foreign tourists, the French often do not see it that way.

I shall miss the quirky pub and the half-size half-colonel, the alleged former SAS assassins, whirling dervishes and all those who made up the strange brew of humanity to be found in Roger's pub. But it is in the nature of things to change, and no more so within expatriate communities anywhere in the world.

Before leaving, we ask Roger to dinner at the weekend. He thanks us but says he is already planning on creating a speciality dish of stuffed pigeon in a wine and truffle sauce. When Donella asks where he bought the pigeon, he says it is free range and he will be catching and not buying it. He has his eye on a big, busty bird which spends its day screeching at and crapping on him from the ridge of the roof and otherwise generally diminishing the quality of his life. He thinks the bird will taste sweeter as he has given it the same name as his wife.

Thursday 3rd

I have been taking revenge on the tree that tried to kill me. The physical exercise and mental demands in dismantling the giant pine without drowning myself or cutting off one of my own limbs made an interesting challenge.

In spite of its attempt on my life, it was sad to see such a huge and otherwise healthy tree lying on its side and waiting submissively for death and dismemberment. I think this was because the sight reminded me of the mortality of our two species. Oaks and yews last centuries; pines, like us, mere decades.

Two of my favourite leisure pastimes are working with woodland and water, and the harvesting of the downed tree in to at least a month's worth of split logs involved both. The job required a basic working knowledge of mechanical engineering, especially in the form of fulcrums, transference of weight by balance, and the generally accepted principals of gravity. Weighing in at the best part of a ton, the tree was laying almost horizontally over the pond with only the base and top branches over dry land. Counterbalanced by the heaviest end, the tree sloped gently upwards to where the tip hung some fifteen foot above the bank. Obviously, the way to move it with minimal damage and danger was to work my way along the trunk from the thin end, lopping off the branches and then cutting the body into manageable lengths which would fall into the pond to be dragged out and sliced up later.

I knew there would be a problem in securing the top of the ladder to the trunk. The problem of securing the bottom of the ladder to the surface of the pond was always going to be a more difficult one. I had already done some stability tests by lowering the base of the ladder into the water while standing on the bank, then pushing it up till the top rested against the horizontal trunk. The weakness of my plan was highlighted when I waded out and started to climb and my weight caused the bottom of the ladder to sink into the ooze. In the race to mount the ladder and tie it off before the top rung sunk below the part of the trunk against which it had been propped, I was the loser. I clung to the top of the ladder for a long moment before joining it flat out at the bottom of the pond, and realised another approach was needed. Recalling how lorries and even tanks had been moved across big stretches of water when circumstances required invention and resourcefulness, I headed for the loft and my 1954 copy of Every Boy's Engineering Wonders of World War II.

*

A couple of hours later I had mugged up on the physics, and, using available materials, had built my first floating bridge. It was a simple but robust construction of scaffold planking and empty plastic petrol containers and catering size olive oil cans. When put to the test it easily took the combined weight of the ladder, me and my chain saw. It was a moment's work to climb the ladder and tie the top rung firmly to the trunk, then fire up the saw.

Remembering all those Laurel and Hardy films, I was sure to make my first cut on the part of the trunk not connected to the base and therefore supporting the ladder. Another minute of the executioner's song of the saw, and the top ten feet of the tree had fallen obediently into the water. All had gone to plan, except my failure to allow for how the sudden removal of a considerable weight from the top end of the tree would encourage the thick end and roots to settle back into the hole from where they had been wrenched. With events around me moving in apparent slow motion in a reminder of when it fell towards me, my end of the tree sprang upwards, taking the ladder and me with it. The top of the ladder being tied to the tree meant it stopped moving at the same time as the tree, while I carried on.

Coming out to investigate what all the screaming and splashing was about, my wife later said she was fascinated to see a hand holding a chain saw emerging from the muddy waters of the pond. I did not appreciate her asking me to hold still while she went for the camera, but was pleased that I had instinctively saved an expensive piece of machinery from a ducking.

Friday 4th

Landerneau is another place which ticks all our boxes as a good place for living in or near. Not far from Brest, the ancient town sits on a broad river which empties into the bay of that name. The estuary also marks the dividing line between the old provinces of Léon and Cornouaille.

Apart from its several other attractions, Landerneau has an increasingly rare architectural treasure in the shape of a *pont vivant*. The Pont de Rohan is certainly alive and lively. Lined with houses and shops and bars, it is a good place to browse or sit on a terrace for a drink or meal as the fast-flowing Élorn surges past below.

We came to Landerneau to see an unusual cottage on the banks of the river and just outside the town. It belongs to a Breton artist and environmental campaigner, and looks it. We knew from the property details it would be too small for us, but we could not resist a visit as the English version of the description said it was made entirely of cannabis. It was almost disappointing to arrive and find that the walls of the property were, though lined with *chanvre* or Indian Hemp, certainly non-smokable. According to the owner, the fibrous texture makes an excellent insulator and you would have to ingest several tons to get any effect. But, as he added with a wink, if there was a serious blaze and the place went up in smoke it would be interesting to see what effect the fumes would have on the neighbours and firemen.

On the way home we called in at a friend's restaurant for lunch and found the lane behind the premises blocked with steamrollers, bulldozers and other heavy plant. Notices informed any would-be users that the lane was undergoing significant repairs and improvements and work could continue for several weeks, and I noted that the anticipated date of completion has been changed four times.

As part of their pay and conditions package, many commune manual workers are given luncheon vouchers. Like all establishments which put on an *ouvrier* (worker's) lunch, our friend's restaurant accepts vouchers and has a very good reputation locally. This may explain why a total of ten men have spent five weeks installing a small concrete channel alongside the lane for a distance of less than twenty yards. In the view of those involved, the job requires the presence of stop-go swing sign holders at both ends of the site, though the two men stand close enough to exchange chat and cigarettes while waiting for the odd tractor to appear. There is also an official clip board holder and several high-visibility jacket-wearing observers, and a timekeeper to ensure that the men down tools from one minute after noon till well after 2pm. The site is apparently one of the most supervised in the area, with a delegation of officials from the regional Highways and Byways Authority arriving every week to see how the work is progressing. As our friend the owner says, the dedication of these officials is evidenced by the fact that they come to check on progress in their own time, and give a whole new meaning to the term 'working lunch'.

Monday 7th

We are reconsidering the appeal of a life aquatic.

As with water and wind mills and lighthouses, many people like the idea of living on a boat. If they get as far as trying it, most wish they had not. Although never having lived on one full time, I have been messing around with boats for half a lifetime. My wife never took to the idea of accompanying me across the English Channel to deliver sailing boats which were not equipped with radio, distress signal devices or life jackets, but is not set against the idea of living on a stretch of water when you can see land very close on either side. Another proviso is that any live-aboard boat we buy must be roomy enough to accommodate all our animals as well as us. I see no problem in fitting a roof garden so she can tend a vegetable plot as well as give the hens somewhere to exercise between landings. It is a beguiling scenario which would see us sailing the rivers and canals and coastal areas of France while staying ahead of our creditors as I write about our adventures afloat.

Perros-Guirec is a hard place to pronounce, but a nice one in which to live. On a part of the north coast known for the natural

273

sculptures, shapes and patterns the sea has hewn from the pink granite, the town boasts three sandy beaches and one very posh marina. It also has a history of fine creative writing as Joseph Conrad wrote his most famous books at his home here. A small apartment overlooking the marina would set you back the same price as a farm and forest inland, and rental prices can be more than a thousand Euros a month. But we are meeting a couple of friends who get the same view and facilities for the equivalent of £20 a week with electricity and water thrown in.

Neil McCartney, his artist wife Amanda and their amiable Airedale Buggalugs live on board the *Chapeau*, a magnificent 46-foot steel Dutch-built sea or river cruiser. For those unfamiliar with boating parlance, it has all the space and home comforts of a very big camper van, and can go where no Winnebago could venture.

The boat used to belong to an American who cruised the waterways of France and wrote about them, so perhaps this is why I feel so much at home on board the *Chapeau*.

When he first came to France after running bars in Spain, Neil sold houses to Britons. Nowadays he is one of those lucky people who have managed to combine a job with a passion. Every month he crosses the Channel to find and buy boats in England which he thinks will sell at a profit in France. If small enough he will bring his new purchase back by trailer on a ferry crossing; if not, he will sail or steam it back. Although he is a seasoned sailor, crossing the busiest shipping lane in the world in a relatively small boat can be challenging, and Neil has had more potentially deadly encounters than Jason and his Argonauts.

His latest close call came when he saw and fell hopelessly for a thirteen-ton Admiralty-built pinnace berthed on the River Severn. The boat was launched in 1964, made of teak planks on a teak frame and designed solely for harbour use. Unable to resist the boat or the challenge, Neil bought it and started the perilous journey across open sea to Perros-Guirec. In a storm-tossed voyage which included near-misses, mutiny at sea and a complete mechanical breakdown, the skipper refused to abandon ship and eventually limped into harbour overseen by a

French coastguard helicopter. Fortunately, he says, there has been no bill for their services as yet.

As not unusual in these matters, there was a bizarre twist to the tale of the newly-named *Bateau de Bois*. Neil sold it relatively quickly, and a month later crossed the Channel to look at a boat moored on the River Severn. Tied up next to the boat for sale was a big craft which looked very familiar. As he drew nearer, Neil saw that it was the same boat he had risked his life sailing to France, and that the *Bateau de Bois* was back almost exactly where it had come from.

Thursday 10th

Port de Foleux could be a dangerous place. Those who should know say the second happiest day in a man's life is when he buys his first boat. The happiest day of his life comes when he sells it. A deciding factor in buying a boat can be its location, and Foleux would be enough to turn the head of the most sensible and confirmed landlubber.

Viewed after a glass of good wine and with eyes half shut, it could be Treasure Island without the pirates and dangerous bugs. So, the boat we are here to look at will look entirely different from how it would appear moored on a mud berth on a rainy day in Scunthorpe. Here, the treeline reaches the water's edge, and the convergence of waterways means you can leave the marina and turn right for the tourist magnet of La Roche-Bernard and then the open sea, or left for Redon and the Nantes-Brest canal and beyond even to the mighty Loire. There is also what is said to be a rather good restaurant overlooking the marina, and an even better one at Bernard's Rock.

We are here with Neil McCartney to look at a boat he thinks might suit us as a starter model. Neil's recommendation is that we buy a riverboat and practice steaming up and down the inland waterways before committing ourselves to a permanent home afloat. Astonishingly, the going rate for a 90-foot Dutch barge can be more than the price of a modest *château*, which defeats the objective if you are looking for somewhere to live on the cheap.

275

His proposal is the Mayfly, a sort of transgender vessel which has changed its identity from a yacht to a river boat by having its mast cut off. It is a no-nonsense, lived-in sturdy vessel with the character of a boat which has been around a bit. Most importantly, Donella likes the general looks and layout of kitchen and toilet, and I like the price.

*

Though not as brazen a hussy as Auray, La Roche-Bernard is not backward in flaunting its watery charms. According to the tourist guide, it was discovered by Vikings in the tenth century, though it is not made clear whether this means the place was founded, settled or pillaged by the visiting Norsemen. A meeting place of sea and river, there is a lock gate, and a sizeable marina which can hold five hundred boats. This is only a couple of hundred less than the permanent population of the village, and shows how popular the place is with visiting yachties.

I could not uncover who Bernard was and why the rock was named after him, but it is a big rock and the port is a pleasant place to stroll around, even at this time of year. There are a number of bars and eating places to suit your mood and pocket, and next to the car park and close to the water is a theatre-cum-restaurant, where you can try an inexpensive dish while watching a play or comedy stand-up session. If you really want to push the boat out, there is also a highly rated and Michelin-starred *auberge* in the hands of Jacques Thorel, one of Brittany's most revered cooks. To put his god-like status under punishing scrutiny, I decide it is only right that we splash out and eat at the *Auberge Bretonne*.

We arrived at La Roche-Bernard under our own steam aboard the Mayfly from Foleux an hour ago, and the crafty Neil persuaded my wife to take the wheel for the best part of the six mile journey. She is already sold on the idea of, if not living on board one, buying a boat as a sort of floating weekend cottage and so we can practise for a life spent mainly on water.

Friday 11th

Sitting on the junction of the Oust and Vilaine rivers, Redon is a major crossroads for the Breton waterways. The Nantes to Brest canal crosses the Vilaine at right angles near the town centre, and a pair of sand barges regularly ran between Redon and the Loire until a long drought in 1976 forced them out of business. The convenient confluence of the two great rivers was exploited from Roman times, and Redon became rich on duties levied from water-borne traffic. The great abbey also waxed fat and became a focus of pilgrimage as, for the faithful travelling from England, Redon was a handy stop on the Compostela trail. Nowadays, the town is sometimes described (mostly by Breton marketing and PR folk) as the Venice of the West. With its town centre port, elevated roads, old buildings and modern outskirts it is certainly a vibrant and aesthetically pleasing place. If we buy Mayfly, this would be a very good place to berth her. I have already spotted several promising restaurants and a lively-looking Irish bar no more than a stagger from the town centre port.

Saturday 12th

Brittany's eastern border abounds with seriously in-your-face fortifications. As with Hadrian's wall, it is a matter of debate and prejudice as to whether they were built to keep invaders out or the natives in.

Combourg looks as if it was designed and built specifically to be a tourist magnet a thousand years in the future. The castle looms high above a lake, with a gaggle of bars and restaurants lining the undemanding climb to the town centre. For once, the castle is exactly that and lives up to its billing. In French, *château* is used to describe any building with lots of rooms and twiddly bits, or by any pretentious Brits who own a house in France which has more than three bedrooms. The castle at Combourg is a proper, full-on *château fort*.

Another satisfying thing about this town is that the ancient buildings are so casually lived or worked in. Amongst and above the modern shop fronts lurk mini-towers complete with witches' hats, arrow slits and even the original outside toilets. Old and new sit comfortably together, and the ultimate example of successful cross-cultural integration and living easily with the past can be found at the Penjabbi Takeaway. The business is housed in a medieval building, and also offers *tartiflettes* and Turkish kebabs along with tandoori chicken and chips.

After I pose for a photograph outside the *Écrivain* (Writer) crêperie and tell the bemused waiter I am in the same line of business, we take a break outside a busy bar opposite the church. The owner clearly revels in the number of customers his business attracts and his ability to serve them all single-handedly, and reminds me of a matador putting on a show for his admirers at the mid-day corrida. He runs from one end of the bar to the other to take or serve an order, and when he jinks his swivel-hipped way through the crowd with our coffee held above his head I see he is wearing running shoes.

There is a threatening roar nearby and my attention is drawn to a gigantic double-trailered cattle transporter which sits thoughtfully blocking the entrance to a car park alongside the church. The engine is running and the driver continually pressing down on the accelerator. To continue the analogy I used for the bar owner, the monstrous vehicle reminds me of an angry bull, pawing its foot and snorting as it waits for a chance to attack.

The door to the bar opens, and a slight, middle aged man limps out. He is wearing the small-town male bar customer uniform of shiny plastic jacket and rumpled trousers, but his feet are encased in surgical boots. He sees me looking, and nods and gives a resigned shrug and half-smile before setting out across the road to the church. As he steps from the pavement, there is a triumphant roar and the cattle transporter lurches forward. Everything rattles and squeals mightily as the driver stamps on the brakes, then blares his horn and shakes a fist at the shuffling man. I do nothing, but would like to drag the driver from his lofty position and invite him to try and think what it must be like to have to walk in his victim's shoes.

We have stopped to take coffee at the French equivalent of a traditional British transport caff. It is of course nothing like a British version except that the customers are mostly heavy goods drivers, and parking facilities, speed of service and quality and price of food come way above décor and health and hygiene concerns.

This classic of its genre is literally right alongside a major express route horizontally bisecting Brittany. The official way of getting to the bar would mean coming off at the next exit and following a road back to the premises for half a mile. Conveniently though, what must have been a very large Euro-lorry has at some time demolished a goodly length of crash barrier between the expressway and bar and in the process created a very short cut. A huge car park behind the ramshackle building indicates the level of traffic and custom come noon, and I count over a hundred covers laid up and ready inside. The owner has obviously cracked the science behind the Tardis syndrome, as the premises look very small from the outside in contrast to what lies beyond the peeling doors. The original building has also been built on to many times over the years, and each addition reflects a different fashion in construction styles. All look as if they have been done without bothering the building regulation or planning authorities. Apart from saving a lot of paper work, this approach is a bonus when business rates based on official size are being assessed and updated, and tax returns on alleged turnover are being filled in.

We do not stay long, as only a lunatic or foreigner would leave his vehicle in the far end of a car park outside a popular *relais routier*-style café. As we leave, the old clock by the bar strikes a quarter to mid-day and the first of a line of lorries navigates the gap in the crash barrier. There is a queue occupying both lanes and causing a logjam, but the trapped car drivers will probably think it is just another demonstration.

As cab doors open and figures swing surprisingly agilely down to the ground, we can see these are heavy goods drivers in more ways than one. This is further evidence of the quality of the food here. Curiously and although none of them could be called slim, the size of the drivers seems in inverse proportion to that of their rigs. Broadly speaking, the bigger the vehicle, the smaller the man driving it. Pulling out of the car park, I narrowly avoid a tiny delivery van barrelling towards us. The driver is probably worried about the proximity of noon, and it is obviously going to be quite an operation to deliver himself to the café. The giant figure behind and enveloping the wheel fills the space so completely that it looks as if he was inflated after getting in.

It would be interesting to wait and see how he is actually going to escape from the tiny cab, and even more interesting to see how he will get back in after a good lunch.

*

Fougères is like Combourg, only more so. For a start, it boasts the largest medieval castle in Europe. It is also another town of two halves, as the medieval bit sits around the castle while the upper town was largely rebuilt following a fire in the 18th century. We found both well worth the visit. Another curiosity is that one of only three belfries in all Brittany is to be found here. Apart from me, great writers who enjoyed visiting Fougères include Chateaubriand, Victor Hugo and Balzac.

Officially, the town grew wealthy as a leading shoe and glass-making centre, but its location also made it a convenient stronghold for salt smugglers. In those times, Bretons were exempt from all centralised taxes and paid their dues directly to their Duke. In the rest of France, the tax on salt was a huge revenue earner. As in Tudor England, salt monopolies were sold by the Crown to the highest bidder and could reach fifty times the going rate in Brittany. This inevitably led to a very organised and highly illegal cross-border trading system, which thrived until the revolution brought the region under the same tax regime as the rest of the country.

We climb to the castle gates, which are firmly bolted as it is off-season. There are a handful of interesting-looking eating places including one described as a medieval crêpe house. Preferring our food a little fresher, we are made very welcome in the buzzy and very friendly Estaminettes, where I resist the

280

landlady's invitation for a free tasting of a new brand of beer called Delirium Tremens.

After lunch we take a walk along the Trail of Discovery, which runs by a stream and takes in the 14th century belfry tower, an impressive botanical garden and the Victor Hugo theatre. An interesting aspect of the tour is how the state of the rear of the oldest houses compare to the face they show the world. An architectural historian friend told me to look at the roof and rear of buildings to see what they once were like, and some of the backs of Fougères' flashest residences look as if they have not seen a lick of paint since they belonged to the town's most successful salt smugglers. The tendency to leave the unvarnished past on show is actually an endearing French trait, and gives the visitor a much better idea of what places were like when they were new. Fougères castle has an original stand-and-deliver toilet overhanging the moat, and it is not only open to public view but, by the evidence, still in public use. Now that really is a practical example of living history.

*

On our way to the final stop on our tour of Brittany's eastern fortress towns, we get lost in the maze of narrow streets connecting lower and upper Fougères. After being tailed at very close quarters by a car for more than three miles, I observe that the driver is probably also lost and hoping we can lead him out of the town. My wife points out that the car has a local number plate, so the driver is more likely enjoying the traditional sport of harrying out-of-town visitors.

Finally escaping on to the arterial road, we clock up our 38th McDonald's sighting of the trip. It is not that we have been looking out for them because we like to eat in the home of Ronald McDonald, but because we cannot help but notice how ubiquitous the outlets are. It tells you something about the difference between old and new France and the changing tastes of the French when you learn that, outside of America, France is Big Mac's most profitable outpost.

It is claimed that Vitré is the best-preserved medieval town in Europe, and I think that may be because those in charge of maintaining the claim go out of their way to dissuade people from visiting it. The town is also a serious contender in my Most Unsuitable Twinning stakes, as its alleged doppelgangers include the little rural town of Lymington in Hampshire and the major industrial seaport of Odessa in the Ukraine.

We get within ballista range of the old quarter of Vitré before a deviation takes us on a tour of the new houses and commercial centres which ring and protect the town more effectively than the original fortress could ever have done.

Having breached the redoubt, we find our tenacity rewarded. History is everywhere in Vitré, and I can't remember seeing such a range of architecture through the ages from middle to modern. There are also so many alleyways, cobbled closes and low, narrow passages which threaten the forehead of anyone of average height that navigating the town on foot can be as confusing as trying to drive through it. Charles VIII of France died suddenly after banging his head on a low doorway, and I reckon it could well have been here.

Eventually, we arrive at the castle, though cannot get closer than the car park, which is being dug up and taken away by giant earthmovers. Across the morass, a cherrypicker platform is holding two men up against one vast wall. I see that they are re-pointing it, filling the gaps between huge slabs with tiny dollops of mortar. As they are using trowels not much bigger than soup spoons, it is clear they at least have a job for life.

On the way back to the car we marvel at the range and condition of buildings, and note probably the only restaurant in France calling itself The Cabbage Soup.

Spotting a sign bearing the silhouette of a teapot, I go in to the café to be confronted by the glinting glasses of a short, fat woman who seems to be chewing a wasp. She denies all knowledge of tea and how to serve it, and when I point my umbrella at a plate of fancy cakes and ask what they are, she completely loses it, grabs my brolly and orders me from the premises. After a spirited tug-of-war, I retreat from the shop and we find somewhere more welcoming.

We end up sitting on the terrace of a brasserie opposite the station, and are served by a beautiful, beaming young and slender woman. I have noticed how happy and friendly the youngest and most attractive waitresses are, but perhaps that is because they have so much more to be happy about.

As we wait for our lemon tea, a heavily-laden pick-up truck pulls up halfway round the roundabout on the main road outside the station, bringing all traffic to a halt. I see the driver reach towards the dashboard and think he is about to ask for directions, then realise he has stopped to roll a cigarette. As the traffic backs up and the hooting starts. I also see that his truck bears the badge, slogan and logo of the town. Perhaps, I idly wonder, he has not brought the traffic to a standstill out of lack of consideration, but, like the lady in the tea shop, is under instructions to dissuade exiting visitors from returning to Europe's best-preserved medieval town.

Monday 21st

We have found our next home in France. Like so many good, bad and tragic events, it happened suddenly and when we were least expecting it.

After almost a year of looking at more than a hundred properties, we have seen one that made our knees go before we got out of the car. This, we know, is a pretty certain indicator that we have found the next place in which we will live. The cottage is in such an idyllic location that it is almost a cliché, has an unexploited business potential, and is almost risibly cheap when compared with similar properties. This is not just an appeal to our instincts for getting something cheap, but means we will be able to afford to pay the full asking price and have money left to put our business plan into action. Also, being able to pay the full price will mean nobody can stop us buying it. If the owner will not agree to the traditional discount of the amount the fees and taxes come to, we can still pay the full price and have some working capital to hand. As we have found, even the best and most

283

original ideas for making money can be doomed if you cannot afford to put them into action without going into debt. This place really is different, and a future conversation-stopper is that what will be our letter box is more than a mile from our front door.

The chain of events started this morning when an agent who we thought had been avoiding us called to say she had just taken on a very unusual place, so thought of us. The lock cottage had only just become available and not yet been advertised for sale, and she advised an early viewing. It will not stay on the market for long, and we might regret it if we do not move quickly. We have heard this classic estate-agent ploy before, but Amanda is not that sort of hard-sell person. Although we had more or less abandoned the idea of paying through the nose for a pokey cottage on the canal, we agreed to meet her at the nearest point of civilisation.

*

Pont-Coblant is one of the few canalside spots in Finistère with moored boats on show. Come to that, it is one of the few villages with any sort of boats on show. The two old river cruisers do not seem to have moved or been worked on since we saw them nearly a year ago, so are probably being used as window dressing.

Although we rather like the usual take-it-or-leave-it attitude elsewhere, it is good to see a community making a play for visitors and their money. Apart from the moored boats, there is a campsite overlooking the water and an *auberge* with a very good name for its range and quality of menu.

As we climbed into Amanda's car, she explained that one of the features making the lock cottage so unusual is that it has no access track. By water or tow path, Buzit is more than a mile away from the nearest road, so the new owner will have to drive along the tow path. In some areas, owners are given permits to do this. In other areas, even the owners are not allowed to drive on the tow path. As Amanda said, this is an important consideration but can be sorted out with the *notaire* later; the important thing was to see if we liked the setting and the house itself.

As we rounded a long and lazy poplar-lined curve, I heard Donella let out a little sigh. This is an even better indicator than the weak-kneed syndrome. Buzit is the first canalside cottage we have seen which is painted snow white, and it really is picture-postcard pretty. It is also bigger and has more twiddly bits than the usual two-bedroomed variety, which might mean it was the residence of a senior lock-keeper. In a place where planning rules are very strict and space a premium, the large wooden cabin in the grounds is another bonus. The property sits right alongside the canal, and large flat arable fields surround it on three sides. The fields are bounded by a thickly-wooded slope, down which runs a tractor track from a distant and unseen farm. Past the lock and thundering weir and on the other side of the canal, there are more open fields and woodland, with not a property in sight. Buzit is clearly in an ideal location and more than ticks all the boxes. Now we were feeling a tingle of trepidation that the Big Problem would shortly manifest itself. In our experience, the price of this little gem must indicate there would be one. It could be regular flooding, an embargo on living in the property except on alternate Thursdays in the summer, or the right of a local farmer to park his tractor and beasts of burden in the sitting room.

After we had clambered eagerly out of the car, Amanda said there was something else she should tell us. Nodding resignedly, and as we braced ourselves for the bad news, our knees collapsed in harmony when she casually announced that the tree-dotted and sizeable island in the middle of the canal went with the cottage.

*

A blissful afternoon at our lock cottage... or what must surely be our lock cottage very soon. We put an offer in this morning, and are waiting for Amanda to report the owner's reply. If he does not accept our bid straight away, I have instructed her to agree to the full price. In fact, I have instructed her to agree to whatever it takes to buy Buzit for us, subject to contract and further investigations. I have not heard of a buyer paying more than the asking price for a property in France, but am quite willing to gazump myself to ensure we get our hands on Treasure Island.

Now we are making plans in a bar near the canal, and even this place seems pretty near perfect. We came through the door to find the clientele having a communal smoke-in, and the landlady had two roll-ups on the go so she could serve at each end of the bar between puffs. She is a big, jolly woman who dishes out huge *relais*-style lunches, the customers seem a friendly lot, and Madame's shaggy mastiff is already mooning over Milly. Apart from all these plus points, the pub is little more than a mile from Buzit by boat or bicycle.

It is strange to feel so young and excited again. Even though we have bought and sold four homes in France, the years have been swept away and I feel exactly the same mix of excitement, anticipation and trepidation as when we saw what was to become our little one-bedroomed cottage in Normandy. Now we are having a celebration lunch and conjuring up plans for putting our stamp on Buzit, and even making money from its unusual location and assets.

Lock cottages with no access road or track are pretty rare; one with its own island is probably unique. The comparative roominess of the cottage will mean Donella can have one of the spare bedrooms for an office, while I will have a writing den on the island. Without the need for planning permission, I will be able to put up a twenty square metre cabin on an area of ancient paving slabs alongside and overlooking the weir. As well as my workplace, the addition of a simple truckle bed, wood-burning stove and a cooker will make it an unusual guest house, or somewhere for me to stay after a row with my wife.

As well as the guest house, we are also planning to have a guest boat. For much less than the cost of extending the cottage, we can ask Neil McCartney to find and buy and deliver to us an old engine-less barge to moor alongside the lock gates. Even better, we can ask Neil to find us two big old boats, and convert one into a pirate ship. I have already reached the planning stage of Phase Two of Operation Buzit, and that will involve turning the acre of grass and trees in the middle of the canal into a real treasure island.

I have noted before how the French do not snack, but as the success of McDonald's has demonstrated, times are on the move. Thousands of cyclists and walkers and their families will pass Buzit every summer, and we will give them a very good reason for stopping for a refreshment break.

The Île de Trésor will be reached by gangplank from the towpath, with tables and chairs alongside the weir and under a shady clump of trees, or in the Tea Barge during inclement weather. While the adults are introduced to the delights of Madame East's bread pudding and carrot cake with coffee, the youngsters will be splicing the mainbrace with pop on board Captain Whitebeard's Saucy Sal. For once, my wife is becoming even more excited than me, and has already come up with some more excellent ideas for cashing in on Buzit's unique location and assets. As she says, I could build a launch jetty on the far side of the island and we could run a kayak and boat hire service. We could also find a characterful old barge and run pleasure cruises as is done with such success on the Midi canal. Thinking more laterally, she adds with a gleam in her eye, we could invest in a big herd of goats and the right equipment for making Treasure Island ice cream.

We look at each other and giggle like children. We both know that most of the schemes we are dreaming up this evening may not materialise, but getting down to the fine tuning of what sort of cutlery you are going to have in the restaurant you will never own is a game everyone likes to play. The beauty of Buzit is that just living there will be reward enough.

The more I think about it, the more I am convinced that fate has brought us here. It explains all the frustrations and disappointments of the past year as we have traipsed around a succession of unsuitable and overpriced properties.

I am also pleased that buying Buzit will mean that once again, and as my Irish grandfather used to say was so important, I will own the ground I pee on. It has been a very relaxing experience to rent for the past year, but we miss having our own home.

Tuesday 22nd

All being well, and I cannot see how it will not be, today is the day. Amanda called last evening to say she had not been able to get in touch with the owner yesterday, but has made an appointment to speak to him this morning. Then we will be able to go to the office of the notary and make an appointment to sign the *compromis de vente*. Unlike the last time we bought a home in France, we will be very pleased to be compromised into buying the picture-postcard lock cottage. I should be beyond such petty pretension, but it will be pleasant to airily tell people who ask where we live that we own a small island on the Nantes to Brest canal.

While we wait for Amanda's call, we are going to look at an English tea and book shop for sale in a pretty town in Morbihan. It will be of no interest to us now we have found Buzit, but we may be able to make an offer to the outgoing owner for some of her stock and catering kit.

*

As the name suggests, Guémené-sur-Scorff sits on the River Scorff. Surrounded by wooded hillsides, the ancient town was the seat of the dukes of Rohan of Pontivy castle fame. A particularly interesting factoid about Guémené is that it is in the running for having the oldest pub in the region. According to the English translation of the website, The Three Merchants is said to have been serving its customer since 1600. Even for France, waiting for service for that long must be some sort of record.

The teashop was a really cute place, and the owner a very nice woman who had decided to make a change. It is a good business in a good setting, but more expensive and not a patch on Buzit, so we will not be putting in an offer.

Wednesday 23rd

Bugger.

It seems we must go back to Plan 'A' and a life on instead of beside the canal.

The phone call from Amanda was to tell us that Treasure Island has been sold, but not to us. Even before our offer to the owner could be made, the *notaire* who would be dealing with the sale had arrived to take the keys back from Amanda, saying he had found a buyer. Working more speedily than any other French lawyer I have known, he had apparently agreed a price between the owner and the anonymous buyer. When we came out of shock, I made a telephone call to his office and enquired about Buzit under another name. There followed a lot of button-pushing and off-air conversations before the receptionist put us on to the negotiator who said it was 'reserved'. As Amanda says, you can never win an argument with a French *notaire*, so, whatever the true facts, Treasure Island is now in effect sold, and no increased offers can be made. The *compromis* commits the signer to buy after a week's cooling-off period, but may also contain any number of suspensive or, in less technical language, get-out clauses. In effect, the *notaire* has blocked anyone else from buying the place until the mystery buyer decides to complete or use a relevant clause as a reason for not completing. The sale may be dependent on the would-be buyer being able to raise the finance, or on any bad news about the structure of the building or use of the towpath to get to and from the cottage. I have even heard of suspensive clauses which allow the buyer to not complete the sale if the weather is bad on the day of signing. I hope the *notaire* did not rush things through because he rather than our agent would be getting the 'negotiation' fee of several thousand Euros, but the government allowing their local legal representative this perk inevitably encourages self-interest and sharp practice, even in France.

I think the main reason we are both so unhappy about losing the property is not whether we have been victims of any dodgy dealings, but that it really did seem that the lock cottage and island had our name on it. Also and perhaps curiously, of all the homes we have bought on both sides of the Channel, Treasure Island is the first property we have made a bid for and then lost.

Even worse was our mistake of making detailed plans for what we were going to do with the cottage and island for the rest of our lives there. In our minds, the walls of the cottage had already been painted a dazzling white inside and out, and my characterful and snug writer's log cabin built on the island next to the weir. In our imaginings, the old boats which would serve as guest quarters and pirate play ship had been found, bought and towed and moored in place, and we had even reached the stage of drawing up a menu for the passing trade.

It is strange to think how dramatically lives can be changed by small events. Had the *notaire* not had another preferred customer up his sleeve, in a month or two we would be living in Buzit, and that apparently inconsequential move across the countryside would have caused an unimaginable number of small but life-changing reactions that will now not occur. As I said to my wife, it could be that living on the canal would have inspired me to write a great novel, or we could have bought a lottery ticket at the local bar at Pont-Coblant and won millions of Euros. As my wife replied, the move might just as easily have caused all sorts of not good things to happen. By not buying a lottery ticket in our local bar because we had moved to the lock cottage could mean that we would have not won the lottery that we might win by staying here. And there could have been much darker consequences of living on the brink of the canal. She had learned yesterday from a local that several people were drowned right alongside Treasure Island a few years ago. Perhaps, as she says, it is just as well that fate or circumstance has intervened and we will never live there, and our family and grandchildren never visit us there.

As usual, my wife is right and we must move on. But I cannot help but think of what might have been, and would sooner never have seen the property. Also, things you do not do always turn out much better than they might have done had you done them. Now I will always wonder how it would have been to have lived with the canal and been the master of Treasure Island.

Epilogue

The pantechnicon awaits, and I have been taking a last walk down to the stone cross. I brought a bag of food, but found out yesterday that I have not been helping keep our fox and its family alive through the winter.

When we had a farewell drink, Alain said that my feeding the fox had long been an open secret and a source of near-disbelief in the neighbouring hamlets. The fox - if it ever existed - had moved on, and the local dogs had been taking advantage of the free food. The owners in the surrounding hamlets were also most grateful for my generosity.

I leave the leftovers, whistle for Milly and walk back to Little Paradise for the last time. There is a slight haze on the moors, the gorse is golden and the signs of a verdant summer to come are all around. Everything seems so familiar, and it is strange to think we have lived here for only a year and that I may never walk this land again.

I see my wife standing in the middle of a knot of figures by the removal lorry, and it seems the entire village has turned out to say goodbye. One of the sweet pains of being a traveller is that you leave so many people and places behind. Life will go on in this tiny community as it has for centuries, a new tenant will move into Little Paradise and it will be as if we were never here. I hope some of our Breton neighbours will remember us with fondness as the years pass. Times will change, but for us, this place and its people will remain forever as they are today.

I wave to my wife and she beckons me to hurry. She is not anxious to leave, but does not want to keep the farewell committee waiting. As I get closer, I see that old Alain has put a tie on in honour of the occasion. He is waving a bottle of moonshine apple brandy, and Mrs Messager is holding a covered tray which I fear may contain a parting gift of rendered beaver. From Alain's yard comes the sound of the Lone Piper tuning up. As he hits the inevitable bum note, I hear my wife telling the driver that our departure may be a little delayed.

Whatever is to come and wherever we go, one thing is for certain. The next place we call home in France will have to go some to be even a patch on Brittany.

Lesmenez, Friday April 15th.

Brief Encounters

These are snapshots of towns and villages reckoned to be amongst the most beautiful in Brittany:

Belle-Isle-en-Terre: I could not work out why an inland place would need to tell you it was sitting on the ground till I discovered there is a Belle-Île-en-Mer. This one approves of visitors, has a rather upmarket air and a good few Brits like to live in or around the town.

Binic: Trendy (for Côtes d'Armor) former fishing port and now seaside town with lots of places to eat. You get your sea lettuce from the beach.

Doëlan: Lovely little Finistèrean fishing port and yachtie haven.

Hédé: A pretty village not far from Rennes and set amongst hills and beside the Ille-et-Rance canal.

Île Tudy: Very quaint fishing village near Pont l'Abbé in the lower reaches of Finistère.

Jugon-Les-Lacs: As the name suggests, a big (4km perimeter) lakeside setting for this historic town.

La Guerche de Bretagne: In Ille-et-Vilaine and renowned for its picture-postcard ancient buildings.

Le Palais: A stunning 16th century Morbihan citadel, tarted up in 1689 by the great marine architect Vauban.

Loguivy de la Mer: A lovely little port in Côtes d'Armor and not far from Paimpol, famous for its signature dish of Coquille Saint-Jacques.

Malestroit: a pleasant little place on the Nantes-Brest canal, with some interesting old buildings and an even more interesting layout of one-way streets which seem to lead to nowhere but themselves.

Paimpol: Popular tourist town with a ferry to the Île de Bréhat.

Plougasnou: Neat little seaside town near to a popular surfing beach at Trégastel. Diben has fresh seafood on offer, and there are some great walks along the cliffs at St-Jean-du-Doigt.

Pontrieux: Côtes d'Armor's answer to Venice; very fetching in a watery way.

Rochefort-en-Terre: Very pretty village in Morbihan overlooking the Valley of Gueuzon.

Tréguier: Very characterful north coast estuarial town with bags of history. The first king of Brittany beat off an invading horde of Vikings here. For more peaceful visitors there's an old church ringed with equally ancient buildings and walkways, and (for some reason) more upmarket wet fish shops than you could shake a dead cod at. There is a marina by the ancient quay, and it is a perfect setting for some stunningly attractive old buildings. At least one sells very good crêpes.

On-line Contacts

There are thousands of tourist attractions in Brittany; any attempt to list all or some of them would inevitably be a compromise or plain bodge. The best thing to do is check out tourist information available on-line or in the flesh at one of the hundreds of official tourist offices dotted around the region. You might even find one where they speak English. Meanwhile, here's a selection of recommended websites for those who want to find out more about Brittany before you visit: The more minor websites can come and go with sometimes alarming rapidity, but these were all alive and well at time of going to press:

www.brittany.angloinfo.com An excellent source of information gathering for those living, having a holiday home in or wanting to visit or live in the region. Just beware of taking any advice from the loonies who infest the forum, which is of course the case with any forum on any website in the world.

www.brittanytourism.com The official website for tourism in Brittany-and it's in English!

www.aikb.fr Stands for Association Intégration Kreiz Breizh. A non-profit organization set up with the sole aim of helping newcomers settle in Brittany. A small yearly membership fee gives access to all sorts of assistance with translation or communication problems.

www.thecbj.com This is the website of the must-have monthly magazine beloved by many expat Brits. Practical articles on all subjects and contains lots of contact details for those interested in moving to Brittany or already here.

www.brittany-france.com Holiday accommodation site which also has some interesting stuff about the region.

www.brittanyferries.com The major ferry carrier to Brittany.

www.france-voyage.com Very helpful site offering handy facts about every region of France.

www.imagesofbrittany.com Lots of pictures and information on the region.

www.marketdaysinbrittany.com Does what it says in the title, which can be very useful information.

www.atasteofgarlic.com A funny site dedicated to Brits who like to write and read blogs and books about France.

www.bretondiary.com The blogosphere of Brittany-based funnyman Keith Eckstein, the editor and creator of the preceding site.

www.brittanywriters.com As the name suggests, a site for those who write or would like to write about the region.

www.frenchpublicholidays.com I still get caught out by closed shops, so handy for any visitor to or resident in France.

www.unevacanceenfrance.com A meeting place for all lovers of Brittany.

Further Reading:

Some of the books I found particularly helpful while researching this one are:

The Horse of Pride   Pierre-Jakez Hélias
Histoire de Bretagne   Jean-Pierre Le Mat
Memoirs of a Breton Peasant   Jean-Marie Déguignet

and:

Central Brittany   Penny Allen
Brittany and Normandy   Rex Grizell
Guide to the Menhirs of Central Brittany   Samuel Lewis
Traditional Fairy Stories of Brittany   Bethan Lewis
Discovering the History of Brittany   Wendy Mewes
Crossing Brittany   Wendy Mewes
Walking the Brittany Coast   Wendy Mewes
The Nantes-Brest Canal   Wendy Mewes

As the list suggests, my main sources of information and inspiration about the region and its history and people were fellow writer and near-neighbour Wendy Mewes and her publisher husband Harold.

To see a full list of Wendy and Harold's books and just how much I stole from them, go to www.reddogbooks.com